Household
Hints for
Singles

Household
Hints for
Singles

A PERIGEE BOOK

Perigee Books
are published by
The Putnam Publishing Group
200 Madison Avenue
New York, NY 10016

Library of Congress Cataloging-in-Publication Data

Heloise.
Household hints for singles / Heloise.
p.   cm.
ISBN 0-399-51811-8 (alk. paper)
1. Home economics.   2. Single people—Life skills guides.
I. Title.
TX158.H4443   1993   93-7925 CIP
640—dc20

Cover design by Mike Stromberg
Back cover photograph © by Michael Vasquez

Printed in the United States of America
1   2   3   4   5   6   7   8   9   10

This book is printed on acid-free paper.
∞

Acknowledgments

So many people and so little space!

As always, Marcy Meffert, my researcher/writer/editor and wonderful friend who lightens my work load with such charm and makes me laugh when I need it. My office magpies, Ruth, Kelly, Joyce, Angie, and Janie, who make the office sing with efficiency.

My team at Putnam, Rena Wolner, Marilyn Ducksworth, Cathy Gruhn, and John Duff, who guided me through the maze from first concept to last stop on the book tour! Thank y'all for being so great to work with!

A big hug and thanks to my stepson, Russell, who puts up with a working stepmom who may not cook much, but always knows how to order pizza, with salad! You will be a single soon and I know you will at least know how to cook, do laundry and iron—maybe not how to pick up your room, but I can't expect perfection, can I?

Of all the important people in my life, my husband, David, who makes it possible for me to be me, home or away!

To my daddy, Mike Cruse, who has always encouraged
me and loved me, even through the teen years!
Thanks for making math fun.
$D + PD = 2XL$

Contents

Introduction

For years people have asked me to write a book for singles. I've always said that most of the hints in my other books apply, so I didn't see a need for a book like this. Well, the more I thought about it, I realized that my fans were right—so I changed my mind and here it is.

We did our homework. We asked bachelors, and bachelorettes, those who were newly single in the later years and some young ones going off to college or into their first apartments: What did they want? The answer: The how to's.

How to shop for food that won't spoil in a few days; how to do laundry when you don't have a full load; how to do everything around the house faster and more easily.

Some of the hints may seem like "Homemaking 101," but for many of you it is survival training. If you didn't learn from your mother or father how to boil water, make an omelet, or do laundry, it's all here.

I remember a friend, a very respected attorney, who was newly single and had to do his own laundry. He called me one day to ask about how to make whites, t-shirt, socks, and underwear really white. His complaint was that after several washings, the clothes would fall apart. I asked how much bleach he was using and he said, "Gee, I don't know. I just kinda pour about half a bottle in with every load."

Heloise's most important hint: Read the directions! The manufacturers spend a lot of money testing their products to be sure they work. More is not always better (especially with bleach)!

And since there's so much more to living solo than household chores, I've covered lifestyle matters from travel to money management to car care . . . plus a few words on the special needs and special circumstances for anyone who is single by choice or by chance.

So, let's sit down for a few minutes and thumb through this book so you can get acquainted with the information here. I am here to help you prevent a problem, solve a problem, or just plain learn a few survival skills.

Never forget to keep a sense of humor. It helps!!!

I would love to hear from you! Write or fax if you have something you would like to share.

Heloise
PO Box 795000
San Antonio, TX 78279-5000
Fax: (210) HELOISE (435-6473)

Household
Hints for
Singles

CHAPTER ONE

Cooking for Yourself

At last! It's your kitchen and yours alone!

You choose the food and you decide how it's prepared—even if "preparation" to you is playing "pick and choose" at the neighborhood deli.

You don't have to eat broccoli anymore, or steak every Thursday, unless that's your choice. You can put jelly on *both* sides of the bread if you feel like being silly. You can lick the ice-cream dish or eat raw cookie dough, too. Who's to know? And, it's your house; your rules!

You can read at the table without interruption or, if you choose, you can eat your meal in front of the TV to see a show of *your* choice—even if you are eating breakfast cereal in a bowl of sloshing milk—for supper!

Pamper yourself! I have a single friend whose favorite "TV dinner" treat is a large Delicious apple, sliced, a large wedge of English Stilton cheese, and a glass of port wine. She showers and changes into her favorite satin lounging pajamas and then serves herself on "good china" and pours the wine into "good crystal" just before settling down to watch a favorite show or a rented movie.

Cooking for one or single-eating with "noncooking" if your style is to buy ready-made foods, can be an advantage if you think positively about it. And, since you *know* you are worth the effort, you'll never think that fixing delicious, nutritious meals for one is just too much trouble.

However, if you don't cook at all and don't want to learn, that's okay, too. Supermarket deli foods and ready-made meals in the dairy or freezer section allow you to heat and eat if you don't like to go to restaurants every day or can't afford to.

Many of my single friends and readers say they'd like to cook for themselves but hate to clean up a mess afterward. Some, who have previously cooked for a family, can't get used to the idea of pleasing themselves and/or cooking in solo portions. That's why the food section is at the beginning of this book; my single readers and friends have said that they need the most help with solo food preparation and kitcheneering.

Kitcheneering is a Heloise word for food-preparation methods that make cooking faster and easier, with less time spent in cleanup. I've also included some of the Heloise Classic Recipes frequently requested by readers which adapt to single cooking and eating and a few recipes to make entertaining less complicated.

Six Heloise Hints for Quick, Less-Mess Solo-Dining

1. If you can't afford to or don't want to eat out, the most important thing is to believe that you and your health are worth the effort to fix a solo meal! While it's okay to eat junk food occasionally, regularly grazing on high-fat and sugary foods makes most of us feel "junky" and less able to get the most out of life.

2. If you pick up meals on the way home from work, learn to make healthy selections from fast-food restaurants (see hints in this chapter) and learn to assemble a tasty, nutritious meal from the hot and cold selections of your supermarket salad bar and deli.

For example, add grated cheese and cooked shrimp or shred a few slices of cold, lean deli meat into a salad bar's pasta-and-vegetable salad (put it over a bed of greens, also from the salad bar) for a do-it-yourself chef's salad. Or, if you prefer, buy a hot entree and add veggie or pasta salads for side dishes and salad-bar fruit for dessert. The variables are endless if you play with different combinations and shop at several markets to get a variety of specialties.

3. Learn to cook, not just to reheat with your microwave, and don't be afraid to experiment. If some of your efforts are a flop, join the rest of the human race—we all mess up occasionally and live to laugh about it!

4. Buy a couple of handled individual-portion (usually 15-ounce size), microwave/conventional-oven–safe ceramic casseroles. Then, you

can heat soup, single portions of frozen vegetables, or other foods in them and eat out of the dish.

You can also make cooked cereal in them in the microwave; the 15-ounce size will usually accommodate the solo portion described on the box without boiling over *if* you follow directions and don't nuke your cereal for more seconds than the directions tell you to.

NOTE: These dishes do get hot, so grab them with a potholder and put a pad beneath them to protect the tabletop when you set them down. (See directions for freezing foods in individual casseroles in this chapter.)

5. Learn how to pan-broil meats in an iron skillet. It's quick and tasty, and you can reheat a starch (potatoes, noodles, rice) on the edges of the pan if it's large enough to accommodate more than one food without crowding. Only one pan or pot to wash! Your best allies for pan-broiling meats are meat tenderizer and nonstick vegetable spray. (See pan-broiling meat directions elsewhere in this chapter.)

6. Make your motto: "Cook once and eat twice . . . or even three times."

If you like to cook, cook enough casserole, stew, soup, or whatever to make your own frozen meals. (See hints and recipes in this chapter.) For example, cook a small roast; eat one portion and freeze the rest to mix with vegetables for quick soups, stews, chili, or sandwiches.

Also, when you chop and slice onions, bell peppers, or celery, prepare extra amounts to freeze in zipper bags for days when you don't have time to fool around in the kitchen. If you never have time to fool around, buy such flavor perks already chopped and frozen or dried. (See the basic pantry shopping list in this chapter.)

7. Organize a pot-luck meal with one or more friends; each person brings one course, home cooked or bought. Or, trade portions of planned-leftover main dishes with a friend so that each of you gets more variety. In either case, getting food buddies will give you social as well as nutritional experiences!

My roommate, Sue, and I had neighbors in college who always cooked great breakfasts but used instant coffee. They liked my fresh perked, so we would swap a half pot of delicious coffee for home-baked muffins, an omelet, etc. The Kutaches are still friends today!

Start-up Shopping Checklists for a Solo Kitchen

Even if you only cook sporadically, you need to have some kitchen equipment. Do check out thrift shops, sales, and discount stores before you spend a lot of money furnishing a kitchen.

Avoid buying "complete-kitchen" sets of pots and pans, unless you really know you'll use all those different sizes and shapes, or buy basic-minimum sets, which usually include two pots of different sizes and one frying pan.

If you've never cooked before and think you'll be making many "burnt offerings" to the "kitchen god," buy your cookware in thrift shops; then if you really cremate something, you won't feel bad if you end up tossing the whole mess out, pan and all!

NOTE: If you are buying cooking equipment for a self-feeding college dorm dweller, first find out what sort of cooking is allowed in the dorm.

Some dorms do not allow any cooking; others permit electric skillets or microwave ovens but not hot plates, and so on. Most allow hot pots which can be used to make soup and canned meals as well as to heat water for coffee, tea, or cocoa. Look for instant water heaters, too, which make hot water for beverages and instant soups.

Some popcorn poppers can be used to fry eggs or make grilled-cheese sandwiches.

When I was in college, our favorite trick was to make grilled-cheese sandwiches with an iron—clothes iron, that is, not waffle iron. We'd wrap our sandwiches in foil, then iron each side for a minute or so, then peel and enjoy!

VARIOUS SIZES OF GLASS AND CERAMIC COOKWARE

Most useful are 1- and 2- or 3-quart sizes, which can double as mixing bowls and casseroles.

Glass and ceramic cookware, which are safe for stove-top cooking or in microwave and conventional ovens, can be used to store the food, too, so you don't have to transfer leftovers to another dish. (I know Mom always said you should put leftovers in a smaller dish, but she needed the pan to cook the family's next meal; you don't have to bother with such things!) Just cover tightly with the pan's cover or with wrap; reheat leftovers by taking out a portion or heating as is if only one portion is left over.

SKILLETS

A good heavy cast-iron skillet or nonstick-coated cast aluminum sauté pan with an oven-proof or metal handle can serve as an all-purpose cooking pan/pot.

Either will go from burner to oven if you need to brown something and finish it off in the oven, and either can be a casserole or stir-fry pan (a wok is nice but not a necessity).

Useful sizes are the smallest (about 6- or 7-inch diameter) for frying an egg, one burger or chop, or for browning a grilled-cheese sandwich, and a 10- or 12-inch one for general use. My grandma and mother made pineapple upside-down cake in an iron skillet, as I do today. Also, look for a pot lid that will fit over several sizes of pots and pans.

NOTE: An electric skillet will cost more but is also an all-purpose cooking pan/pot that you will keep forever. Most come with recipe books containing one-dish meals and provide instructions that will get you started if you've never cooked before.

HINT: The tricks of pan-grilling anything are:

- a hot-enough pan
- patting food dry with paper towels before grilling
- preventing sticking with vegetable spray or by applying vegetable oil/margarine to pan and/or food
- not crowding the food in the pan to allow the excess liquid that bubbles from the food as it cooks to evaporate.

HINT: To stir-fry without fat, "fry" in bouillon.

Spray the pan with nonstick spray and add enough bouillon to cover the pan's bottom about an inch deep, then add foods and stir-fry quickly at high heat. After meat bits are cooked, add veggies. Stir-fry veggies should be crisp, so it takes only a few minutes. (Please see stir-fry and one-dish meals in the recipe chapter.)

1-QUART POT

A heavy nonstick 1-quart pot is big enough to heat up solo portions of soups, stews, and other main dishes. A pot, such as one of heavy-grade thick aluminum, also lets you melt cheese without the bother of a double boiler. You can cook one cup of dry rice, which is enough for several meals, in this size pot—but you will need a larger pot for noodles, which tend to boil over.

3- OR 4-QUART POT

To boil pasta; and, if it's a heavy, nonstick pot, it will be ideal for making soups or stews if you want to make your own and have leftovers to reheat. A large pot also doubles as a mixing bowl if you have company!

INDIVIDUAL-PORTION–SIZED CERAMIC CASSEROLES WITH HANDLES

To heat individual portions of food in the microwave or conventional oven.

NOTE: These are not usually suitable for stove-top cooking; foods are likely to burn if you try it.

HINT: To freeze single portions of leftovers for reheating in individual casseroles, line the casserole with foil or heavy plastic wrap before pouring in the food, then freeze. After you have a frozen, casserole-shaped food-block, remove the block, wrap airtight with foil, plastic freezer wrap or in a zipper bag, label and return to the freezer. Then, when you want to reheat the food-block, it will fit perfectly in the casserole, which you will still be able to use in the meantime.

OTHER MICROWAVE-SAFE DISHES

1. A 4-cup glass measuring pitcher, which can be used, in addition to measuring, to boil water and to cook just about anything in the micro-

wave and for a mixing bowl. A 1-cup measuring pitcher used as noted above for smaller amounts.

2. A 9- or 10-inch-diameter pie plate or flat glass microwave-safe "pizza" plate for cooking things that have to be arranged in a circle, such as broccoli, or for cooking meats. (These are usually also safe for conventional-oven cooking.) Also, a 1- or 2-quart casserole for cooking and for use as a mixing bowl.

OTHER USEFUL COOKWARE

1. An 8-inch square and/or 9-by-13-inch rectangular, oven-safe glass or aluminum pan for general-purpose baking.

HINT: No cookie sheet? Bake cookies on the underside of an aluminum rectangular baking pan.

2. Cookie sheet(s) for general-purpose baking as well as cookies. Jelly-roll pans, which look like cookie sheets with half-inch sides, are useful for baking chicken pieces with sauces or meat juices that might spill over.

3. Bread loaf pan made from glass or metal for meat loaf, quick breads, or casseroles.

HINT: Save on cleanup by mixing meat loaf in clear plastic take-out containers. To add the egg, make a well in the middle and then mix all with a fork or your fingers before pressing the mixture into a nonstick vegetable-sprayed pan.

NOTE: Meat loaf will cook faster if you flatten it in an 8-inch square pan instead of baking it in a loaf tin. You will get four flat, square pieces to eat hot or save for cold sandwiches. Or, make four mini–meat loaves from one recipe. If you begin with about a pound or so of ground meat, the mini-loaves will bake in 20 to 25 minutes at 350 to 375 (moderate) degrees F. Freeze or refrigerate leftovers. (See meat loaf recipe in chapter 2.)

UTENSILS

- can opener
- wire whisk (can substitute for an electric mixer)
- large and small spatulas/pancake turners for turning foods in the

pan and for serving such foods as lasagna (plastic or wood for nonstick cookware; any kind for iron or stainless-steel cookware)

- several heat-proof plastic or wooden spoons (to prevent burned fingers when stirring hot foods and for protecting nonstick cookware)
- rubber spatula for removing all of anything from a bowl or other container
- wood-handled, long-tined fork for turning meats in the pan or for testing baked potatoes
- a "spaghetti grabber" (handle with "fingers") to lift noodles, veggie hunks, and other foods out of hot liquids and/or a slotted spoon for removing food from liquid
- sieve and/or colander for straining foods and draining noodles.

HINT: For quick straining, look in gadget departments for a plastic pot-drainer which you can hold across the edge of a pot to drain away liquid such as water from noodles. After draining, you let the noodles slide back into the pot; add sauce or veggies and grated cheese and you've saved yourself the washing of another dish!

CUTTING IMPLEMENTS

1. Buy a cutting board to protect kitchen surfaces and your fingers, too! Nonwooden ones, such as nylon or plastic, can go into the dishwasher.

Wooden cutting boards need to be scrubbed well with soap and hot water to avoid accumulation of bacteria and then seasoned with mineral oil every so often—not salad oil, which can get rancid.

You can serve cheese and crackers or a loaf of bread on your cutting board if you don't have serving dishes.

2. Several good knives: buy the best you can afford!

Good knives can replace any fancy cutting or chopping appliance and, with care, will last indefinitely; they should be washed by hand and not in the dishwasher to prevent heat damage to the metal and harsh-washing damage to the handles.

HINT: Try holding the knives to see if they fit your grip before buying them. The new-style padded, fat-handled knives and other utensils are a blessing to those of us who are a bit fumble-fingered.

Include:

- A small paring knife
- a French chef's knife for chopping
- a slender boning knife for general purposes
- and a serrated-edge knife for cutting bread, tomatoes, and some meats.

NOTE: If you don't have a garlic press, you can mash garlic by pressing it with the side of a large wide knife. If you are handy, you don't even have to bother peeling the garlic first!

3. A knife sharpener—you are more likely to cut yourself forcing a dull knife through food than when you cut neatly and quickly with a sharp one.

4. A pizza cutter for pizza or lasagna, for cutting crusts off sliced bread, for cutting refrigerated or homemade cookie dough into squares, and for cutting noodles if you're feeling "gourmetish" and want to make your own.

MEASURING EQUIPMENT

Like my mother, I measure mostly by "eye" and taste. However, if you bake or if you are a newcomer to the kitchen, you may want to measure as directed in recipes until your eye knows how to please your taste buds.

When you measure, you usually use glass measuring cups to measure any kind of liquid and dry measuring cups for flour, sugar, shortening, etc.

Measuring spoons are needed for such ingredients as salt, spices, etc. You use standard measuring spoons when the recipe calls for less than 1/4 cup. "Dash" in a recipe means less than 1/8 teaspoon. Here are some equivalent measures to help you when you shop for recipe ingredients:

One-Pound Equivalents

2 cups butter
4 cups all-purpose flour
2 cups granulated sugar
3½ cups powdered sugar, packed
2¼ cups brown sugar, packed
(*Always pack brown sugar tightly into the measuring cup.*)

Liquid Measurements

1 cup = 8 fluid ounces
2 cups = 16 fluid ounces
4 cups = 32 fluid ounces
2 cups = 1 pint
2 pints = 1 quart
1 quart = 4 cups
4 quarts = 1 gallon

Dry Measurements

(*When abbreviated, tsp. = teaspoon and tbsp. = tablespoon; oz. = ounce and lb. = pound*)

3 teaspoons = 1 tablespoon
4 tablespoons = ¼ cup
16 tablespoons = 1 cup
2 tablespoons = 1 ounce
4 oz. = ¼ pound
16 oz. = 1 pound
1 lb. = 454 grams (metric)

Metric Measurements

1 teaspoon = 5 milliliters
1 tablespoon = 15 milliliters
1 cup = 240 milliliters
1 ounce = 28 grams
1 pound = 454 grams

APPLIANCES

High on my list for quick and no-mess cooking aides, if you can afford them, are:

1. Microwave oven (the higher the voltage the quicker the oven cooks). Save the books that come with your microwave; they are the key to successful cooking with it!
2. Toaster oven or wide-opening toaster that will accommodate English muffins, bagels, and frozen waffles that serve as a base for more interesting sandwiches and breakfasts. Toaster ovens can bake potatoes and broil meats, too, without heating up the kitchen the way conventional ovens do, as well as toast whatever needs toasting or browning.
3. A blender to make fruit and yogurt shakes and fruit/veggie juices or to do the usual chopping and blending.
4. Water heater to make coffee, tea, cocoa, or instant soups, if you don't have a microwave to boil water in the cup.

POTS, PANS, COOKING UTENSILS, HEALTH CONCERNS

New types of cookware have caused health concerns about nonstick coatings and base metals of pots and pans. If you are buying new-tech cookware, here's information from the American Institute for Cancer Research to help you.

Nonstick Coatings

Some nonstick coatings may abrade and chip after heavy or improper use, but the particles chipped off have not been found to cause health problems. When cooking, make sure the pot or pan contains enough liquid and that temperatures are moderate. Wooden or plastic utensils and nonabrasive cleaning materials protect the surface.

Anodized Aluminum

Such surfaces are hardened and sealed by an electrochemical process for a nonstick, scratch-resistant surface to allow for fat-free cooking. This ware is durable and the cookware materials don't leach into food, which tends to cook evenly and quickly.

Aluminum

Always a favorite for heat conduction, most of today's aluminum cookware has been anodized or treated with nonstick coatings. There has been concern about aluminum cookware safety but research has shown that high levels of aluminum in Alzheimer's patients' brains are not caused by aluminum ingestion but by accumulation as a result of the disease.

Cooking and storing food in uncoated aluminum cookware daily results in ingesting only a minute amount of aluminum, but high-acid or salty foods like spaghetti and tomato sauce or cabbage and sauerkraut may allow more aluminum to be absorbed by the food. It's not a good idea to store high-acid or salty food in aluminum for a long time, anyway, because it can cause the surface to pit.

Ceramic and Enamel Cookware

Slow cookers and other kinds of microwave cookware are in this category. Some glazes on ceramic cookware may carry small amounts of lead, but FDA studies show that U.S.-made ceramic cookware doesn't exceed safety standards. However, be wary of imported ceramics, especially from Third World countries where regulations are not so strict.

Basic Pantry-Stocking Shopping Checklist

While fresh onions, peppers and herbs are very nice, solo cooking often means wasting the leftovers.

Frozen chopped onions and peppers are terrific for cooking, and you can freeze fresh leafy herbs, too; but if you have a tiny freezer, you'd be better off with dried bottled food enhancers. The spice shelves of supermarkets have all sorts of flavoring substitutes that keep well in the cupboard.

Salt, Pepper

The most basic! However if you are avoiding salt, consider salt substitutes, lemon juice, and various other herbs and spices to perk up the taste of your food.

Bouillon

Cubes, powder, or liquid make a cup of soup anytime you want one. Anything cooked in water will taste better cooked in bouillon; remember to decrease salt because bouillon is salty and can be a salt substitute.

Dried Onion Soup

There is no rule that says you have to use the whole bag at once. Keep in a zipper bag or tightly closed jar after opening and add a tablespoon or so to add extra flavor to soups, stews, or other foods cooked in liquid. Use like bouillon for flavoring.

Onion Powder, Garlic Powder

Or, onion or garlic salts or juices.

Dried Seasoning Veggies Such as Dried Green Peppers, Tomatoes, Dried Mixed Vegetables

They perk up soups and other dishes. You can soak these in water for fifteen or twenty minutes or so before adding to a salad like tuna or chicken. They keep nicely on the shelf, and you won't end up with slimy peppers, onions, etc., in the fridge when you don't use up fresh ones quickly.

Dried Onions, Sliced or Chopped

Use in place of fresh onions in all recipes. If you are careful, you can brown dried onions in a frying pan. Watch them closely, as they brown very quickly.

When adding dried onions to salads like tuna fish, the mixture needs to wait in the fridge for a while so that the onions absorb liquid from the recipe; otherwise they will still be crunchy. You can also soak them in water for about fifteen minutes or so and use them like fresh onions.

Dried Garlic Bits

Can replace fresh garlic. (See notes for browning dried onions and be extra cautious to prevent charring them, or just sprinkle them on the food to be cooked.)

Dried Chives, Dried Green-Onion Tops

Flavor baked potatoes and other vegetables; add color.

Dried Parsley

Adds flavor and color to foods.

Dried Celery Leaf

Flavors salads, soups, meat loaves, and stews.

Imitation Bacon Bits

Sprinkle on potatoes, cooked veggies, scrambled eggs; add to omelets or fried rice; sprinkle over salads. Add flavor and crunch if added at the last minute.

Mixed Dried Salad Toppings

Use like bacon bits.

Butter Sprinkles

Moisten and flavor potatoes and flavor cooked vegetables.

Liquid Butter Substitute

Moistens potatoes and substitutes for a butter sauce on vegetables or parslied boiled potatoes. (Boil potatoes, sprinkle with dried parsley, pour on imitation liquid butter, and serve.)

Butter-Flavored Vegetable Spray

Keeps foods from sticking to pans and dishes. Spray on raw or frozen vegetables before cooking in microwave for delicious flavor. Spray lightly on popcorn to avoid the fat calories of melted butter or margarine.

Olive Oil–Flavored Vegetable Spray

1. Keeps foods from sticking. Gives Italian flavor to foods fried in it.
2. Spray on salad instead of adding oil; sprinkle on a bit of vinegar and you have oil and vinegar dressing.
3. For Italian-style but low-cal broccoli, spray dish with olive oil–flavored vegetable spray, place several pieces of cut fresh garlic or dried garlic bits on the dish, lay broccoli spears on the garlic, spray again with olive oil–flavored vegetable spray, add a few droplets of water, and nuke in the microwave according to directions for that amount of broccoli—fresh or frozen. For added zip, sprinkle on a bit of dried oregano before serving.

NOTE: Don't overcook the broccoli; it's better if there's some crunch left. If you wish, you can cook the flowered ends and save the stalks, which can be peeled and eaten raw for a snack or sliced for salad or stir-fry dishes.

Juice in Plastic Lemons or Limes

Handy when you want fresh-tasting lemon or lime juice to flavor iced tea, vegetables, and salads.

HINT: You'll save fat calories if you sprinkle lemon or lime juice on your fruit or vegetable salad instead of commercial salad dressings.

Paprika

Sprinkle on potatoes, salads, and other pale-colored foods to make them look better without altering the taste.

NOTE: The above are basic, but if you like Italian flavors, add oregano; if you like Tex-Mex, add ground cumin (comino); if you like Indian, add curry powder; and, if you like Simon and Garfunkel, be sure to get parsley, sage, rosemary, and thyme . . . then you can sing "Scarborough Fair" while you cook.

Pasta and Rice

These pantry staples can be side dishes or main courses when topped with sauces and/or grated cheese. Cook single servings or, to save time later, cook extra to use as the base for stews or soups or to mix with vegetables and low-fat dressing to make pasta salads.

NOTE: Add canned beans of different types to leftover rice or noodles for tasty main dishes. They substitute for meat protein in vegetarian meals. Here are some examples:

1. Reheat leftover rice and top with canned black beans spiced with chili powder or other peppery seasonings to make a Caribbean-style dish.

2. Reheat leftover rice and top with red beans seasoned with Cajun mixed spices and/or sliced smoked sausage which has been browned briefly in the same pot before you heat up the beans. Mash a few beans on the side of the pot so that you have a "bean sauce" to stir in, and moisten it all.

3. Mix black-eyed peas and rice to make the traditional Southern "Hoppin' John."

4. Add kidney beans, chickpeas or other canned legumes to a pasta salad for flavor and as a meat-protein substitute.

COUPON CHECKLIST

- Keep in envelope and write list on outside.
- File according to expiration date.
- Put in envelope in order of aisles.
- Don't use coupons for items you wouldn't normally buy.
- Highlight the expiration date on the coupons.
- Go to stores that offer double coupons.
- Leave unwanted coupons on store shelf.
- Exchange coupons with friends, family, or coworkers.
- Buy an extra newspaper or magazine for extra coupons.

Miscellaneous Kitcheneering Basics

Save the booklets that come with kitchen appliances and the stove so that you get the most and best possible use from your appliances. The manufacturers spend a lot of money on researching the proper use of their appliances, so you may as well take advantage of their expertise.

If you are making up a recipe, look in the appliance recipe book for one that compares to yours with amounts and ingredients; it will take some of the guesswork out of possible cooking times.

You will save money on service and repair if you check out the troubleshooting hints in the appliance manual before calling to arrange for a service person.

HINT: To save embarrassment as well as service costs, the first question to ask yourself if an appliance won't go on is: "Is it plugged in?" You may laugh, but you'd be surprised at how many people write to me to tell me that they didn't check the obvious!

Microwave Oven Cooking Hints

A microwave oven is one of your best kitchen helpers, especially when cooking small portions. It allows you to cook in and eat from the same dish, shortens food-preparation time, keeps kitchens cool in summer, and is easier to wipe clean than a conventional or toaster oven. Here are some microwave cooking hints:

ALL FOODS, COOKING METHOD

Since microwaves penetrate from the outer edges in, place food so that the thicker or denser parts are toward the outer edge of a circle. For example, when cooking a vegetable like broccoli, arrange pieces in a circle on a microwave-safe plate or pie dish with the stems pointed outward; when cooking corn on the cob, arrange the cobs so that the pointed ends are toward the center.

CAUTION: Whenever lifting covers of microwaved foods *always* open wraps *away* from you to prevent steam burns.

ALL FOODS, COOKING METHOD

Because microwaves cook from the outside in, cut-up veggies and some other foods are best made in a ring mold or bundt pan. To make one, place a glass ovenware custard cup, microwave-safe glass, or preserving jar in the center of a microwave-safe round casserole that has the proper diameter. Usually, a small 4-ounce juice glass will fit in the center of a 1-quart dish and a custard cup or pint jar will fit in the center of a 4-quart dish. Or buy a plastic microwave "bundt" pan.

HINT: Buy single-serving packages of vegetables to microwave and eat them out of the pack for a snack or veggie lunch. Or, buy frozen vegetables in 1-pound bags, cook what you need for a single serving, and close the bag with a spring clothespin for storing in the fridge or freezer. If you buy several types of frozen bagged vegetables, you can mix up your own favorite combinations.

ALL FOODS, COOKING TIME

It's better to cook for the shortest time period and then add a few seconds or a minute more than to cook at the longest recommended time.

Also, the food continues to cook for a few seconds after the oven stops; it's called residual cooking time. Most of the bad results such as cardboard bread, bouncy rubber meatballs, and hockey-puck chicken breasts occur when foods are overcooked.

CEREALS, MILK, OR CREAMY MIXTURES

These tend to boil up quickly and overflow; allow plenty of head room. *Heloise hint:* place on a cheap paper plate just in case! Containers should be two to three times the volume of the ingredients to avoid messy boil-overs. A 4-cup microwave-safe glass measuring pitcher is a good "pot" for heating liquids in the microwave.

COFFEE, TEA, COCOA

When boiling water in a cup or mug for instant coffee, tea, or cocoa (usually two to three minutes on HIGH), wait a second or two after removing the mug from the microwave before dunking a tea bag or stirring vigorously; the microwave action continues for a few seconds, and disturbing the water can cause it to overflow and burn fingers if they are in the way.

Also, when reheating beverages, wait a few seconds before sipping to avoid burning your lips.

NOTE: Although some of the new coffee bags instruct you to place the bag in the cup of water and then zap in the microwave, you can't do this with all tea bags. I know of an instance when the metal staple of a tea bag ruined a microwave oven.

FISH

One of the best ways to cook fish is in the microwave oven.

Place the thickest parts toward the outside, cook for a few minutes, and then take the fish out of the microwave and cut a small slit in the thickest part. When the flesh starts looking barely opaque, remove the fish from the microwave. *Important note:* let stand a minute or two, and it will finish cooking. Unless the fish is crumb coated, cover it with wax paper or plastic wrap to retain moisture.

NOTE: It's best to undercook fish slightly because it continues to cook when removed from the microwave oven; as with other foods, you have to allow for residual cooking time.

HEAT-SUSCEPTOR PACKAGING

As this is being written, the FDA is researching heat-susceptor materials. It says that high temperatures such as 400 to 500 degrees F. may cause harmful chemicals in heat-susceptor packaging to get into the food. Heat-susceptor materials include the thin, aluminum-containing package inserts usually found in microwave-cooking pizzas, french fries, fish sticks, Belgian waffles, and popcorn. Until the final results of the FDA research come out, take these precautions:

1. Don't microwave products any longer than instructed to on the package; that's what increases the chance of the temperature going too high.
2. Don't eat foods such as popcorn if the package has become very browned or charred—signs that the food may have been overheated.
3. Don't reuse containers with heat susceptors or remove them for use with other foods.

POTATOES

Stick three or four wooden toothpicks into one of the long sides of a potato before placing it in a microwave to make a "stand" that allows the potato to cook evenly.

ROLLS

Warm rolls or bread on a low setting and inside a terry-cloth towel to prevent sogginess. Also put a cup of water in the microwave to help replace lost moisture.

SWEET ROLLS

To avoid soggy bottoms of sweet rolls, place them on a paper (that's real paper, not foam) plate or paper towel/napkin when heating them in the microwave.

WASSAIL (MULLED WINE)

Can be heated nicely in the microwave in a microwave-safe serving pitcher or bowl.

WRAPPERS

If you recycle bread bags, don't use them as food covers in the microwave. It's possible that lead in the paint on the wrapper's outside could get into the food you are cooking.

NOTE: Also, if you recycle bread bags to wrap food items, don't turn them inside out for the same reason.

Microwave Cookware

TEST TO DETERMINE IF A DISH IS MICROWAVE-SAFE

Place a glass measuring cup of water next to the empty dish to be tested. (*Never* metal or silver or gold-trimmed dishes!) Heat on full power for one minute, then check the temperature of the dish.

If the dish is cool and the water very warm, the dish can be used. If the dish is slightly warm, it can be used for short-term cooking only. If the dish is hot and the water is cool, do not use the dish. A hot dish means that the utensil is absorbing the rays instead of permitting them to pass through as they should for safe cooking.

NOTE: Place an indelible mark with fingernail polish or a pen for marking glassware, etc., on the rim of a casserole or pie plate. Then, when you place the container in the microwave oven, make it a habit to center the mark at "twelve o'clock" so that if you have to give it quarter or half turns during cooking, you'll know how much of a turn you've made.

MICROWAVE COOKING BAGS

Twist ties contain metal and can cause "arcing" sparks that can damage your oven. Tie microwave cooking bags closed with dental floss and *always* open bags *away* from you to prevent steam burns.

HINT: Check out your favorite housewares department to find a plastic dome lid. These lids are perforated to let steam escape and are big and high enough to cover most dishes that fit into a microwave. You'll be helping the environment because you'll have less waxed paper and plastic wrap in the trash and, most of all, you'll always have a handy lid to prevent spatters. (Unless you are more efficient than most people and always remember to buy waxed paper and plastic wrap when the packaging warns you that you're about to run out!)

WAXED PAPER

When covering food containers with waxed paper, crumple the paper slightly so that it won't blow off.

MICROWAVE COOKING TIMES

Directions on microwave meals give a time range because the time needed is determined by your oven's wattage. You may need to add time if your oven is less than 600 watts. Best results in ovens with less than 500 watts come with use of HIGH or maximum power, even when directions say 50 percent power because HIGH on ovens with less than 500 watts equals 50 percent on 600- or 700-watt ovens. Microwave ovens work best if they are the only appliance running on an electrical circuit; competing with other appliances can reduce available wattage.

Here's a way to find out what the wattage is on your microwave oven so that you can decide which time given on the directions is best.

Fill a microwave-safe glass measuring cup with exactly 1 cup of tap water. Microwave on high uncovered until water begins to boil.

If water boils in:	Your wattage is:
less than 3 minutes	600 to 700
3 to 4 minutes	500 to 600
more than 4 minutes	less than 500

Kitchen Odors

COOKING ODOR–CAUSING FOODS

Add a bit of vinegar to the water while boiling corned beef and cabbage or other odor-causing foods to keep the house (and visitors!) from being overpowered.

FISHY ODOR ON HANDS

Apply lemon or lime juice and wash.

HINT: When you go fishing, soak small hand towels in a mixture of lemon juice and water, put the wet towels in plastic self-sealing bags (two per bag), and store the bags in the freezer. Take as many bags as you think you'll need and put them in a cooler. At the end of the fishing day, the towels are thawed and ready to wipe away fish odors from hands and freshen your face, too.

GARBAGE-DISPOSAL ODORS

Grind grapefruit rind or lemon or lime pieces left over from iced tea and other drinks through a garbage disposal to dispel odors. Always run lots of water afterward.

LUNCH-BOX ODORS

To keep a lunch box fresh, place a piece of paper towel or stale bread dampened with vinegar in the lunch box and allow to remain overnight. Wash in the morning, and it will smell fresh.

ONION ODOR, AVOIDING IT ON HANDS

When you grate onions, put your onion-holding hand in a plastic bag. Then when you are finished grating, put the bag around the onion without touching it. The onion is ready to cook and leftovers ready to refrigerate, and your hands don't smell!

ONIONS, REMOVING ODOR FROM HANDS

After peeling or slicing onions, sprinkle a bit of salt on your damp hands, work it in, and rinse. Or, to remove onion and other odors from your hands, rinse them with mouthwash or scrub with toothpaste.

HINT: Next time, wear rubber gloves to avoid the problem.

Food Storage

One of the Heloise food-shopping rules is "Never shop when you are hungry." However, many people have to shop on the way home from work, so they are bound to be hungry. Try promising yourself a reward—something special from the supermarket deli or salad bar if you manage to curb those urges to buy impulsively whatever catches your eye or the urge to buy too much of anything.

HINT: Buy salad for one meal at the salad bar and single-meal portions of deli foods or single-portion canned soups and stews to avoid leftovers. Instead of buying packaged meat from the counter display, have the butcher wrap up only one chop or steak.

If your supermarket has a bakery, don't buy a whole package of anything; get one or two of your favorite muffins or rolls so you won't be tempted to overeat lest the goodies go to waste. A lot of people "get fat for shame" as in "It's a shame to throw that out, so I'll eat it before it spoils."

However, if you do like to cook or shop only sporadically and you want to keep a variety of foods on hand, here are some guides for storage times to help you get the most for your money by avoiding spoilage.

STORING CANNED FOODS

Canned and packaged foods are staples when you cook for one, but they do have a shelf life and don't keep forever. Some people write the date of purchase on the can with a marker as an added shelf-life note. Here's help from the USDA on pantry storage life:

1. Store canned goods in a cool, clean, dry place below 85 degrees F.
   Low-acid canned foods such as canned meat, poultry, stews, corn, carrots, and peas will keep in a cabinet for two to five years. High-acid foods like tomato-based products, fruits, juices, vinegar-based salad dressings, and sauerkraut should be used in nine to eighteen months.
2. When canned goods get frozen (in a car, basement, or cabin) seams can be damaged from freezing and swelling of contents. Move frozen cans immediately to a refrigerator and allow to thaw. After thawing, cook and use the food or cook and refreeze. If cans didn't thaw in a refrigerator or if you suspect that they may have frozen and thawed more than once, discard!
3. You can store most nonacidic opened canned foods in the can in the refrigerator safely, but doing so may affect flavor.

HINT: Wash well and recycle those mayo jars and margarine tubs for storing leftovers! Then, if the leftovers spoil, you can discard them in the disposable containers without having to smell or touch anything disagreeable.

NOTE: Lead has nearly been eliminated as a metal used in the canning industry. The percentage of food packed in lead-soldered containers has dropped from more than 90 percent in 1979 to 3 percent in the first quarter of 1990.

4. The new shelf-stable entrees that you can heat in the microwave are in plastic and paper containers which are considered "flexible cans." The contents have been sterilized with heat to make them shelf stable. If there are no breaks or tears in the package, they should maintain quality for more than a year if stored in a cool, dry place.
5. For proper storage, read labels carefully to check "Sell-by" or "Use-by" dates and look for "Keep refrigerated." The chances are that

if the package was bought off the shelf, it doesn't need refrigeration until it's been opened.

6. Place newly purchased foods behind older ones in the cupboard or turn new cans upside down so you will use the oldd ones first.

7. *Caution*: When in doubt, throw it out! That's the main rule for leftovers in the fridge or for foods stored in the freezer or cupboard. *Never* eat food from cans or glass jars with dents, cracks, or bulging lids. *Always* discard any food that's off-color or has a bad odor or appearance. Food poisoning is not worth taking a chance!

Also, wrap such discards securely and dispose of them carefully to protect curious children or animals who might play in the trash.

STORING FROZEN FOODS

Freezers can be time and money savers if you cook when you are in the mood or have the time and then make your own single-portion frozen dinners.

If you buy frozen dinners, check out the "Use-by" dates and keep those that should be eaten first in the front of the freezer. You can also mark the date of purchase on food packages with a marker. A "grease" or china marker works well on slick surfaces.

Here's some advice from the American Frozen-Food Institute:

1. Make sure your freezer stays at 0 degrees F. Fluctuating temperatures cause frozen foods to lose moisture at a faster rate than normal and result in their becoming rough and dry.

2. A full freezer maintains its temperature better than a half-empty one.

HINT: Fill up the freezer with bagged ice from the supermarket or recycle clean water-filled plastic milk jugs or soft-drink bottles if you don't fill the freezer with food. You'll always have enough ice cubes, and with the milk jugs or 2-liter soft-drink bottles, you have a way to chill foods in a picnic cooler and have ice water to drink as the ice thaws.

3. Don't freeze too many items at one time; the heat given off by nonfrozen foods can raise the freezer temperature.

4. Try to place lukewarm products away from those already frozen to avoid heating up frozen products. (Many new refrigerator-freezers have a freezing shelf that's extra cold for quick-freezing.)

5. Keep items most used in the front or on the door so that you don't have to dig around while the freezer "loses its cool."

6. To keep food at its edible best and to preserve nutritional value, packaging should be moisture- and vapor-proof.

Rigid containers and plastic bags need airtight seals, and wrapped foods should be stored in extra-heavy aluminum foil, pliofilm, or polyethylene-lined paper. Seal the edges of rigid containers with freezer tape. Squeeze air from bags before sealing. When you have foods from which you eat only portions at one time, like ice cream in rigid containers, place a piece of plastic wrap directly over the food surface to prevent crystals from forming and to preserve flavor; then replace the lid.

7. No food can be stored forever. Make note of "Use-by" dates on packaged foods and if you freeze foods yourself, freeze them as quickly as possible when they are as fresh as possible. It's as your first computer instructor said, "Garbage in; garbage out!"

8. Use thawed food immediately after thawing. Not all bacteria are killed by freezing; bacteria get active as food thaws, so food not used soon after thawing will begin to lose nutritional value and spoil.

9. In case of power failure, a filled freezer will stay frozen twice as long as a half-filled freezer. Avoid opening the freezer door and prevent spoilage by packing the freezer with dry ice if possible. *Caution*: Don't handle dry ice with bare hands; it burns.

10. Foods that have reached temperatures of 40 or 45 degrees F. are not likely to be worth refreezing and may be unsafe to eat as well as have deteriorated in quality.

Fruits, vegetables, and meats that have not completely thawed and have some ice still on them—or that have been thawed for a short time and have been refrigerated—can be refrozen, but they will have lost quality and flavor. Refrozen vegetables toughen. Refrozen fruits become soft and mushy, which makes them suitable for cooking but not for eating uncooked.

Low-acid foods like vegetables and meats spoil rapidly after thawing and reaching 45 degrees F.; it's not advisable to refreeze them. Acid foods, like most fruit and fruit products, are likely to ferment after thawing and reaching 45 degrees F. Slight fermentation of acid foods may spoil the flavor, but they are not unsafe to eat.

GENERAL EMERGENCY POWER-OUTAGE ACTION

(From the USDA Food Safety and Inspection Service, "Food News For Consumers," Spring 1992.)

Foods to Keep

The following foods should keep at room temperature (above 40 degrees F.) for a few days, but you still should discard anything that gets moldy or has an unusual look. The foods in this group include butter, margarine; fresh fruits and vegetables, dried fruits and coconut; opened jars of salad dressing, peanut butter, jelly, relish, taco sauce, barbecue sauce, mustard, ketchup and olives; hard and processed cheeses; fruit juices; fresh herbs and spices; flour and nuts; fruit pies; bread, rolls, cakes, and muffins.

Foods to Discard

Discard the following foods if kept over two hours at above 40 degrees F.: raw or cooked meat, poultry and seafood; milk, cream, yogurt, soft cheese; cooked pasta, pasta salads; custard, chiffon or cheese pies; fresh eggs, egg substitutes; meat-topped pizza, lunch meats; casseroles, stews, or soups; mayonnaise and tartar sauce; refrigerator and cookie doughs; cream-filled pastries.

NOTE: The FDA says you can refreeze thawed foods that still contain ice crystals or feel cold.

GENERAL FROZEN-FOOD HINTS AND INFORMATION

1. Frozen fish may be of better quality than some so-called fresh fish because it can be frozen aboard the fishing ships or within four hours of being caught, whereas some fish sold in supermarkets can be as much as ten days old by the time you buy it. The bonus is that the frozen fish often costs less than fresh.
2. If you freeze one-quarter to one-half loaf of sliced bread, it won't get moldy or go to waste. Toast frozen slices or thaw them in

the microwave for about ten seconds per slice. If you prefer tor-tillas instead of bread, they, too, can be frozen and thawed in the microwave at ten to twenty seconds per tortilla. Some types of pita bread may crumble after storage in the freezer.

3. Line a cook-and-serve dish with foil or plastic wrap; pour in a portion of soup, stew, or casserole; and freeze. Then, after the food is solid, remove it and wrap the food-block airtight for storage. The meal will fit into the cook-and-serve dish when it's time to thaw, and you will still have the use of the dish in the meantime.

4. Keep a clean 1-quart recycled plastic container in the freezer and pour all leftover vegetables into it. When it's full, brown a chopped onion (and a pressed garlic clove, too, if you like garlic), add the leftover-vegetable ice-block together with enough liquid to cover it up to about an inch or so, and a chicken- or beef-bouillon cube or its equivalent for each cup of total liquid which includes any liquid frozen with the veggies. Simmer for about twenty minutes to make semi-homemade vegetable soup. Add salt and pepper (and other seasonings or herbs) to taste. Before serving your soup, you can add leftover noodles or rice, if you have them. Sprinkle the top of each portion of soup with grated Parmesan cheese for extra flavor.

Or: You can mix a package of dried onion soup with the vegeta-bles, adding enough water to get the liquid required in the soup-package directions; simmer to blend flavors.

NOTE: *Always* mark packages with the date and to identify con-tents; so many things look the same when they are frozen into a lump that identification for any reason is a challenge. And, like the rule for canned foods, "When in doubt, throw it out"—if a food has an "off" odor or appearance, discard it.

SUGGESTED FREEZER STORAGE TIMES FOR SELECTED FOODS

1. Beef: Six to twelve months

2. Cooked Foods: Varies greatly according to product and prepara-tion.

3. Fish: a. Moderate-to-high oil content (like mackerel, mullet, croaker), one to three months

b. Low oil content (like flounder, red snapper, redfish, trout), three to six months

4. Fruits and Vegetables: One year or less

5. Lamb: Six to nine months

6. Liver: One to two months

7. Oysters: One to two months

8. Fresh Pork: Three to six months

9. Sausage: One to three months

10. Poultry: Six months

11. Shrimp: a. In shell, six to twelve months. (Remove heads, which contain fat that tends to get rancid.)

b. Peeled and deveined, three to six months

STORING FRESH FOODS

Here are some hints from my files and from Howard Hillman's *Kitchen Science* (Boston: Houghton Mifflin Co., 1981 and 1989).

1. All Fruits and Vegetables: If stored in an airtight environment, such as the tightly closed plastic bag from the supermarket, fruits and veggies will use up all the available oxygen and expel carbon dioxide. As a result, they actually "suffocate" and then lose color, flavor, texture, and nutrients.

HINT: On the bottom of the fruit and vegetable crispers in your refrigerator, place several paper towels to absorb excess moisture or a plastic doily, if you can find one, to help air to circulate.

2. Bananas and Oranges: Bananas too green to eat? Store them in a paper bag with apples, which give off the ethylene gas that accelerates ripening.

NOTE: Forget the old commercial jingle that said you should never put bananas in the refrigerator. If the bananas are beginning to turn brown before you can eat them, put them in the fridge to slow down the ripening process. The cold will kill cells in the skin and make it brown, but the banana inside will stay fresh for several more days.

3. Carrots and Celery: An ice-water soak will restore limp carrots and celery sticks; but, when celery is fresh, soaking can have the opposite effect.

HINT: For instant celery- and carrot-stick snacks and broccoli and cauliflower bits ready-cut for salad, check out the bagged veggies in the produce section. Many supermarkets have the four vegetables in combination, bags of ready-to-eat baby carrots and celery, or baby carrots alone. They will keep well in the bag. If you want to store the veggies for longer than a few days, you can place them in a flat, sealed container with a wet paper towel placed over the top of the veggies to add moisture without soaking the vegetables.

HINT: If you are lucky enough to have received a floral gift from a florist in a tall pressed-glass vase, you have the perfect crisper for whole celery stalks. Just separate the stalks, wash, cut off the leaves to freeze for flavoring stews or soups, and then poke the whole lot into the vase with some water for a "snack bouquet."

4. Lettuce: Salad is a standby vegetable course or main meal when you cook for one. The meal is merely assembled on the plate, and cleanup is minimal.

Iceberg lettuce keeps longer than other types. Store for up to two weeks unwashed in a sealed plastic bag with a paper towel until ready to use.

NOTE: Never store unwrapped lettuce near such ethylene-producing fruits as apples, bananas, and pears because ethylene speeds up decay in lettuce. Leaf lettuces should also be stored unwashed in a plastic bag, but they will keep for only about a week.

HINT: If you don't feel like tearing up greens for a salad each day, here's a trick with leaf lettuce such as Boston, Bibb, red tip, romaine, etc.: Separate leaves and wash under running water; gently shake off water.

Tear up leaves in bite-sized pieces and place in a plastic bowl that can be sealed tightly. The bowl should be large enough so that the pieces aren't packed. Place two or three paper towels on top, then store the bowl of lettuce *upside down*. The towels will absorb the excess moisture so that the salad dressing will adhere. When you store the bowl upside down, each time you remove a portion, you will be removing the "bottom" layer, which has held the weight of the other leaves; the other leaves will keep longer because they were not bruised.

Green salad stored in this way will be fresh and crisp for four to five days. To make a salad, just grab a handful or two and put it in a bowl, replace the wet paper towels to keep the remaining lettuce moist, reseal, and return the bowl to the fridge.

5. Onions and Potatoes: Don't store onions and potatoes together. Onions give off gases that alter the flavor of the potatoes, and the potatoes' moisture makes the onions sprout.

6. Potatoes: Potatoes should not be stored in the refrigerator, because the starch in them turns to sugar.

If you buy a bag of potatoes, add an apple to the potato bag for storage. Apples give off ethylene gas, which helps prevent sprouting.

NOTE: Prolonged exposure to light causes potatoes to become tinged with green. Green-tinged potatoes (and potato sprouts) have a bitter taste, and the tainted areas will contain at least some level of toxic solanine—not enough to kill you, but enough to make you wish you hadn't eaten that potato! So cut it away if you want to use that potato.

Test to Determine Your Nutritional Health

Are your eating habits in a rut? And is that rut not a path to nutrition? When you don't have anyone else to please with food selections, it's easy to fall into a pattern of food choices that may or may not be healthy.

The following test is from the "Tufts University Diet and Nutrition Letter," May 1992. It was developed and distributed by the Nutrition Screening Initiative, a project of the American Academy of Family

Physicians, the American Dietetic Association, and the National Council on Aging. It gives the often-overlooked warning signs of poor nutritional health.

Read the statements, add up the points shown in parentheses for all of the "yes" answers, then compare your nutrition score to the key scores shown at the end:

- I have an illness or condition that made me change the kind and/or amount of food I eat. (2)
- I eat fewer than two meals per day. (3)
- I eat few fruits or vegetables or milk products. (2)
- I have three or more drinks of beer, liquor, or wine almost every day. (2)
- I have tooth or mouth problems that make it hard for me to eat. (2)
- I don't always have enough money to buy the food I need. (4)
- I eat alone most of the time. (1)
- I take three or more different prescribed or over-the-counter drugs a day. (1)
- Without wanting to, I have lost or gained ten pounds in the last six months. (2)
- I am not always physically able to shop, cook, and/or feed myself. (2)

If your nutritional score is:

0 to 2: *Good!* Recheck your score in six months.

3 to 5: You are at *moderate* nutritional risk. Find out what you can do to improve your eating habits and life-style. Your health department or local office on aging, senior nutrition program or senior citizens center can help. Recheck your nutritional score in three months.

6 or more: You are at *high* nutritional risk. The next time you see your doctor or other qualified health or social-service professional, take this checklist along. Discuss your problems and ask for help to improve your nutritional health.

REMINDER: Warning signs suggest risk but do not represent diagnosis of any condition.

NOTE: Senior citizens are the fastest-growing population segment. By the year 2030, the youngest of the baby-boom set will celebrate their sixty-fifth birthdays, and more than one of every five people in the U.S. will be seniors. The concern is that the elderly are the single largest high-risk group for malnutrition because an older person's body doesn't correct nutritional imbalances as well as a younger person's; about 45 percent take multiple prescriptions that can affect nutrient absorption and appetite; age diminishes taste and smell and therefore the satisfaction from food, which results in a decreased appetite.

New FDA Nutrition Guidelines

The basic-food-group nutritional guidelines per day have changed from an emphasis on protein foods (meats, poultry, fish) to a greater emphasis on the bread, cereal, rice, and pasta foods and the inclusion of less fat (20 percent [ideal] to 30 percent [maximum] of total intake). Instead of the old basic four food groups in a square, the new guidelines take the form of a pyramid.

1. Base Food Group, Foundation of the Diet

6 to 11 servings of breads, cereals, and other grain products (including whole-grain products); rice and pasta.
One serving can be: 1 slice of bread; ½ hamburger bun or English muffin; a small roll, biscuit, or muffin; 3 to 4 small or 2 large crackers; ½ cup cooked cereal, rice, or pasta; 1 ounce of ready-to-eat breakfast cereal.

2. Next Tier of the Pyramid

2 to 4 servings of the fruit group; 3 to 5 servings of the vegetable group.

Fruit Group (includes citrus, melon, berries, and other fruits)
One serving can be: a whole fruit such as a medium apple, banana, or

Food Guide Pyramid

A Guide to Daily Food Choices

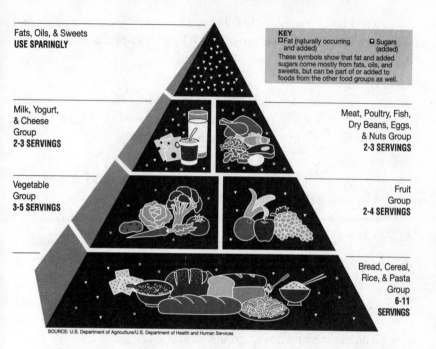

Fats, Oils, & Sweets
USE SPARINGLY

KEY
☐ Fat (naturally occurring and added)   ☐ Sugars (added)
These symbols show that fat and added sugars come mostly from fats, oils, and sweets, but can be part of or added to foods from the other food groups as well.

Milk, Yogurt, & Cheese Group
2-3 SERVINGS

Meat, Poultry, Fish, Dry Beans, Eggs, & Nuts Group
2-3 SERVINGS

Vegetable Group
3-5 SERVINGS

Fruit Group
2-4 SERVINGS

Bread, Cereal, Rice, & Pasta Group
6-11 SERVINGS

SOURCE: U.S. Department of Agriculture/U.S. Department of Health and Human Services

Sources for Dietary Pyramid Foods: *Preparing Foods & Planning Menus Using the Dietary Guidelines,* a booklet from U.S. Department of Agriculture, Human Nutrition Information Service, Home and Garden Bulletin no. 232–8.

orange; a half grapefruit; a melon wedge; ³/₄ cup of juice; ¹/₂ cup of berries; ¹/₂ cup of cooked or canned fruit (best canned in juice instead of heavy syrup); ¹/₄ cup dried fruit.

Vegetable Group (includes dark-green leafy, deep-yellow, legumes such as dry beans and peas, starchy and other vegetables)
One serving can be: ¹/₂ cup of cooked vegetables; ¹/₂ cup of chopped raw vegetables; 1 cup of leafy raw vegetables, such as lettuce or spinach.

Include all types regularly and eat dark-green leafy vegetables and dry beans and peas several times a week.

3. Third Tier of the Pyramid

2 to 3 servings of meat, poultry, fish, and alternatives of dry beans and peas, eggs, seeds and nuts group; 2 to 3 servings of the milk, yogurt, and cheese group.

Meat Group
One serving can be: Amounts to total 5 to 7 ounces of cooked lean meat, poultry, or fish a day. Count 1 egg, ½ cup cooked beans, or 2 tablespoons peanut butter as 1 ounce of meat.

Dairy Group
One serving can be: 1 cup of milk; 8 ounces of yogurt; 1½ ounces of natural cheese; 2 ounces of process cheese.

4. Top Tier of the Pyramid

Avoid or use sparingly fats, oils, and sweets. If you drink alcoholic beverages, do so in moderation.

NOTE: Many foods contain fats, oils, and sweets (obviously or hidden), so you can get adequate amounts of them without adding them to your diet if you eat the other food groups as suggested.

Restaurant Eating with the New Dietary Guidelines

Although fast-food restaurants tend to have set food-preparation methods, chefs in more expensive restaurants usually try to accommodate the needs of their customers—it's good business.

If you have very special dietary needs, ask if they can be met when you make reservations. For example, if you are a vegetarian, ask if you can have a special vegetarian meal; a creative chef will see it as a challenge!

Don't forget that you can order special meals on airlines if you call in advance. Ask about low-fat, vegetarian, Kosher, diabetic meals, etc., when you make your flight reservations; most airlines require special-menu requests to be submitted twenty-four to forty-eight hours in advance.

APPETIZERS

Select steamed seafood, raw vegetables, or fruit. Go easy on rich sauces, dips, and batter-fried foods such as cheese sticks, vegetables, and chicken pieces. Avoid filling up on high-fat and/or salty foods such as chips, peanuts, and pretzels.

SOUPS

Order a cup instead of a bowl of soup if it's the appetizer course. Or, order soup and a dinner salad instead of an entree. Broth or tomato-based soups are lower in fat than creamed varieties. Soups made with lentils, beans, or split peas offer added starch and fiber. Most soups are high in sodium.

BREADS

Along with other baked goods, breads vary greatly in amount of fat or sugars. Croissants, biscuits, and hush puppies are higher in fat than most other breads. Sweet rolls and sticky buns are higher in sugars and fat than loaf bread. Butter and spreads add fat and calories. Note also that many crackers are high in fat and sodium.

ENTREES

1. Select meat, fish, or poultry that has been broiled, grilled, baked, steamed, or poached instead of fried. But, because many broiled or grilled entrees may be prepared with a lot of fat, ask to have your entree cooked without added fat or ask to have lemon juice, wine, or just a bit of fat used.

2. Choose dishes flavored with herbs and spices instead of smothered in rich sauce, gravy, or dressing.

3. If fried foods are the only choice, remove the skin or breading and take a smaller helping to avoid fat and sodium. Steamship round of beef

is leaner than prime rib or spareribs, and stir-fried mixtures are usually made with less oil.

4. Ask if you can be served only a half portion, or eat what you want and ask for a take-home bag.

VEGETABLES/SALADS

Look for vegetables seasoned with lemon, herbs, or spices instead of fat and salt. Have a tossed salad or baked potato instead of fries or chips. Go easy on prepared salads containing a lot of mayonnaise, salad dressing, or oil.

DESSERTS

It's best to wait to order dessert until after you've eaten your dinner. Then, you'll know if you really want one or if you are already too full to enjoy dessert. If fruits aren't available, try sherbet, fruit ice, or sorbet. If you decide to have a rich dessert such as pie, cake, or pastry, get a friend to split it with you. Or, just have a cup of tea or coffee instead of dessert. Even if you add a teaspoon of real sugar to satisfy your sweet tooth, you will have added only 16 to 20 calories instead of hundreds of calories from a rich dessert.

BEVERAGES

Water really does quench your thirst, and it's low-cal, too! Or, have a nonalcoholic "cocktail" of fruit juice mixed with seltzer or mineral water or a glass of tomato juice with a twist of lemon or lime.

If you drink alcoholic beverages, order liquor mixed with water or seltzer instead of sweetened mixers. Have a glass of wine instead of a carafe or try a wine spritzer (wine and seltzer water).

FAST-FOOD SELECTION

Fast-food restaurants are making efforts to reduce the fat content in their products, however some foods still have an extremely high fat content. Here are ten ways to cut at least some of the F-A-T from F-A-S-T foods:

1. Substitute mustard, taco sauce/salsa or, diet salad dressings for mayo or special sauces on burgers or broiled chicken sandwiches. Also, order the smallest-portion burger and look for grilled lean burgers or grilled chicken instead of fried. Ask for your sandwich to be garnished with lettuce, tomato, onions, and pickles instead of bacon strips and cheese.

2. Put light dressings on salads. If the fast-food restaurant you frequent doesn't offer them, buy small individual-portion packets of light dressings and carry a selection of them in a zipper bag in your purse or briefcase.

3. Order low-fat fruit-sweetened muffins such as apple bran instead of Danish; choose a bagel instead of a croissant or biscuit.

4. If you order a taco salad, don't eat the shell that holds it. A bean burrito has as many calories but less fat and saturated fat than a serving of nachos. It is salty, though.

5. Top your pizza with mushrooms, peppers, and onion instead of pepperoni or sausage and ask for half the cheese.

6. A salad from the salad bar is a low-fat meal until you add high-fat dressings, potato/macaroni salad, or slaw dripping with mayo, olives, high-fat cheeses, real bacon bits, etc.

7. Order a baked potato or mashed potatoes instead of fries. When you order a baked potato, one pat of margarine provides less fat than such toppings as cheese, chile/cheese, bacon/cheese or broccoli/cheese. Try topping your potato with diet salad dressing to moisten and flavor it.

8. Peel the skin off fried chicken. The center breast is the leanest part; fattest parts are thighs and wings; drumsticks and side breasts are in the middle range, fat-wise.

9. Instead of a milk shake, order a diet soda, plain tea, or coffee, low-fat milk or juice.

10. Instead of a fried pie or other pastry for dessert, have a nonfat frozen yogurt or nonfat soft-serve ice cream. At the ice-cream shop, order sorbet or ice instead of ice cream; the smaller sugar cone has fewer calories than the larger waffle cone.

KITCHEN HINTS CHECKLIST

- Put foil on the bottom of the toaster oven for easy cleaning.
- Put a red dot on the oven controls to mark "off" button.
- Have one shelf in the fridge just for leftovers.
- Tape a list of leftovers on the fridge door.
- Buy in large quantities and separate when you get home.
- Buy a cookbook specially designed for singles.
- On your day off, make several dinners and freeze.
- Put leftover coffee in fridge for quick iced coffee.
- Use toaster oven for smaller meals to save electricity.
- Use baking soda in place of abrasives for cleaning.
- Don't add salt to dried beans; it causes them to toughen.
- If you've added too much salt to a dish, add raw potato slices, cook until soft and remove.

CHAPTER TWO

Quick and Easy Recipes

Breakfast

There's no excuse for not getting a good start with a healthy breakfast. Just check out the supermarket frozen-food sections for toaster treats and microwavable goodies! Also, cooked cereal is easy if you make one portion in the microwave according to the directions on the cereal box.

Try adding yogurt to your cold cereal instead of milk for extra nutrition and a different texture and taste. Or, try adding dry oatmeal to your fruit yogurt for a filling "power breakfast." And, there are no "breakfast police" to arrest you if you prefer sandwiches or last night's dinner (reheated or cold) to start off your day. However, I wouldn't rationalize like an acquaintance of mine who eats cake for breakfast because, she says, "it has eggs in it and eggs are breakfast food!"

Cake really isn't a good breakfast, but a shake can be. Try the California Sunrise Surprise below.

CALIFORNIA SUNRISE SURPRISE

I discovered this recipe on a menu in California. In print, it seems pretty unappetizing but trust me when I say that it's a good-tasting, filling, and portable breakfast-in-a-hurry "shake."

METHOD:

1. In a blender, mix 8 ounces yogurt (standard container), about ¼ to ½ cup low-fat milk (enough milk to thin the yogurt), about ¼ cup of any breakfast cereal you like, and some sweetener or honey (or berries, if you are lucky enough to have some) to taste.

2. Swirl for just a few seconds, and it's ready to drink.

NOTE: One of my friends said that this recipe sounded like a Heloise homemade beauty facial, but then she tried it and liked it—to drink, that is, not as a facial!

HINT: Quick-clean your blender by filling it about half full of cold water and adding a drop or two of liquid dishwashing detergent, put on the top, then whirr a few seconds. Rinse and let dry.

EXOTIC EXTRACT COFFEES

When you live alone, buying a bag of expensive gourmet coffee is a nice thing to do for yourself, but then you have a choice—drink your hazelnut-mocha coffee until you never want to see a nut or a mocha ever again or keep the gourmet coffee in your freezer and bring it out only when you are in the mood.

Here's a Heloise alternative: Keep several flavored liquid extracts on hand such as chocolate, black walnut, rum, brandy or vanilla to add to your regular coffee when you're in the mood for something different. The extracts keep for a long time on the shelf and can be added to regular high-octane coffee or decaf for flavor without extra calories or extra cost.

NOTE: You can substitute cocoa for chocolate extract. For extra-rich flavor, you can substitute a tablespoon or so of ice cream (vanilla or chocolate) for milk or coffee cream.
For 1 cup: Add a couple of drops of your favorite extract to taste to coffee.
For 8 cups: Add ½ teaspoon extract to the pot of coffee.

Eggs

Eggs can be a nutritious substitute for meat/protein (one egg substitutes for 1 ounce meat, fish, or poultry) in a vegetarian diet or just plain quick-and-easy basics for a variety of quick one-pan meals.

If you are restricting eggs in your diet, try replacing eggs in your favorite recipes with egg substitutes; use proportions suggested by directions on the egg-substitute carton.

NOTE: If you must restrict cholesterol levels in your diet, egg yolks are usually restricted but egg whites can be freely eaten. Generally, two egg whites or two egg yolks can substitute for one whole egg in a recipe. One-fourth cup egg substitute equals two egg whites or one whole egg. In baking, replace one whole egg with two egg whites; for each whole egg replaced, add 1 teaspoon oil and reduce liquid in recipe by 1⅓ tablespoons.

(One large egg contains 80 calories, 6 grams of protein, less than 1 gram of carbohydrate, 5 grams of fat [56 percent of calories], 1 gram polyunsaturated fat, 2 grams saturated fat, 2 grams monounsaturated fat, 215 milligrams cholesterol and 65 milligrams sodium.)

Here are some easy egg-cooking methods and recipes from the American Egg Board:

HOW TO HARD-BOIL AN EGG

1. Gently put eggs in a single layer into a deep saucepan that has a cover.

2. Add water to 1-inch depth above the eggs, cover the pan, place over high heat, and let water come to boil. ("Boil" is defined as the point when large, breaking bubbles form in the water.) After the water is at boil, turn off the heat; remove pan from burner if you have an electric stove.

3. Let stand fifteen to seventeen minutes, uncover the pan, and run cold water over the eggs until they are cool, about 5 minutes. Remove eggs from the pan and refrigerate.

To Peel: Tap egg on all sides on the countertop, roll the egg gently between your hands to crackle the shell, and start peeling at the large end of the egg. Hold it under cool running water to help get the shell off quickly.

CAUTION: DO NOT microwave eggs in shells; they will explode.

HINT: When boiling eggs, add a few drops of food coloring and vinegar to the water so you'll know which eggs are boiled when you look in the fridge. You can celebrate Easter any time of the year in *your* house!

SCRAMBLED EGG

1. Beat one egg and 1 tablespoon milk with a fork or wire whisk until well mixed.

2. Melt butter/margarine in a small skillet or spray it with nonstick spray and heat over medium temperature. If using margarine or butter, roll the pan so that the bottom is covered.

3. When the skillet is hot, add egg mixture and push it around the pan with a pancake turner until it looks cooked but is still shiny.

NOTE: Eggs will continue to cook while standing, so don't overcook them.

MICROWAVE SCRAMBLE METHOD

1. Beat egg and milk in a small, microwave-safe bowl until well mixed.

2. Cover with paper towel and cook on HIGH for about one minute, thirty seconds, stirring when you see the egg beginning to cook around the edges. Stir and check for doneness about every thirty seconds and remove when it puffs up around the sides of the dish.

3. Let stand a few minutes to finish cooking.

SCRAMBLED-EGG SANDWICH VARIATIONS

1. Spread peanut butter and/or jelly on bread (or peanut butter on 1 slice and jelly on the other) and add egg.

2. Heat a tortilla (flour or corn) in the microwave for fifteen to twenty seconds just while the egg is standing; place egg into the tortilla and add taco sauce/salsa before folding the tortilla. *My favorite San Antonio breakfast!*

3. Put catsup on a hot dog or burger bun, add egg.

HUEVOS CASAS

Vegetable spray or butter
1 egg
1 teaspoon water
1 tablespoon shredded low-moisture, part-skim mozzarella cheese
1 (7-inch) corn tortilla
2 tablespoons prepared salsa or taco sauce
Shredded lettuce

METHOD:

1. Spray 7-to-8-inch omelet pan or skillet with a light coating of vegetable spray or lightly grease with butter. Over medium-high heat, heat coated pan until just hot enough to sizzle a drop of water.

2. Break and slip egg into pan and immediately reduce heat to low. Cook until edges turn white, about 1 minute. Add water, cover pan tightly to hold in steam, and cook 3 minutes.

3. Sprinkle with cheese, then re-cover pan and continue cooking to desired doneness.

4. Place on tortilla and top with salsa and lettuce.

For ease in eating, lap edges of tortilla over egg to form a roll.

MICROWAVE METHOD:

1. Omit water.

2. Break and slip egg into a lightly greased glass pie plate, saucer, or custard cup. Gently prick yolk with tip of knife or wooden pick. (*Note:* If you don't prick the yolk, it may explode!) Cover with plastic wrap. Cook on 50 percent power just until egg is at almost desired doneness, about 2 to 2½ minutes.

3. Remove from oven and sprinkle with cheese. Let stand, covered, until desired doneness, about 30 seconds to 1 minute.

4. Place tortilla on serving plate, then cook on full power until warm, about 15 to 30 seconds.

5. Top with egg, salsa, and lettuce.

For ease in eating, lap edges of tortilla over egg to form a roll.

(Total fat is 8 grams; cholesterol 216 milligrams.)

EGGS IN POTATO NESTS

Makes 1 or 2 servings.

2 servings prepared instant mashed potatoes
2 tablespoons chopped tomato, well drained
1 tablespoon finely chopped green onion with top or *1 teaspoon instant minced onion*
3 slices canned sliced jalapeños, drained and chopped
2 eggs
1 to 2 tablespoons shredded Monterey Jack cheese

METHOD:

1. Stir tomato, onion and jalapeños into prepared potatoes.
2. In lightly greased pie plate, with spoon, shape potato mixture into two nests, making each center about 2½ inches in diameter.
3. Break and slip one egg into each nest. Sprinkle with cheese, then cover with foil or another pie plate.
4. Bake in preheated 375-degree F. oven until eggs are desired doneness, about 12 to 18 minutes.

MICROWAVE METHOD:

1. Prepare potato nests and slip in eggs as above.
2. Gently prick yolks with tip of knife or wooden pick, then sprinkle with cheese and cover with plastic wrap.
3. Cook on full power until eggs are desired doneness, about 3 to 4 minutes.

PASTA-VEGGIE SCRAMBLE
For egg lovers on cholesterol-lowering diets.

Makes 2 servings.

½ cup halved thin zucchini slices (about 2 ounces)
⅔ cup chopped green onions with tops
⅓ cup julienned sweet red pepper
2 whole eggs
4 egg whites
2 tablespoons grated Parmesan cheese

1 teaspoon garlic salt
³/₄ teaspoon Italian seasoning
¹/₈ teaspoon ground red pepper
4 ounces fettucini or linguine, cooked and drained
4 cherry tomato halves

METHOD:

1. Spray 10-inch omelet pan or skillet with nonstick pan spray. Add zucchini, onions, and red pepper. Cover and cook over medium heat until zucchini is crisp-tender, about 3 minutes.

2. Meanwhile, beat together whole eggs and whites, cheese, and seasonings. Pour over vegetables. Add fettucini and tomatoes. As egg mixture begins to set, gently draw an inverted pancake turner completely across the bottom and sides of pan. Continue until eggs are thickened but still moist. Do not stir constantly. Serve immediately.

(Contains 233 calories; 212 milligrams cholesterol; 268 milligrams sodium; 7 grams fat; 2.7 grams saturated fat; 2.7 grams dietary fiber.)

EGGS FU-YUNG

(adapted from the USDA booklet *Shopping for Food and Making Meals in Minutes Using the Dietary Guidelines*)

Makes 2 patties and 2 tablespoons sauce for each.

EGG MIXTURE:
2 eggs
1 cup fresh bean sprouts
¹/₃ cup chicken or beef, cooked and diced
1 or 2 ounces canned mushrooms, stems and pieces, drained
1 teaspoon instant minced onion
1 teaspoon oil

SAUCE:
¹/₃ cup water
1 teaspoon soy sauce
¹/₂ tablespoon cornstarch

METHOD:

1. Beat eggs with electric mixer or whisk until very thick and light, about 5 minutes. Fold in bean sprouts, chicken or beef, mushrooms, and onion. Heat oil in frying pan over moderate heat. Pour egg mixture by half-cupfuls into the pan to form patties. Brown on one side; turn and brown on other side. Keep warm while preparing sauce.

2. Mix sauce ingredients in small saucepan until smooth; cook over low heat, stirring constantly, until thickened.

3. Serve sauce over patties.

How to Reduce Fat in Recipes for Egg Lovers

You can reduce fat in most recipes by substituting different ingredients for old standbys and by cutting the amounts of other higher-fat ingredients. While a "classic" omelet is made with bacon drippings, bacon, and regular cheddar cheese, the low-fat version will cut fat by more than half with tasty substitutions.

OMELET

2 eggs
2 tablespoons water
Nonstick vegetable spray
¹/₄ cup chopped turkey ham
2 tablespoons shredded low-moisture, part-skim mozzarella cheese

METHOD:

1. Beat together eggs and water. In a 7-to-10-inch omelet pan or skillet over medium-high heat, heat nonstick vegetable-sprayed pan until just hot enough to sizzle a drop of water.

2. Pour in egg mixture. (Mixture should set immediately at edges.) With an inverted pancake turner, carefully push cooked portions at edges toward center so uncooked portions can reach hot pan surface, tilting pan and moving cooked portions as necessary. When top is thickened and no visible liquid egg remains, fill with

bacon or turkey ham and cheese. With pancake turner, fold omelet in half and slide onto plate.

(Contains 228 calories; 15 grams fat; 5 grams saturated fat.)

FILLINGS: Omelets cook so fast that you need to have the fillings ready before you start the eggs. Almost any food can fill an omelet and turn it into a complete meal. Generally, you add one or more filling ingredients to total about $1/3$ to $1/2$ cup for each two-egg omelet (two whole eggs, equivalent amount of egg substitute, or four egg whites). Flavorings can vary, too. Add about $1/8$ to $1/4$ teaspoon of your favorite herb or spice or seasoning blend (salad dressing, soup, or other flavoring mix).

HINT: Some of my readers and other sources suggest filling your omelets with a dollop of yogurt, peanut butter, or jelly, or with diced/sliced fruit when you are bored with traditional fillings.

Be sure to heat refrigerator-cold fillings to serving temperature or to cook raw foods fully before you begin cooking the omelet.

NOTE: A traditional omelet is made with beaten eggs cooked in a pan and rolled or folded; it can hold or be topped with any food from caviar to leftover meat loaf.

A *frittata* is an unfolded Italian version of the omelet and may contain any combination of cooked vegetables, seafood, meat, chicken, or cheese you choose.

MICROWAVE OMELET

1 teaspoon butter
2 eggs
2 tablespoons water
$1/8$ teaspoon salt
Dash pepper

METHOD:

1. In a 9-inch glass pie plate, cook butter on full power until melted, about 45 seconds. Spread to coat bottom of plate.

2. Beat together remaining ingredients until blended. Pour into plate and cover tightly with plastic wrap.

3. Cook on full power about two to three minutes, rotating one quarter turn each thirty seconds. Do not stir. When center is set but still moist, fill, if desired. (It's better to fill omelet when it's slightly underdone; heat retained in eggs completes the cooking.) With a pancake turner, fold omelet in half or roll and slide from pie plate onto serving dish. (You could eat it from the pie plate, but the retained heat of the dish might continue cooking the omelet and make it overcooked and tough.)

NOTE: To make a tender, easily rolled microwave omelet, the secret is to have a tight-fitting cover. Trapped steam helps it cook evenly; no need to stir. Cooking times in this recipe are based on an oven with 650 watts. Consult the book that came with your microwave oven for cooking times. See microwave wattages information in chapter 1 to find out about your oven's wattage.

Potatoes

Potatoes can be a starch course or the whole meal, depending upon what you do with them. The trick with one-serving cooking is to make several potatoes at one time when you boil or bake so that you have leftovers ready and waiting in the fridge for quick meals.

HINT: You don't always have to peel boiled thin-skinned potatoes, such as "new" or red-skinned ones, just because Mom did. Potato skins, boiled and baked, add fiber and nutrition to your diet, and not peeling adds extra minutes to your leisure time. Do scrub potatoes with a vegetable brush before cooking.

QUICK-AND-EASY BAKED-POTATO MEAL

METHOD:
Scrub potato(s), pierce with a fork or ice pick, and cook:

MICROWAVE METHOD:
1. Wrap in waxed paper and bake according to your micro-

wave's directions—usually about 4 minutes on HIGH for one medium to large potato.

To bake more than one potato in the microwave, consult the instruction book that came with your oven; usually it's twice the time for two potatoes, but times vary for more than two potatoes.

HINT: To prevent waxed paper from unfolding from around the potato, use a sheet big enough to allow you to double-fold the lengthwise edges of the paper over each other (like a French seam, if you sew) and to twist the ends shut. (Use this same wrapping method for microwaving corn-on-the-cob.) Then, after the potato is cooked, lift it carefully to the plate and tear off the twisted ends to let steam escape safely; they will rip off easily, so don't attempt to lift a very large potato out of the microwave oven by holding only the twisted paper ends.

HINT: If you can't deal with waxed paper, wrap the potatoes with plastic wrap and pierce. However, be aware that when opening the tighter seal of plastic wrap, escaping steam can burn.

CAUTION: ALWAYS open all wraps and lids from microwave-cooked foods away from your face and protect your hands with mitts.

TOASTER OVEN METHOD:

1. Bake in a toaster oven according to the manufacturer's directions, usually about the same as a conventional oven.

CONVENTIONAL OVEN METHOD:

1. Bake several potatoes at one time in a conventional oven so that you have leftovers—about forty-five minutes to one hour at 375 to 400 degrees F., depending upon potato size.)

HINT: If you don't pierce potatoes with a fork before baking, they will most likely "explode" while baking and make a big mess.

2. When the potato is done (test with fork) cut it in half and "rake" the cut surface with a fork to allow flavorings to penetrate and to "plant" crunchy dry toppings so that they don't fall off as easily.

3. Top with combinations of the following ingredients: yogurt, dried chives, imitation bacon bits, crunchy salad toppings (usually found near the bacon bits in supermarkets), shredded or

grated cheese of choice, heated bottled cheese sauce, canned creamed soup, cooked vegetables or anything else that makes the potato a nutritious meal.

HINT: If you want only dried chives and bacon bits on your potato, you can make the potato moist without adding margarine or butter if, when you cut the potato open and it's still steaming, you sprinkle the surface with imitation butter powder (some are cheese flavored), drizzle on liquid butter substitute, or spray lightly with butter-flavored vegetable spray (the same stuff you use to keep foods from sticking to the pan).

PEKING (DOUBLE-BAKED, STUFFED) POTATOES—A HELOISE CLASSIC RECIPE

This recipe is often requested by readers. It's one of my mother's favorite creations and is true to her style of cooking: Seasonings to taste, a bit of this and some of whatever else you prefer. Enjoy!

Baking potatoes
Milk to moisten
Drop or two yellow food coloring
Bit of margarine
Salt and ground black pepper to taste
Choice of grated cheese
Grated raw onion

OPTIONAL INGREDIENTS:
Garlic juice or salt, to taste
Chopped chives
Sliced tops of green onions
Pimientos

METHOD:

1. Poke holes in potatoes and bake in a conventional or microwave oven until done. (If baking in a microwave, you may want to crisp the skins by baking a few minutes—five or so—in a 400-degree F. conventional oven or toaster oven so that the skins are easier to handle and hold the stuffing better.) Cut each one in half, scoop out the centers with a spoon, and place pulp in a

mixing bowl. Mash while *dry.* (I use my beater for this, but a potato masher will do; so will a fork if you have only a couple of potatoes.) Add a little milk to moisten, a drop or two of yellow food coloring, margarine, and salt and pepper to taste.

2. Grate cheese and raw onion using coarsest holes of the grater or a food processor. Add cheese and onion to mashed potatoes and stir well with a fork. Do *not* beat or use mixer or masher for this. Then refill each baked potato half-shell with this mixture, place in a baking dish, and reheat in a conventional or toaster oven. The potato skins tend to lose their crispness in the microwave oven, but if crisp isn't important to you, reheat in the microwave.

3. To serve, heat until thoroughly warm. After rebaking the potatoes and just before removing them from the oven, I like to sprinkle Parmesan cheese or another cheese on top and let it melt slightly to a brown tinge. Or, add a dash of paprika to give it zing.

If you like garlic, add the optional garlic juice or salt to the mixture before filling the shell or sprinkle the garlic on top before reheating the potatoes. Chopped chives, green onion tops and pimientos are colorful garnishes for these delicious potatoes.

If you bake extra potatoes when you are oven-cooking a meal, you can use them for this recipe without heating up an oven just for one cooking project.

MOTHER'S POTATO SALAD—A CLASSIC HELOISE RECIPE

My mother cooked by taste instead of measure, so this recipe is just a guideline; adjust it to your own taste and the amount you want to make. You can boil a batch of potatoes, make this salad, and then save the rest of the potatoes to add to soup, stew, or to fry when you pan-broil meats.

Potatoes (boiled in jackets)
Enough mayonnaise to moisten
Bit of vinegar to taste
Celery salt to taste

Seasoned salt to taste
A nice amount of chopped pimiento
Dash of pepper
Some chopped hard-boiled eggs
Dab of prepared mustard
Bit of chopped onion (*optional*)
Several chopped stuffed olives (*optional*)
Sprinkling of paprika

METHOD:

1. Boil potatoes in their jackets until done, then peel (or not, if you don't want to) and dice them.

2. In a separate bowl, mix mayonnaise, prepared mustard, vinegar, celery salt, seasoned salt, pimiento, and pepper together and pour over warm potatoes. Add eggs, olives, onion and mix all ingredients carefully but thoroughly.

3. Sprinkle with a bit of paprika for color before serving.

REHEATING LEFTOVER COOKED POTATOES

METHOD:

1. Slice a boiled or baked potato (about one-half inch thickness) and pan-fry slices in the same pan used to pan-broil a steak or other meat. (See "No-Fail Method to Pan-Broil Meat for One," p. 77).

2. Spray the pan with vegetable spray (flavored or not) before adding food to prevent sticking, then spray the tops of the potato slices with the vegetable spray before turning them to brown both sides; the spray will prevent sticking and drying out.

HINT: Add extra flavor to the fried potato rounds or halves by sprinkling them with onion or garlic powder or other herbs and spices.

HINT: If you use garlic or onion powders instead of garlic or onion salts, you can control your salt intake and save money with the less expensive powders.

Chicken

Chicken is relatively inexpensive, easy to cook, and terrific as leftovers. Here are several of my favorite chicken recipes.

PAN-BROILED BONELESS CHICKEN BREASTS

Serves 1.

2 boneless chicken-breast halves
1 or 2 small cloves of fresh garlic, sliced or chopped, or dried garlic bits
Italian-seasoned or plain bread crumbs (optional)
1 teaspoon olive oil, margarine, or other oil
Nonstick vegetable spray

METHOD:

1. Heat a pan that has been sprayed with nonstick vegetable spray, preferably butter- or olive oil–flavored.

2. When the pan is hot enough so that a droplet of water sizzles, sprinkle the pieces of fresh garlic on the areas where you will place the chicken pieces on the pan. Place the chicken breasts on the garlic pieces; they will stick to the meat as it browns.

OPTIONAL METHOD:

If you wish, you can also roll the chicken breast in Italian or plain bread crumbs for extra flavor before frying. (If you substitute dried garlic bits for fresh, sprinkle them on the chicken breasts instead of on the pan because they tend to burn if put on the pan alone.)

1. Spray the top sides of the chicken-breast pieces with vegetable spray to keep them moist and to prevent sticking when you turn them over to brown the other sides. If the meat looks too dry, add about a teaspoon of olive oil, margarine, or other oil. Fry until juices are cooked; don't overcook, or it will be stringy and dry.

2. Serve as a meat course or in a sandwich on a hamburger bun, or on French or other bread. You can top the chicken with bottled sauces of choice if you wish, such as pizza, spaghetti, steak, barbecue, or other favorite sauce.

CHICKEN QUARTERS (LEGS AND THIGHS) FOR MORE THAN ONE MEAL

Chicken quarters
Nonstick vegetable spray
Barbecue or other favorite sauce or *choice of seasoning salt/blend*
   (*Cajun, Mexican, Italian, homemade, or other*)

METHOD:
   1. Cover with foil a pizza or jelly-roll pan (flat like a cookie sheet with half-inch sides to hold juices) and spray foil with nonstick vegetable spray.
   2. Place chicken quarters, drumsticks, or thighs on foil, skin-side up. Drizzle barbecue or other favorite sauce over the chicken pieces. Or, sprinkle chicken pieces liberally on both sides with your favorite seasoning salt/blend before baking.
   3. Bake at 375 to 400 degrees F. (Four to six chicken-leg quarters will take about an hour, depending upon their size.)

HINT: Save energy by baking white or sweet potatoes at the same time, enough for this meal and for leftovers.

NOTE: If seasoning salt is used instead of sauce, these chicken pieces are delicious cold and make good lunch-box sandwich substitutes, if you can refrigerate your lunch until you eat it or if you use a small cooler as a lunch box.

NOTE: This recipe gives you about an hour to pamper yourself with a relaxing bath or to just sit down and put your feet up! If you are very hungry, make and eat your salad or veggie course to stop yourself from snacking on junk food filler-uppers.

BAKED ITALIAN CHICKEN

1 cut-up chicken or equivalent in chicken parts
Nonfat Italian salad dressing
1 onion, sliced
Sliced potatoes (one, medium, per person or meal), with or without
  skin

METHOD:
1. Spray casserole dish with nonstick spray.
2. Place chicken in dish and drizzle on Italian dressing. Top with sliced onions and sliced potatoes, and drizzle on additional dressing.
3. Bake at 350 degrees F. for about one hour until done.
Serve with a salad.

BAKED ORIENTAL PINEAPPLE CHICKEN

1 cut-up chicken or equivalent in chicken parts
2–3 tablespoons low-sodium soy sauce
20-ounce can of juice-packed chunk pineapple
Paprika, garlic, and onion powder to taste

METHOD:
1. Spray casserole dish with nonstick vegetable spray.
2. Place chicken in dish and sprinkle with paprika, garlic, and onion powder.
3. In a separate bowl, mix soy sauce and juice from pineapple. Baste chicken with the mixture. Pour pineapple chunks over the chicken.
4. Bake at 350 degrees F. for about an hour.
Serve over rice with a salad.

HINT: If you cook a large quantity of rice early in the week, you can reheat leftovers in the microwave when you need them.

Ground Meat

FIFTEEN-MINUTE FRENCH HERB PATTIES
(from the National Livestock and Meat Board)

¹/₂ lb. ground beef (80 percent lean)
¹/₄ teaspoon each of coarse ground black pepper and dried
　rosemary and thyme leaves
1 tablespoon butter
2 small onions, sliced and separated into rings
1 tablespoon Dijon-style prepared mustard

METHOD:

　1. Shape ground beef into two patties, each ¹/₂ inch thick.

　2. Combine pepper, rosemary, and thyme; gently press into both sides of patties.

　3. Melt butter in a small nonstick skillet over medium heat. Cook onions six to eight minutes or until transparent and tender. Stir in mustard. Remove onions and divide evenly between two plates; keep warm.

　4. Place patties in same pan; cook four minutes. Pour off drippings. Turn patties; continue cooking four minutes or to desired doneness. Season with salt, to taste.

　5. Place patties over onions; top with additional Dijon-style mustard, if desired.

NOTE: This makes two servings. To adapt this recipe to make one serving, you could shape the ground beef into two patties, press the herbs into them as directed, then cook one patty and freeze the second one for another meal. You can also slice the onions, wrap one portion in plastic wrap, put it in a zipper bag with the patty, and freeze. Frozen onions can't be eaten raw but can be cooked like fresh ones from the frozen state. To cook the second patty meal, thaw meat patty (not the onion) and follow directions beginning with heating the skillet. Meat thaws most safely in the refrigerator. Take it out in the morning and refrigerate all day until you cook it for dinner.

FIFTEEN-MINUTE MINI-BEEF LOAVES WITH YOGURT-DILL SAUCE
(from the National Livestock and Meat Board)

Makes 2 servings.

BEEF LOAVES
8 ounces ground beef (80 percent lean)
2 tablespoons dry bread crumbs
1/2 small onion, minced
1 tablespoon milk
1 egg, slightly beaten
1 1/2 teaspoons prepared horseradish
1/4 teaspoon each dill weed and salt
Paprika

METHOD:
1. Combine ground beef, bread crumbs, onion, milk, egg, horseradish, dill weed, and salt, mixing lightly but thoroughly.
2. Divide beef mixture into two equal portions; shape into small loaves. Arrange loaves in microwave-safe dish. Sprinkle each loaf lightly with paprika. Cover with waxed paper; microwave at high four to four and one-half minutes, rotating dish one-half turn after two minutes. Let stand five minutes.
3. Top with Yogurt-Dill Sauce.
Serve with assorted vegetables, if desired.

YOGURT-DILL SAUCE
1/4 cup each chopped seeded cucumber and plain yogurt
1 teaspoon minced onion
1/8 teaspoon each dill weed and garlic powder

METHOD:
1. Combine all ingredients.
2. Season with salt, if desired.
3. Cover; refrigerate.

SLOPPY JOES
(Untidy Josephs)

Measuring for this favorite is also "sloppy" because it's one of those "add anything that tastes good" recipes.

1 lb. or so lean ground beef or turkey
1 can vegetable soup, undiluted
Catsup or barbecue or steak sauce, to taste

OPTIONAL INGREDIENTS:
Dried or fresh onion, green pepper, garlic bits
Worcestershire or soy sauce
Tablespoon or so of dried onion soup
Dried mixed vegetables and bouillon (substitutes for canned vegetable soup)
Substitute Denver Brew (p. 80) for bottled barbecue sauce

METHOD:
 1. Brown meat; drain off excess fat.
 2. Stir in other ingredients. Simmer ten to twenty minutes or so to blend flavors and to allow extra liquid to evaporate and thicken the mixture.

Serve on French bread or a bun, over sliced bread (this is too sloppy to stay between two slices of regular bread) or on a baked potato. Store leftovers in the fridge for another meal.

NOTE: This recipe is for either ground beef or turkey. You can substitute low-fat ground turkey in many recipes; to give turkey a "beefier" taste, add crumbled beef bouillon cubes (about 2 cubes per pound of turkey) or the equivalent of beef bouillon granules/powder to the turkey while it's browning in the pan. Remember that bouillon adds salt to a recipe, so adjust the amount of salt you add.

NO-FAIL METHOD TO PAN-BROIL MEAT FOR ONE
(in an iron skillet)

1. Sprinkle a $1/2$-to-1-inch-thick steak or chop (pork, lamb, veal) with meat tenderizer and, if you wish, garlic powder or mixed unsalted seasoning. Allow tenderizer to work as directed on the label; some require fifteen minutes or so to work, and others are instant.

2. Spray an iron skillet with nonstick vegetable spray; heat on high until droplets of water "dance" and sizzle in the pan.

3. Place the meat on the hot skillet. Turn to broil the other side when the meat juices bubble up and show on the surface of the meat. (About four to six minutes, depending upon thickness of the meat and heat in the pan.) To cook rare, turn as soon as juices show; for well-done, turn when juices appear cooked, grayish and opaque. The more well-done, the less tender the meat, but using tenderizer helps prevent toughness and shrinkage.

HINT: You may need to give the skillet a quick spray as you turn the meat to prevent sticking; it depends upon how seasoned your skillet is.

HINT: If you are frying cooked potato slices at the same time, use a large skillet and place the potatoes on the perimeter of the frying pan so they won't crowd the steak or chop when you put it in the pan. Start cooking the potatoes while the pan is getting hot enough for the meat, especially if they are cold from the fridge, because they will take longer to heat and brown than it will take to fry the meat. You can zap the potatoes in the microwave to heat them up before browning them with the meat to speed up the process.

ROAST BEEF HASH
(from the National Livestock and Meat Board)

Makes 4 cups hash.

1 lb. cooked beef, cut into $1/2$-inch pieces or cubes
1 cup chopped green, red, or yellow bell pepper
$1/2$ cup chopped onion

1 tablespoon oil
¹/₂ lb. all-purpose potatoes, peeled and cut into ¹/₂-inch pieces
¹/₂ teaspoon black pepper
¹/₂ cup prepared brown gravy

METHOD:
1. Heat oil in large frying pan.
2. Sauté bell pepper for 3 minutes at high heat. Add cooked beef and potatoes. Stir in ground pepper and gravy.
3. Reduce heat to medium. Cook for twelve to fifteen minutes until potatoes are done, stirring occasionally and pressing down with spatula near the end of cooking time to brown potatoes.

NOTE: Make a full recipe and reheat leftovers or just prepare half of each ingredient listed in the recipe.

SUBSTITUTIONS HINT: If you don't have leftover cooked beef, substitute deli roast beef and leftover boiled or baked potatoes for the raw potato in the recipe. If you don't have any canned gravy on hand, you could add catsup or barbecue sauce for a different flavor.

ITALIAN STIR FRY
(from the National Livestock and Meat Board)

Makes 2 servings.

8 ounces beef round tip steaks, cut ¹/₈ to ¹/₄ inch thick
1 clove garlic, crushed
1¹/₂ teaspoons olive oil
1 small zucchini, thinly sliced
¹/₂ cup cherry tomato halves
2 tablespoons bottled Italian salad dressing
1 cup hot cooked spaghetti
Grated Parmesan cheese

METHOD:
1. Cut beef steaks crosswise into 1-inch-wide strips; cut each strip crosswise in half.
2. Cook and stir garlic in oil in large nonstick skillet over medium-high heat for one minute. Add beef strips; stir-fry one to

one and one-half minutes. Season with salt and pepper. Remove with slotted spoon; keep warm.

3. Add zucchini to same skillet; stir-fry two to three minutes or until crisp-tender. Return beef to skillet with tomato halves and dressing; heat through.

Serve beef mixture over hot pasta; sprinkle with Parmesan cheese.

NOTE: This is an example of a recipe that makes enough for a second reheated meal or, if you wish, you could use only 4 ounces of meat and then you would have a single meal with a greater proportion of pasta and vegetable, if that's your preference. Too often, new cooks are afraid to adjust recipes. Playing with a recipe often yields something better than the original, so feel free to be creative with any recipe in this chapter or in any other book! You are cooking for YOU!

TEN-MINUTE BEEF TENDERLOIN STEAKS WITH BLUE-CHEESE TOPPING
(from the National Livestock and Meat Board)

2 beef tenderloin steaks, cut 1 inch thick, about 4 ounces each
1 tablespoon cream cheese
2 teaspoons crumbled blue cheese
2 teaspoons plain yogurt
1 teaspoon minced onion
Dash white pepper
1 clove garlic, halved
¼ teaspoon salt, divided
1 teaspoon chopped Italian parsley

METHOD:

1. Thoroughly combine cream cheese, blue cheese, yogurt, onion, and pepper; reserve.

2. Rub each side of beef tenderloin steak with garlic. Place steaks on rack in broiler pan so surface of meat is 2 inches from heat source. Broil first side of steak for five to six minutes. Season with half of the salt. Turn; broil second side of the steak for three to

four minutes. Season with remaining salt. Top each steak with half of the reserved cheese mixture. Broil an additional one to two minutes.

3. Garnish with parsley and serve immediately.

NOTE: Two steaks, about 4 ounces each, serve two; for solo dining, make one steak, 4 to 6 ounces, and half of the topping. Salt for one steak would be about ⅛ teaspoon or a mere pinch. Salting meat lightly prevents loss of juices. You can always add more salt after the meat is cooked. If you don't like the cheese topping, use other sauces with the same cooking method.

TEN-MINUTE ANTIPASTO-ON-A-STICK
(from the National Livestock and Meat Board)

A terrific lunch-box idea!

Serves 1.

2 slices cooked lean beef (about 3 ounces), cut into 1-inch strips
3 pitted ripe olives
2 small cherry tomatoes
2³/₄-inch cubes provolone cheese
2 marinated artichoke heart quarters, drained
2 tablespoons Italian dressing
1 cup torn romaine lettuce

METHOD:

1. Roll up beef strips (pinwheel fashion). Alternately weave beef pinwheels, olives, cherry tomatoes, cheese and artichoke heart quarters on two 9-inch bamboo skewers. Place kabobs in a carry-along container; pour dressing over kabobs.

2. Place lettuce in separate carry-along container.

3. Refrigerate several hours or overnight. Transport in an insulated bag. To serve, remove antipasto from skewers and arrange on top of lettuce. Pour remaining dressing over lettuce.

HEARTY VEGETABLE-BEEF SOUP
(from *Shopping for Food and Making Meals in Minutes Using the Dietary Guidelines*, USDA)

This soup can be adapted with substitutions of planned leftovers from your freezer or refrigerator such as chicken for the beef, leftover vegetables instead of the commercial frozen mixed vegetables, or leftover cooked noodles or rice for the uncooked noodles.

NOTE: If adding already-cooked noodles or rice to this recipe, which requires cooking the noodles in the soup, just add the leftover noodles at the end of the cooking time and cook only long enough to heat them through.

Makes about four 1-cup servings.

10½-ounce can unsalted chicken broth
½ cup water
2 cups frozen mixed vegetables for soup
16-ounce can tomatoes, broken up
1 cup beef, cooked and diced
1 teaspoon thyme leaves, crushed
Dash pepper
¼ teaspoon salt
1 bay leaf
2 ounces (about 1¼ cups) narrow-width noodles, uncooked

METHOD:
1. Heat broth and water. Add vegetables, meat, and seasonings. Bring to boil, reduce heat and boil gently, uncovered, for fifteen minutes.
2. Add noodles; cook until noodles are tender, about ten minutes. (If adding already-cooked noodles, simmer for ten minutes after the fifteen-minute gentle boil for a total of 25 minutes; add the cooked noodles during the last five minutes or so of the cooking time.) Remove bay leaf before serving. (Bay leaf, if swallowed can choke a person if it gets stuck, so always remove it!)

COLESLAW WITH YOGURT

This recipe is a low-fat version of traditional slaw.

$^{1}/_{2}$ *cup nonfat plain yogurt*
1 small sweet pickle, minced, or 1 tablespoon pickle relish
2 tablespoons minced green onion
1 teaspoon fresh lemon juice
$^{1}/_{8}$ *teaspoon freshly ground black pepper*
1 cup shredded cabbage
$^{1}/_{3}$ *cup shredded carrot*

METHOD:

1. Combine yogurt, pickle, green onion, lemon juice, and pepper in a bowl.

2. Mix in cabbage and carrot, making sure the yogurt mixture is evenly distributed and all the cabbage and carrot gets well coated.

3. Chill before serving.

NOTE: You can buy packaged shredded cabbage and carrots at some supermarkets and salad bars.

SUMMER FRUIT SALAD
(from the California Raisin Advisory Board)

While this is called a salad, it could be a delicious breakfast, too, or brunch if you can't mix things early in the morning before work. And it can be made with ready-cut fruit from supermarket salad bars to allow minimum waste and spoilage.

Serves 4.

$^{1}/_{4}$ *cup orange juice*
1 tablespoon honey
Equal parts (up to 1 cup of each) strawberry halves, red and/or green grapes, melon balls or hunks
1 banana, sliced
$^{1}/_{4}$ *to* $^{3}/_{4}$ *cup raisins*

TOPPING FOR EACH SERVING:
¹/₄ cup granola cereal
¹/₄ cup vanilla yogurt

METHOD:

1. Measure orange juice and honey into a large bowl and mix. Add fruit.

2. Spoon fruit mixture into serving bowl; top each serving with granola and yogurt.

3. Garnish with a whole strawberry if desired.

HELOISE'S HUMDINGER OF A SALAD

I cook the way my mother did—without exact measurements. You can change the proportions of the ingredients, too, depending upon your taste. I have a friend who uses a smaller can of tuna but makes up for the volume with shredded carrots or cooked peas because she likes veggies more than meat or fish.

6¹/₂-ounce can tuna, chicken, or turkey
3 celery stalks
1 egg, hard-boiled and diced
4-ounce can sliced mushrooms
10 or 12 black olives
Mayonnaise or salad dressing to bind mixture
1 to 2 tablespoons prepared hot mustard, to taste
Salt, pepper, and celery salt, to taste

METHOD:

1. Slice the celery stalks very thin on the diagonal, instead of chopping.

2. Slice the black olives, using any amount you like.

3. Add seasonings to taste and just enough mayonnaise or salad dressing to bind the ingredients. (The amount of dressing is a matter of taste; add about 2 tablespoons to start and then add a tablespoon at a time until you get the salad as moist as you like it.) Mix together.

Serve on a bed of lettuce, sprinkle with a dash of paprika for extra garnish. This salad tastes better if refrigerated for a few hours but can be eaten at once, and it sure stretches a can of tuna, chicken, or turkey!

TEN-MINUTE BEEF SALAD WITH CURRY DRESSING
(from the National Livestock and Meat Board)

Serves 2.

6 ounces thinly sliced cooked beef, cut into $1/2$-inch strips
2 cups torn leaf lettuce
$1/4$ cup shredded carrot
2 tablespoons raisins
2 tablespoons reduced-calorie mayonnaise
2 tablespoons plain low-fat yogurt
$1/2$ teaspoon curry powder, or to taste
1 teaspoon fresh lemon juice

METHOD:

1. Place cooked beef strips, lettuce, and carrot in medium bowl. Toss lightly; sprinkle with raisins. Cover tightly; chill.

2. Combine mayonnaise, yogurt, curry powder, and lemon juice. Cover tightly; chill.

3. To serve, pour dressing over salad; toss.

NOTE: To make only one serving, use half of each ingredient. Or, adjust the amounts to have more of whatever you like; for example, if you like to fill up on lettuce, just use half of the meat and all of the other ingredients.

Heloise's Classic Quick-and-Easy Sauces

MUSTARD SAUCE FOR FISH

6 tablespoons butter or margarine, melted
3 tablespoons fresh lemon juice
2 tablespoons Dijon mustard

METHOD: Heat butter, lemon juice, and mustard in a small sauce pan and mix thoroughly. Serve on grilled fish.

HINT: To save extra dish cleanup, make the sauce in the microwave in a flat microwave-safe oven-to-table dish and then place the grilled fish on the sauce. Then, "present" the dish to yourself the way many restaurants do these days with the entree on the sauce instead of under it.

NOTE: When pan-broiling, broiling, or cooking fish in the microwave, fish is done when it flakes if you cut it with a fork. Cooking times depend upon how thick the pieces are.

RED CHILI SAUCE

A perfect piquant sauce to serve with meats, on a baked potato, or to dip raw veggies in.

Makes ²/₃ cup.

¹/₂ cup dairy sour cream
2 tablespoons mayonnaise
1 tablespoon chili powder
¹/₂ teaspoon ground cumin

METHOD: Mix all ingredients in a blender until smooth. Refrigerate in a small container for up to five days.

DENVER BREW
(barbecue sauce for meats)

*A hearty sauce to use for barbecue or when baking chicken parts.
(See recipes in this chapter.)*

Makes 1¹/₃ cups.

1 cup dark beer
¹/₄ cup vegetable oil
2 tablespoons plus 1¹/₂ teaspoons Dijon mustard
2 garlic cloves, minced
¹/₂ teaspoon salt
¹/₄ teaspoon freshly ground black pepper
¹/₄ teaspoon sugar

METHOD: In a medium bowl whisk all ingredients together. Use
immediately or pour into a container with a tight-fitting lid. Cover
tightly; refrigerate up to seven days.

Rice and Pasta

Rice can be a nutritious low-fat staple if you cook enough for more than
one day's portion and then save the leftovers for fried rice, for adding
filler to soup or bouillon, or for mock rice-pudding dessert. (Add a bit of
milk, cinnamon, and sugar to taste, some raisins or other dried fruit bits,
and reheat in the microwave.) Cooked rice, covered tightly, keeps for
about a week in the fridge.

COOKING RICE

One cup of white or brown rice cooks to a volume of 3 or 4 cups. Follow
package directions given for the kind of rice you've bought.

Generally, you put twice as much water than rice into the pot (2¹/₂
times as much for brown rice); add a bit of margarine or butter or, if you

are avoiding fat, spray the pot with vegetable spray before adding the rice and water; stir, cover and simmer (without picking up the lid to peek inside).

Simmer times vary according to the type of rice. Usually fifteen minutes for instant rice; twenty to twenty-five minutes for parboiled rice; and up to forty-five minutes for brown rice. Simmer until rice is tender and liquid is absorbed.

NOTE: For extra flavor in rice main dishes, cook rice as usual but substitute bouillon for plain water (2 cubes or 2 teaspoons of dried or liquid bouillon for 2 cups of water).

CHICKEN ITALIANO WITH BAKED RICE

This recipe from the Rice Council saves energy—yours and electricity, too. Bake the rice during the last half hour of baking the chicken.

Makes 6 servings.

THE RICE
1 cup uncooked rice
2 cups boiling water
1 tablespoon butter or margarine
1 teaspoon salt

METHOD:
1. Combine ingredients in a buttered (or nonstick sprayed) casserole. Stir. Cover with a tight-fitting lid or heavy-duty foil.
2. Bake at 350 to 375 degrees F. for 25 to 30 minutes or until rice is tender and liquid is absorbed.

THE CHICKEN
12 choice chicken pieces, 2¹/₂ to 3 pounds (drumsticks, thighs, and/or breast halves)
1 envelope (1³/₈-ounce) onion soup mix
10 ³/₄-ounce can condensed cream of mushroom soup
¹/₂ cup dry sherry or chicken broth (make with bouillon)
1 cup drained canned tomatoes

METHOD:

1. Place chicken pieces in a buttered or sprayed large shallow baking dish (about 9 by 13 inches). Sprinkle with soup mix.

2. Blend soup and sherry. Pour over chicken. Add tomatoes.

3. Cover (with foil) and bake at 375 degrees F. for 1 hour or until chicken is tender.

Serve over beds of fluffy rice.

NOTE: Served with yellow squash, a tossed green salad with Italian dressing, and garlic toast, this could be an easy company meal when you don't feel like solo dining. When you make it for yourself, it's delicious if you refrigerate leftovers for other meals.

MOTHER'S FRIED RICE—A HELOISE CLASSIC RECIPE

My mother got this recipe while she lived in China, and it's one of our family favorites. Here, it's adapted to serve one person generously or make two smaller servings.

¹/₂ cup cooked rice
(Use rice that has been cooked and cooled a day ahead or earlier in the day. It's better if it's had a chance to dry out a bit.)
2 slices bacon (diced), with drippings
2 eggs
2 cut green onions (or scallions), tops and all
Leftover bits of pork, beef, or ham, chopped into small pieces (optional)
Soy sauce to taste

METHOD:

1. Brown bacon in a heavy skillet until crisp. Remove bacon and turn down heat.

2. Slightly beat eggs and pour them into the hot bacon drippings. Add rice and onions; mix together. Add bacon and leftover meat. Mix. Add soy sauce until the rice is as brown as you like it.

3. Stir well and cook on low heat 15 to 20 minutes.

Makes one hearty main course portion or two smaller ones.

CONFETTI RICE
(adapted from a Rice Council recipe)

Serves 1.

2 slices bacon
(Or substitute 1 tablespoon butter or margarine and fold in a
   sprinkle of bacon bits just before serving the finished rice)
1 cup cooked rice, cooked in chicken broth
4-ounce can or less sliced mushrooms, drained
$1/3$ to $1/2$ cup cooked green peas
2 tablespoons diced pimientos
1 to 2 teaspoons chopped chives
Salt and black pepper to taste, about a dash

METHOD:
   1. In a skillet, cook bacon until crisp (or heat butter or margarine).
   2. Drain off fat.
   3. Add remaining ingredients to skillet and heat thoroughly.

NOTE: You can play with this recipe and add other meat bits; chopped green, red, and yellow peppers; and green or other onions.

PEPPERONI-MUSHROOM PIZZA
(from the Rice Council)

Makes 4 servings.

$1 1/2$ cups cooked rice
1 egg, beaten
$1/2$ cup (2 ounces) shredded Cheddar cheese
$1/2$ to $3/4$ cup tomato sauce
$1/4$ teaspoon each basil leaves, garlic powder, and ground oregano
1 tablespoon grated Parmesan cheese
1 cup shredded mozzarella cheese, divided
2 ounces pepperoni, thinly sliced
$1/2$ cup sliced mushrooms
1 tablespoon snipped fresh parsley

CONVENTIONAL OVEN METHOD:

1. Combine rice, egg, and Cheddar cheese. Press into buttered (or sprayed) 12-inch pizza pan or 10-inch pie pan. Bake at 400 degrees F. for four minutes.

2. Combine tomato sauce, basil, garlic powder, and oregano. Spread over rice crust. Sprinkle with Parmesan cheese. Layer 1/2 cup mozzarella cheese, pepperoni, and mushrooms. Top with remaining 1/2 cup mozzarella cheese and parsley.

3. Bake at 400 degrees F. for eight to ten minutes.

MICROWAVE METHOD:

1. Combine rice, egg, and Cheddar cheese. Press into buttered (or sprayed) micro-proof 12-inch pizza pan or 10-inch pie pan. Cook uncovered on MEDIUM (50 percent power) for two minutes.

2. Combine tomato sauce, basil, garlic powder, and oregano. Spread over rice crust. Sprinkle with Parmesan cheese. Layer 1/2 cup mozzarella cheese, pepperoni, and mushrooms. Top with remaining 1/2 cup mozzarella cheese and parsley.

3. Cook uncovered on MEDIUM for seven minutes. Let stand five minutes.

GREEN CHILES AND RICE FRITTATA
(adapted from a Rice Council recipe)

Serves 1.

2 tablespoons finely chopped onions
1 tablespoon butter or margarine
2 eggs
2 tablespoons milk
Dash salt
1/4 teaspoon Worcestershire sauce
1 drop hot pepper sauce, optional
1/2 cup cooked rice
1 ounce chopped green chiles, undrained
1/4 medium tomato, chopped
2 tablespoons grated Cheddar cheese

METHOD:

1. In a skillet over medium-high heat, cook onions in butter until tender.

2. In a bowl, beat eggs with milk and seasonings. Stir in rice, chiles and tomato. Pour into skillet.

3. Reduce heat to medium-low. Cover; cook until top is almost set, about five or minutes so. Sprinkle with cheese.

4. Cover, remove from heat, and let stand a few minutes until cheese melts and blends in.

Rice Cakes

Packaged rice cakes can be the base for quick meals, especially if you are counting calories. If you've previously thought rice cakes were too bland, try them again! Here are some recipes from the Rice Council for cooking with rice cakes. The recipes each make four servings. If two servings would be a full meal for you, just use half of the ingredients.

MEXICAN RICE CAKES

A delicious, easy snack or meal with only 87 calories per serving.

Makes 4 servings.

4 rice cakes
1/4 cup picante sauce
1/4 cup refried beans
1/3 cup shredded Cheddar cheese
1/4 cup sliced jalapeño peppers

CONVENTIONAL OVEN METHOD:

1. Place rice cakes on baking sheet.

2. Spread refried beans evenly on each rice cake; top with picante sauce, cheese, then with peppers.

3. Bake at 400 degrees F. for ten minutes. Serve immediately.

MICROWAVE METHOD: Prepare rice cakes as directed above on micro-proof baking sheet. Cook uncovered on HIGH (maximum power) for one and one-half minutes (less time if you make only two servings); rotate after one minute. Serve immediately. (Each serving is only 87 calories, if you are counting!)

PIZZA RICE CAKES

Makes 4 servings.

4 rice cakes
¹/₃ cup pizza sauce
¹/₄ cup each sliced ripe olives, diced green pepper, and sliced mushrooms
¹/₃ cup shredded mozzarella cheese

METHOD:
1. Place rice cakes on baking sheet.
2. Spread pizza sauce evenly on each rice cake; top with remaining ingredients.
3. Bake at 400 degrees F. for ten minutes. Serve immediately.

NOTE: Unlike the Mexican version, microwave directions were not suggested for this recipe.

Pasta

If your favorite starch is pasta, you can substitute it for rice in many recipes. Noodle leftovers also can be cooked in advance and reheated in the microwave or placed in a sieve and reheated by dipping the sieve into boiling water until the noodles are heated. One cup uncooked macaroni or spaghetti (in pieces) weighs about 4 ounces and will about double in bulk when cooked. Most other noodles swell only about one fourth when cooked. So, about 2 cups uncooked (8-ounce bag) yields about 4 cups cooked macaroni or about 6 servings.

HINT: Check out the new-style lasagna noodles which have directions for cooking the noodles in the pan with the sauce to save extra mess.

Lasagna reheats well; in fact, some people think it tastes better the second time around!

NOTE: Cooking pasta in the microwave is possible, but it doesn't really save much time because cooking time is almost the same as on top of the stove.

ORIENTAL NOODLES

This is a very casually measured, play-with recipe because it uses up leftovers and bits of vegetables remaining from salads. Spaghetti, linguini, or vermicelli work best for this recipe, but you can also substitute flat egg noodles if that's all you have cooked.

Salad oil (peanut oil is best)
Cooked leftover vegetables, sliced or diced
Ham, turkey ham, cooked beef, pork, or chicken, cut in bits
Cut up green onions

OPTIONAL INGREDIENTS (about ½ cup each to serve one vegetable lover):
Sliced celery, bok choy, Chinese cabbage
Green, red, or yellow peppers
About ½ to 1 cup leftover noodles
Soy sauce
Bouillon, about 1 cup or less
Oriental sesame oil, hot or mild

METHOD:

1. Heat oil in pan, add cooked veggies or meats, and brown; add fresh veggies and stir-fry until a bit less than crisp; add cooked noodles (you may need to add a bit more oil at this point to prevent sticking).

2. After noodles are heated, add soy sauce to taste. Add bouillon if this mixture is too dry for your taste.

3. Heat thoroughly and serve.

Add sesame oil, if you wish, to the finished recipe.

CAUTION: If this is your first experience with hot sesame oil, be aware that it really is *hot* so be conservative and taste after stirring in only *one drop* or two!

NOTE: I like to spray pans with nonstick vegetable spray when the recipe includes rice or noodles in addition to adding oils; it helps prevent starches from sticking to the pan.

Sandwiches

With all the good grain breads available in stores, a sandwich can be a very fast, easy, and nutritious meal.

Here are some Heloise Classic sandwich fixings that you can make and store in the fridge to be handy when you need them for sack lunches, quickie meals at home, and finger-sandwich or cracker-spread snacks when you have unexpected guests.

NOTE: When the recipe says "salad olives" or "cheapest olives," it's a hint from my mother who taught me that when you plan to chop up the olives anyway, you don't need "premium" or "fancy" olives. Look for green olives labeled "salad olives." These money-saving lower-grade olives compare to "seconds" since there will be bits and pieces of olives mixed in with the whole ones. Of course, sometimes this nonpremium grade will be almost all whole olives anyway, so you can eat the whole olives and save the less-than-perfect ones and pieces for salads.

HINT: If you are cutting calories, spread sandwich fillings on a lettuce leaf or in the groove of a celery stalk.

HINT 2: If you don't like to mix up batches of anything, check out the cheese spreads in the dairy case of your supermarket or shop on Saturdays when many supermarkets dispense samples of various quickie foods. I have a friend who says eating lunch on her supermarket-shopping Saturdays is a matter of "grazing" the free-sample counters.

HELOISE CLASSIC OLIVE-NUT SANDWICH SPREAD

6 ounce softened cream cheese (or low-cal)
1/2 cup mayonnaise (or diet mayo)
1/2 cup finely chopped pecans
1 cup sliced salad olives (see note above)
2 tablespoons olive liquid from the jar
Dash pepper (but no salt)

METHOD: Mix all ingredients well. This spread is better the second day and keeps in the fridge for weeks.

HELOISE CLASSIC PIMIENTO-CHEESE SPREAD

1 pound boxed processed soft cheese
1 cup mayonnaise
1/2 cup super-finely chopped sweet or sour pickles
4 ounces of the cheapest pimientos on the shelf

For variations, add:
Juice from 1 jar of pimientos

*4 ounces chopped salad olives (or, if you have no pimientos, use the
    cheapest pimiento-stuffed green olives on the supermarket shelf)*
Chopped onions to taste

METHOD:

1. Grate cheese coarsely with the large openings of a grater or food processor.

2. Now the kitchen-play part: Layer ingredients as if you are making lasagna on a large piece of waxed paper or plastic wrap. Place wrap on the counter, then start layering. Put down a layer of grated cheese, mayonnaise, pimientos, and handful of pickles. Use a spatula to fold it over and over, starting from the bottom, or knead the layers together with your hands.

NOTE: You could stir up the ingredients in a bowl, but it's easier to work the mixture on a waxed paper–covered flat surface.

3. Repeat the process, folding again and again until you have

used all your ingredients. I divide this up into two batches. Put it in jars, seal well, and pop into the fridge.

If you want a thinner, gooier spread, add the juice from one jar of pimientos and mix well. Vary the spread by adding chopped cheap salad olives and onions.

HELOISE'S CLASSIC PINEAPPLE–CREAM CHEESE SPREAD

8 ounces softened cream cheese
1/3 cup undrained crushed pineapple
1 teaspoon vanilla
Dash of salt
Sugar, to taste (optional)

METHOD: Mix all ingredients thoroughly and spread on fresh sourdough or French bread.

MEDITERRANEAN RAISIN TAPENADE SANDWICH SPREAD
(from the California Raisin Advisory Board)

THE SPREAD:
1/2 cup pitted ripe olives
1/4 cup golden raisins
1 clove garlic
2 tablespoons fresh chopped basil leaves or *2 teaspoons dried basil*
1 tablespoon drained capers
2 tablespoons olive oil
1 teaspoon red-wine vinegar
1/4 teaspoon pepper

THE SANDWICHES:
4 large crusty sandwich rolls
4 lettuce leaves
1/2 pound sliced Jarlsberg or Swiss cheese
2 small tomatoes, sliced
1/2 cup drained, prepared, roasted red peppers

METHOD: In a food-processor bowl, puree olives, raisins, garlic, basil, and capers. Add olive oil, vinegar, and pepper; pulse to combine.

Will keep up to two weeks in the refrigerator.

TO MAKE SANDWICHES: Halve a crusty sandwich roll horizontally; spread each cut side with 1 tablespoon tapenade. Layer bottom half with 1 lettuce leaf, 2 ounces sliced Jarlsberg or Swiss cheese, half a sliced tomato, and 2 tablespoons red pepper. Cover with top of roll, cut-side down.

TEN-MINUTE ONION-'N-PEPPER BEEFSTEAK SANDWICHES
(from the National Livestock and Meat Board)

8 ounces beef round tip steaks, cut ¹/₈ to ¹/₄ inch thick
2 teaspoons vegetable oil
1 small onion, cut into ¹/₄-inch wedges
1 medium jalapeño pepper, cut crosswise into rings (To reduce heat of jalapeño peppers, membranes and seeds may be removed.)
1 small clove garlic, minced
¹/₈ teaspoon salt, if desired
2 kaiser rolls, split
¹/₄ cup chopped tomato

METHOD:

1. Heat oil in large nonstick frying pan over medium-high heat. Add onion, jalapeño pepper and garlic; stir-fry for three to four minutes or until lightly browned. Remove from frying pan; reserve.

2. Add beef round tip steaks to frying pan and cook over medium-high heat for one to two minutes, turning once. Do not overcook. Season with salt, if desired.

3. Place equal amounts of beef on bottom half of each kaiser roll. Top with equal amounts of reserved onion mixture and tomato.

NOTE: This makes two servings. However, if you wish to have one generous meat serving, you could put it all on a large French roll.

FIVE-MINUTE MICROWAVE FRANKFURTER PIZZAS
(from the National Livestock and Meat Board)

Makes 2 servings or 1 hearty serving, especially in a college dorm!

2 beef frankfurters
1 English muffin, split and toasted
1 tablespoon pizza sauce
1 slice (1 ounce) mozzarella cheese, cut in half
¹/₈ teaspoon dried oregano leaves

METHOD:

1. Place muffin halves on paper plate; spread cut sides with equal amount of pizza sauce. Carefully make 5 crosswise cuts into frankfurters, spacing ³/₄-inch apart and cutting almost through. Arrange frankfurter in a circle on each muffin half; cover with a half slice of cheese. Sprinkle with oregano.
2. Microwave at HIGH for 1 minute.

SANDWICH HINTS

1. If the sandwich is to be eaten later, as in noon lunches, butter both bread slices (inner side, of course!) thoroughly to prevent the sandwich filling from making the bread soggy.

NOTE: Cream cheese (regular or diet) can substitute for margarine or butter with some fillings.

2. Save time by buying peanut butter and jelly already mixed and ready to spread.
3. No jelly? Spread peanut butter on both bread slices and sprinkle with cinnamon sugar, drizzle with honey, or sprinkle with 1 to 2 ounces of raisins. Press slices together gently to embed the raisins in the peanut butter.
4. No celery to add crunch to tuna salad? Substitute diced sweet

onion, cabbage core, water chestnuts, apple, pickle, shredded cabbage, or carrots or nut pieces.

5. No tuna? Substitute canned mackerel, sardines, salmon, or shrimp.
6. No time to boil eggs for egg salad? Scramble eggs firm and then chop; use as usual. This makes a tasty quick breakfast or lunch sandwich!

Vegetables

FRESH

If you are accustomed to cooking for a family, remember that fresh veggies won't keep forever. Buy only what you need. Solo portions are easily cooked in the microwave or stir-fried in a bit of oil or bouillon. Please see the microwave cooking hints in chapter 1.

SALAD-BAR VEGGIES

Mix and match salad-bar offerings. Dress with either plain lemon juice, a mixture of two parts vinegar to one part oil, or bottled low-fat dressing.

Add fruits to green leafy and other salad-bar vegetables. For example: Curly endive, romaine, Chinese cabbage, red leaf lettuce shredded and mixed with any of the following: apples, tomatoes, cucumbers, straw-berries, zucchini, carrots, beets, drained canned grapefruit sections, mandarin oranges. Don't be afraid to mix fruits and vegetables. Some good combinations are pineapple chunks with fresh snow peas; orange segments and sliced red onion; apple slices and spinach leaves.

FROZEN

There are two schools of thought on frozen veggies. Some think it's easier to buy single portions of vegetables which come in square, microwave-ready packs. (You can eat out of the pack if you want; Mom's not watching!) The single portions were designed for family dining when not everyone likes the same vegetables but are bought mainly by solo diners for convenience even if they are more costly than other size packages. Others, especially folks who are watching their pennies, think it's better to buy bags of vegetables and just close the bag with a clothespin after removing one portion.

Whatever your system, it's important to eat your daily nutritional requirement of vegetables; and if buying the individual microwave cook-in-the-pack helps you do it, it's certainly worth the extra pennies.

I like the single portions and often make more than one for a meal. After they are cooked, you can sprinkle on Parmesan cheese, imitation butter sprinkles, imitation bacon bits, or any herbs and spices that make your daily vegetables taste less humdrum.

CANNED OR COOKED

Mix several kinds of canned or cooked, chilled beans (kidney or lima beans, green or wax beans, chickpeas or pigeon peas, or others) with thinly sliced onion and celery and a reduced-calorie salad dressing or vinaigrette. Serve on torn bits of green, leafy vegetables.

SALAD-BAR VEGETABLE MEDLEY
(adapted from the USDA booklet *Shopping for Food and Making Meals in Minutes Using the Dietary Guidelines*)

Makes 2 servings, about 3/4 cup each.

1 tablespoon water
1/2 pound or 2 1/2 cups mixed salad-bar fresh vegetables (See note below.)
1/4 teaspoon marjoram leaves
1 tablespoon reduced-calorie French or Italian salad dressing

METHOD:
1. Heat water in frying pan. Add vegetables; sprinkle with marjoram. Cover and cook 5 minutes or until vegetables are tender-crisp.
2. Drain, if necessary.
3. Toss vegetables with salad dressing.

NOTE: Select vegetable pieces that are fairly similar in size, such as broccoli and cauliflower florets, carrot slices, green pepper strips, sliced celery, mushrooms, zucchini slices, etc.

VEGETABLE PANCAKES
(from the National Livestock and Meat Board)

A vegetarian meal feast!

Makes 4 vegetable pancakes.

1/2 cup finely shredded carrot (or shredded zucchini)
1/2 cup finely shredded potato
1 tablespoon minced onion
1/8 teaspoon salt
Dash pepper
1 teaspoon butter
1 teaspoon olive oil
2 tablespoons plain yogurt
1/4 teaspoon grated lemon peel

METHOD:

1. Combine carrot, potato, and onion. Pour off liquid, if necessary. Stir in salt and pepper.

2. Heat butter and oil in large nonstick frying pan over medium heat. Spoon 4 equal portions of vegetable mixture into frying pan and flatten with a spatula.

3. Cook four to six minutes, turning once.

4. Meanwhile combine yogurt and lemon peel. Garnish pancakes with lemon-yogurt mixture.

Heloise's Homemade Seasonings

HINT: You can mix up batches of these seasonings and save them in clean, recycled old spice jars or baby-food jars (supplied by a willing friend). Whenever you mix up a batch for yourself, you can divide the mixture into the jars and give the extras to your friends.

HINT: Never store spices near the stove—they lose their zip.

NO-SALT SPICE

This salt substitute helps if you are avoiding salt in your diet but still want flavorful food. Note that it uses onion and garlic powders, not salts.

5 teaspoons onion powder
1 tablespoon garlic powder
1 tablespoon paprika
1 tablespoon dry mustard
1 teaspoon thyme
¹/₂ teaspoon white pepper
¹/₂ teaspoon celery seeds

METHOD: Mix all ingredients and store in a tightly covered container in a cool, dark place.

SEASONED SALT

This replaces commercial seasoning salts and lets you have the spices you like best.

1 cup salt (or salt substitute, if you avoid salt)
2 tablespoons onion powder
1 teaspoon garlic powder
1 tablespoon celery seed, well ground
2 teaspoons paprika
1 teaspoon chili powder
¹/₂ teaspoon cayenne pepper
1 teaspoon dried parsley flakes, well ground

METHOD: Mix all ingredients together well and store in a screw-top jar. Put the remainder in a salt shaker for table use.

Solo Desserts

Fruit eaten out of your hand, combined with ice cream or yogurt, cooked or baked, can be a simple no-fuss, no-mess dessert. *Try*: A melon wedge topped with a small scoop of fruit sherbet; ice milk or frozen yogurt topped with fresh unsweetened strawberries or other fruit. Or, fruit slices spread with cheese; fruit served with cheese, such as pears with Swiss, apples with Cheddar, grapes with just about any cheese.

BASIC FRUIT SALAD

Any combination of cut-up fruit that you like with or without salad dressing.

For example: Combine 1/2 cup unpeeled apple, 1/2 cup sliced banana, 1/2 cup grapefruit sections (cut up), about 2 tablespoons juice from grapefruit or pineapple, 1/3 cup halved grapes, and 1/3 cup drained juice-packed pineapple tidbits. If you mix the apple, banana, and grapefruit sections with juice, it prevents darkening of the apple and banana, then add grapes and pineapple and chill.

Substitute other fruits such as peaches, nectarines, melon, berries, or apricots as you wish when they are in season. You can buy seasonal fruits already cut up at some supermarket salad bars if you don't want to bother cutting up your own.

Add zippy flavor to your fruit salads and keep some fruits from darkening by sprinkling them with lime or lemon juice (fresh or from a "squirt" plastic container of lime or lemon juice). Or, add flavor with ground nutmeg, cinnamon, or crushed gingersnaps.

FRUIT SALAD PARFAIT

Alternate layers of fresh fruit with plain lowfat yogurt (or vanilla-flavored yogurt) in a parfait glass. Sprinkle top with cinnamon and/or crushed ready-to-eat cereal of your choice.

Combine a variety of diced fresh fruits, toss lightly with a bit of fruit juice such as apple or orange, sprinkle with ground nutmeg, cinnamon, or crushed gingersnaps.

BAKED FRUIT

Bake or broil fruits such as pears, bananas, apples, peaches, or grape-fruit halves and enhance the flavor with a sprinkle of cinnamon or nutmeg.

NOTE: Bake a whole ripe banana, with peel on, on a cookie sheet at 350 degrees F. for twenty minutes. Split baked fruit with a knife and sprinkle with cinnamon or nutmeg.

BAKING WITH FRUIT

If you bake muffins, pancakes, or quick breads, try adding dried apri-cots, raisins, bananas, blueberries, or apples for extra flavor and fiber. Bake double batches and freeze for a lazy Sunday.

READY-MIX FOR BAKING BISCUITS OR MUFFINS
(from the USDA booklet *Shopping for Food and Making Meals in Minutes Using the Dietary Guidelines*)

Makes about 8 cups.

BAKING MIX
3 cups whole-wheat flour
3 cups all-purpose flour
3 tablespoons baking powder
1 1/2 teaspoons salt
3/4 cup nonfat dry milk
3/4 cup vegetable shortening

METHOD: Mix dry ingredients thoroughly. Cut in shortening with pastry blender, mixer, or two forks until fine crumbs are obtained and shortening is evenly dispersed. Store, tightly covered, in refrigerator. Use within 3 months for biscuits or muffins as di-rected below.

BISCUITS (USE READY-MIX, ABOVE)

Makes 8 biscuits.

¹/₃ cup water
1¹/₂ cups Ready-Mix

METHOD:

1. Preheat oven to 425 degrees F.
2. In a large bowl, add most of the water to the mix. Add the rest of water as needed to make a dough that is soft but not sticky. Shape dough into a ball.
3. Pat or roll dough into a rectangle about 8 by 4 inches; cut into eight pieces.
4. Place on an ungreased baking sheet and bake until lightly browned, about fifteen minutes.

APPLESAUCE MUFFINS (USE READY-MIX, ABOVE)

Makes 8 muffins.

1¹/₂ cups Ready-Mix
1 tablespoon sugar
¹/₂ teaspoon ground cinnamon
1 egg white, slightly beaten
¹/₂ cup applesauce, unsweetened
¹/₄ cup water

METHOD:

1. Preheat oven to 400 degrees F.
2. Grease muffin tins.
3. In a large bowl, stir mix, sugar, and cinnamon together. Mix egg white, applesauce, and water thoroughly; add to dry ingredients. Stir until dry ingredients are barely moistened (batter will be lumpy).
4. Fill muffin tins two thirds full and bake until lightly browned, about 20 minutes.

HANDY SUBSTITUTIONS

When the recipe calls for	*You can substitute*
one small onion	one teaspoon onion powder or one tablespoon dried minced onion
one cup tomato juice	one-half cup tomato sauce plus one-half cup water
one square unsweetened chocolate	three tablespoons unsweetened cocoa powder plus one tablespoon shortening or cooking oil
one cup of refined sugar	one cup packed brown sugar or two cups sifted powdered sugar
one teaspoon baking powder	one-half teaspoon cream of tartar plus one-fourth teaspoon baking soda
one cup whole milk	one-half cup evaporated milk plus one-half cup water, or one cup water plus one-third cup nonfat dry milk powder
one tablespoon cornstarch for thickening	two tablespoons all-purpose flour
one cup bread crumbs	three-fourths cup cracker or cereal crumbs
one-eighth teaspoon cayenne pepper	four drops of hot pepper sauce
one cup cream cheese	blend one cup low-fat cottage cheese with one-fourth cup of margarine.

CHAPTER THREE

A Home of Your Own: Setting Up a New Home, Storage, and Simple Home Repairs

It's fun to have a home of your own, to do with as you wish to please yourself! Good taste has no price tag, and you can develop your own style when decorating your home if you buy and display things and colors that you like to live with. Decorating accents—such as art, pillows, knickknacks, or rugs—depend upon your budget, and there are many ways to accent a room without devastating your checkbook.

ART ON A BUDGET

Framed or mounted on poster board, posters and calendar pictures can be inexpensive art "collections."

COLLECTIONS

It seems that if something exists, somebody collects it—buttons, dolls, toys, glass, china, wood carvings, etc. (I know someone who collects photos of interesting signs and another person who collects photos of street musicians whenever she travels.) Whatever your collection, grouping similar objects on a table, shelf, or a wall is a good decorating trick to give your home a more personal look and your room a focal point.

You don't need to focus on the monetary value of a collection but you should buy what you like to live with. However, if you buy the most rare and best examples of whatever you collect, the value is more likely to remain constant or increase.

PHOTO COLLAGES

Make a collage from photos of family and/or friends, put it in an appropriately sized frame, such as an inexpensive poster frame, and hang it on the wall. If you can't afford a frame, try double-stick taping your favorite photos on a poster board in a color that matches your room.

WALL HANGINGS

Quilting is an American folk art. To display a quilt on the wall, attach wooden rings to the quilt and hang it from a wide, wooden rod. Or, if you don't want to sew on rings or the quilt is too heavy to hang from rings, put the rod on brackets that extend a few inches from the wall and just drape the quilt over the rod.

HANGING ONE PICTURE

If the picture isn't too heavy, hold it by its wire, decide where it will go, then wet a fingertip and press it on the wall to mark the picture wire's inverted "V" point. The fingerprint mark will stay wet long enough for you to drive in the nail or hook. If the picture will conceal the nail/hook hole, you can make a slight mark by rubbing the picture wire's upside-down "V" point on the wall—wire will make a black mark on painted walls or some wallpapers.

HANGING PICTURES/GROUPINGS

Here are several ways to position a single picture or hang a grouping without making unnecessary holes in the wall:

1. To determine the position of a single picture or mirror on the wall, trace the outline of the frame on a piece of paper, then stick it to the wall with a straight pin or two so that you can step back to check the

positioning. Straight pins won't leave very visible marks if you have to move your pattern several times. Then, please see 3, below.

2. Cut paper patterns to the exact size of the pictures or other items to be hung in the group. If the wall area is large, tape together several newspaper pages to make a pattern for the hanging area, such as the area above a sofa. Position the paper-picture patterns on the larger piece of paper "wall" until you get the arrangement you like. Then, see number 3 below.

3. After you know where the pictures will hang on the wall, here's an easy way to determine where nails will go: Position each picture pattern on each picture's back side and pull up taut the picture's hanging wire so that you see an inverted "V." Mark the "V" point on the pattern and poke a hole through the pattern at the marked point to show where the nail needs to be. Do this for each picture in the grouping.

When you hang a single picture, place the pattern on the wall, and use the "V"-point holes to make pencil marks showing exactly where the nails should go.

For a grouping, tape the picture patterns on the larger sheet, pin the large sheet to the wall, and drive the nails through the holes in the paper patterns. Then, tear away the paper. The pictures will all hang precisely where you want them.

HINT: To prevent crumbling plaster: Before driving a nail or hook into the wall, first form an "X" over the nail spot with two strips of masking or transparent tape.

WHEN A PICTURE WON'T HANG STRAIGHT

1. Wrap tape on the picture wire to make "stoppers" on both sides of the hook so that it won't see-saw back and forth.

2. Or, install parallel nails and hooks a short distance apart; two hooks are really better than one for keeping pictures straight, especially if they are heavy.

3. Or, stick squares of double-faced tape or wads of masking tape to the frame's two lower back corners, which will then stick to the wall.

DECORATING TO MUFFLE NOISE

1. Quick fix: Place rubber vibration and sound-absorbant mats beneath typewriters and computer and other home-office equipment, and put stereo speakers on resilient mats.

2. Next step: Line walls of noisy rooms with soft or textured surfaces, filled bookcases, wall hangings like draperies and rugs, and add upholstered furniture.

3. Major effort: Line walls/ceilings of noisy rooms with acoustical tiles or cork panels and install thick carpet and padding on the floors.

NOTE: The idea is to separate noise producers from hard, resonant surfaces like walls, ceiling, and floors that can amplify sounds. Remember, you can hang draperies on a wall to serve as sound absorbers even if there is no window behind them.

STUDENT BOOKCASE VARIATIONS

Instead of board shelves supported by cement blocks or bricks—the traditional student bookcase—try substituting colorful plastic "milk-carton" crates for bricks or blocks. Or just gather enough of the crates to stack together and hold your possessions so that you don't need board shelves.

HOME OFFICE

Make a desk by placing a plain, hollow door (from a home-improvement center or lumberyard) over two two-drawer file cabinets. The doors come in various widths to meet your needs. You can paint or stain the "desktop" if you wish or just leave it as is. If it slips on the file tops, anchor with double-sided sticky carpet tape.

QUICK-FIX FILES

Plastic milk-carton crates will hold files neatly. You can also get "freebies" when office-supply houses give away empty cartons; the boxes from computer paper, file folders, and some other paper supplies are the right size for file storage boxes and some will even hold hang-file folders.

DAYBED COVERS

Daybeds are popular for efficiency apartments. Instead of buying an expensive spread, get sheets, pillowcases (four king-sized pillows will cover the back and corners/sides of a typical daybed), add a dust ruffle in coordinating colors, and you have instant cover-up upholstery.

Many of the new dark-colored print sheets come in designs that look like upholstery anyway. The bonus is that your "upholstery" or "slip-cover" can easily be removed and washed! And, when you get tired of looking at the pattern or color, the bedding can be bedding again.

HINT: The trick to sleeping on a daybed in an efficiency apartment is to pull out the lower bed for sleeping—then "making your bed" in the morning is a matter of flattening the bedding and just pushing it back under the top bed which still has all its pillow piles and spread intact!

CREATIVE DECORATING TO STORE EVERYDAY ITEMS

1. Place dishes on a wooden rack or buy a plate holder or two for your kitchen counter, such as those used to display antique plates, and keep your everyday plate, saucer, and cup displayed on the counter.

2. Wooden or plastic racks can be attached beneath cupboards to hold stemmed glassware—never mind that your "crystal" came from a flea market or garage sale. "Junque" can be your personal style!

3. A mug tree or cup hooks attached to cabinet undersides will display those cute mugs you've collected through the years. It'll keep them off the counter and free up valuable cupboard space.

4. Extra pillows: Cover bed pillows with zippered pillow shams or pillowcases in colors that coordinate with your sofa. The bonus is that they'll be handy for a comfy snooze.

NOTE: If you can't find a matching color, and many are available in corduroy, try dyeing or painting designs with fabric paint on zippered cotton pillow cover/protectors (often found reasonably priced in either white or beige in linen departments of discount stores).

If you can sew, close up the neck and armholes of a school-emblem or other favorite T-shirt to make a decorative pillowcase for a dorm room.

Storage When Space Is Limited

STORING BEDDING

Store extra bedding (folded flat) between the mattress and box springs of your bed. Store hide-a-bed sheets on the hide-a-bed mattress with a fabric-softener sheet tucked in the fold to maintain a freshly laundered scent. The bonus here is that the bed is already made for unexpected guests. See #4 above for storing extra pillows.

HANGING LINENS

Hang table linens and bedding on plastic hangers if you have more closet than shelf space. If you can, put the hangers on a nail or hook fastened to the back wall of your closet so they don't take up closet pole space.

CLOTHING STORAGE

1. Look for "under the bed" storage boxes or zipper bags at variety stores. They are frequently on sale and are helpful when closet or dresser-drawer space is limited.

2. Storing out-of-season clothing in large, clean plastic garbage cans keeps it clean and out of the way. The bonus is that you can put a round wooden or sturdy cardboard "table top" on the can, add a round floor-length table cloth, and you'll have an end table! Here's how I get seventeen skirts, seven blazers, four vests, and eleven sweaters in one thirty-gallon clean, plastic garbage can:

Lay the garbage can on its side. Roll skirts vertically until you have a long, thin roll. Place the hem against the bottom of the can. If the waistband extends out of the can, it's OK.

Next, fold blazers, lining-side out, and roll. Place hem-side down on top of the skirts. Continue with vests, slacks, dresses (fold from waist and roll). If you put all hem ends down, the wider top part of the can allows more room for bulk like shoulder pads in blazers.

When the can is full, stand it up and fold over skirt tops. Place an inventory list on top of the clothing and drop in a few mothballs placed in an empty margarine tub with holes in the top. If you are not putting the plywood over the top to make a table, seal the can with its lid and place it in the back of your closet, attic, or dry basement.

CAUTION: Do not store clothing in damp areas. Also, be aware that if mothballs are placed in with clothing having certain types of plastic beads or buttons, there will be a chemical reaction that damages the plastic.

HINT: To remove mothball odors from clothing when you bring it out of storage, allow it to air outdoors if possible, but to avoid fading, don't hang noncolorfast garments or fabrics in the bright sun.

To remove mothball odors from dresser drawers, lightly sand the inside of the drawers and vacuum up any dust. Then if needed spray evergreen-scented spray, such as the type used for artificial Christmas trees, in the drawers; take them outdoors and leave in the fresh air for a day.

3. Never store furs, leather, or leather-type garments in plastic bags; they need to "breathe." Covering them with old cotton pillowcases or sheets will prevent dust from collecting on such garments. You can also buy special "breathing" bags for furs and leather in notions departments for a few dollars—not an extravagance when you consider the price of fur or leather clothing.

4. Never store dirty clothing; odors will collect in your closet, and soiled garments attract fabric-eating insects.

5. In some climates, almost any closet harbors fabric-eating insects. Silverfish and firebrats like materials high in protein, sugar, or starch such as cereals, flour, paper with glue on it, or starch in clothing and rayon fabrics.

6. If you like to air clothing outdoors or inside, hang it away from direct sunlight or strong artificial light. Some brighter-colored fabrics and many silks can oxidize and fade in strong light.

Simple Home Repairs

WALLS: QUICK-FIX REPAIRS FOR SMALL HOLES OR NICKS

1. Fill nail holes in white walls with white toothpaste or a paste of crushed aspirin and water pushed into the hole. Apply neatly with an old ice-cream stick.

2. On colored walls, do the above and touch up the repair with watercolor paints or colored typewriter correction fluid after the toothpaste or aspirin dries completely.

NOTE: Some blue or mint green toothpastes will match pastel painted walls.

3. Typewriter correction fluid will fill tack or small nail holes in walls if you dab it on so that some flows into the hole. If you're careful and can get a good color match, it can also cover up small nicks in painted woodwork.

4. Fill holes in wood paneling with an inexpensive kit found at hardware stores. The kit contains several colors of filler "crayons" that you simply rub over the hole.

5. To quick-repair larger holes, such as those in a ceiling if you remove a swag hook (from plants or swag lamps), plug the unsightly hole with a cork pushed flush to the surface. Then paint the cork end to match the ceiling.

FAUCET AERATORS

When water squirts out of your faucet instead of bubbling out, the aerator may be clogged with mineral deposits and hard-water buildup.

1. *Quick fix*: Unscrew the aerator, take the screen out, and rinse it.

HINT: If you have to use pliers to loosen the aerator, avoid scratching the faucet by wrapping the chrome with a heavy rubber band or double layer of plastic electrical tape before attacking it with any tools.

2. Next step: If it's totally clogged, soak the aerator screen in vinegar

to remove the mineral deposits and then put all the parts back together and screw it back on.

3. Major problem: If neither step 1 nor 2 works, buy a new aerator; they are relatively inexpensive. But, notice whether the aerator screws over the edge of the faucet or into the faucet opening. Some aerators have adaptors to work on all faucets; some don't. It's a good idea to take the old aerator along when you shop for a new one.

CLOGGED DRAINS

1. Quick fix: Clean a slightly clogged drain by flushing boiling water down into it.

2. Next step: Pour down the drain a quarter-cup baking soda followed by one cup vinegar, then three gallons of hot water. Or, unclog a more seriously clogged drain with a "plumber's helper" (plunger).

NOTE: A plumber's helper works better if its rubber cap is covered with water. To keep from spattering the walls, yourself, the sink countertop, and everything else in the room when "plunging" a small sink, make a tent from a bath towel that covers the plunger and the sink.

3. Major solution: Call a plumber.

HINT: To keep drains clear, use the following drain cleaner once monthly. Mix one cup baking soda, one cup table salt, and one-fourth cup cream of tartar in a small bowl. Store your "drain cleaner" in a clean, dry, *well-marked*, and tightly covered jar. Pour one-fourth cup of the powder into a drain, then immediately add one cup of boiling water. Wait ten seconds, then flush with cold water for at least twenty seconds.

Furniture Assembly and Repair

You can save money by buying unfinished, assemble-it-yourself furniture and then painting or staining it yourself. Here are some helpful hints:

1. A long screwdriver gives you more turning power, but a short one is easier to control.

2. To start a screw in hard-to-reach places, push it through a slit in a piece of masking tape, adhesive side up. Then, place the screwdriver tip into the screw slot and fold up tape ends to secure the screw to the screwdriver. Pull off the tape after the screw is started.

3. Always start a "pilot" hole for the screw; you can do this by making a small nail hole. You can make the screw go in more easily by lubricating the screw threads with wax. Soap isn't a good lubricant because it can cause corrosion.

4. Adding glue to threads increases the screw's holding power, but don't do this if you expect to dismantle the piece later.

5. Tighten a loose screw by inserting wooden toothpicks or matches into the hole, or squeeze wood filler into the hole; then, drive in the screw before the filler dries. Or, wrap thread or fine string around the screws before inserting them.

6. Remove a stubborn screw with locking grip pliers or, if you have one, heat the screw with a soldering iron. The screw will expand from the heat, slightly enlarging the hole, and when it's cool, the screw will come out more easily.

7. Quick-fix furniture scratch cover-up: Cover the scratch with matching liquid or paste shoe polish (a pipe cleaner or cotton-tipped swab can be your "paintbrush"); rub a broken pecan or walnut over a scratch; "color" with matching crayon or artist's paints.

8. Remove heat-caused white marks on finished wood surfaces, such as those that have been varnished, by rubbing the area with mayonnaise; allow to remain on the area for a while, and then polish with a clean cloth. Next time, remember to protect the surface with a pad!

Shopping List for Simple Home Repairs and Chores

1. Hammer, pliers, screwdrivers (for Phillips and standard screws of different sizes).

NOTE: If you get a multihead screwdriver with different sizes of Phillips (for screws with an "X" on the top) and flat screwdriver heads, you only need one.

2. Packs of different sizes of nails, screws, nuts, and bolts.
3. Picture/poster hangers relating to the weight of items to be hung.
4. Typewriter correction fluid in colors to match the walls.
5. Yardstick or retractable metal measuring tape.
6. Heavy-duty scissors.
7. Single-edge razor-blade holder and extra blades or craft knife.
8. Multipurpose glue.
9. Masking, electrical, transparent, and duct tapes.
10. Miscellaneous items for special jobs such as: stick-on felt and/or plastic "feet" for bottoms of items that might scratch floors or tabletops; paint and brushes; steel wool or sanding pads; etc.

CHAPTER FOUR

Cleaning House for Yourself

When you live alone, all the mess is yours and the only picking up and cleaning is after yourself. So, if you acquire a few neatophile habits, serious cleaning will be only a sometime thing!

You will notice that most of the cleaning hints involve those old Heloise standbys vinegar and baking soda. Both are cheap, effective, and environmentally safe. Why waste money on a shelf full of special cleaners for specific jobs? A jug of generic white vinegar, a large-size box of baking soda, and a can of petroleum-based prewash spray will get the whole house sparkling clean quickly with minimum effort and expense.

Of course, if a home has been severely neglected, such as a totally encrusted shower-door track, you may have to buy stronger commercial cleaners. The trick is to maintain a comfortable level of cleanliness by cleaning as you go or cleaning regularly so that you can avoid a major effort.

Bathroom Cleanup

CLEAN-AS-YOU-GO QUICK FIXES

1. Bathroom Sink and Fixtures: Wipe with excess squeezed-out toothpaste. Speed-shine chrome fixtures with facial tissue or cotton saturated with alcohol or mouthwash.

2. Shower Walls: Wipe down the shower walls with your used towel or keep a squeegee handy to eliminate soapy buildup.

3. Commode: Clean the commode by tossing in a denture or antacid fizz tablet. (Denture tablet ingredients include cleaning and bleaching agents.)

4. Shower Stalls, Glass-and-Aluminum Shower Doors, Ceramic or Stainless-Steel Sinks, Chrome Fixtures: A favorite Heloise hint for quick-cleaning these and other water-spotted, soap-scummed areas is to spray on petroleum-based prewash spray. It cleans and shines in one quick application; an easy wipe-off polishes the surface. Water just beads off those scuzzy shower doors for several days. Used regularly, it keeps the shower door track from hard-water buildup. If it's really bad, water buildup can be removed with a full-strength white vinegar soak or commercial cleaners.

NEXT-STEP, DEEP CLEANING

NOTE: Always ventilate the room while cleaning with vinegar.

1. Shower Walls, Sink, Toilet Bowl: Scrub shower walls and sink with baking soda (it's cheap, safe and environmentally friendly) sprinkled on a wet sponge. Sprinkle baking soda into the commode, brush, and flush.

2. Hard-Water Deposits in Tubs, Showers, Shower-Door Tracks, Sinks, Toilet Bowls, and Chrome Fixtures: Spray or apply with rag/sponge full-strength white vinegar; rinse and dry. If there is a heavy deposit, allow vinegar to remain for ten minutes or so, then rinse and wipe. If it's the commode, soak then flush. If there is too much deposit for vinegar to tackle, you may have to buy a commercial cleaner.

3. Shower Curtain: To quick-clean soap film and mildew from a shower curtain, pour full-strength vinegar on it and rinse.

You can also wash plastic shower curtains (and rubber bath mats, too) in the washing machine with a load of terry-cloth towels. The towels will scrub the curtain automatically. Add one half cup detergent and one half cup baking soda to the wash cycle and one cup vinegar to the rinse cycle. After washing, if the shower curtain is wrinkled, let it fluff in the dryer on low heat for only two to four minutes to "iron" out the wrinkles, remove from the dryer and hang immediately.

4. Commode: To clean and deodorize, pour in undiluted white vinegar, let remain for about five minutes and flush. Major cleaning: To remove lime deposits on the toilet bowl above the waterline, line the bowl with three or four thicknesses of toilet paper and pour vinegar over the tissue to saturate them. You may have to add vinegar to keep the paper moist until the deposits dissolve and you can brush the toilet clean again.

NOTE: This technique also works for sink fixtures with lime deposits; just wrap the fixtures with paper towels and proceed as with the toilet bowl.

Kitchen Cleanup

Wipe often is the key phrase for the whole kitchen. If you wipe up after each food-preparation session and every time you spill anything anywhere, your major cleaning sessions need only occur when you need scrub-hard therapy to get rid of life's frustrations.

HANDY HOMEMADE CLEANING SOLUTIONS

I mix homemade solutions in a recycled clean gallon jug and then put some of them into recycled pump-spray or squirt containers as needed.

1. Mix a solution of equal parts white vinegar and water in a spray bottle for general cleaning of windows, sinks, chrome fixtures, countertops, to deodorize your hands, the sink drain, to make glasses sparkle and eliminate water spots, and on and on. This solution also helps eliminate odors when your pet has an accident on the rug.

2. A solution of one part vinegar to two parts water will remove fingerprints and dirt from varnished woodwork or paneling. Wring out the cleaning rag well, wipe, polish with a clean dry cloth. This solution can also be used to clean some furniture surfaces. Test on an inconspicuous place.

3. Mix one half cup white vinegar with enough water to make a gallon of cleaner for wet-mopping tile and most bathroom and kitchen flooring surfaces.

4. Mix one half cup vinegar, one pint rubbing alcohol, and one teaspoon of liquid dishwashing detergent with enough water to make a gallon of cleaner for more heavily soiled windows and bathroom fixtures and tiles.

5. Mix one half cup sudsy ammonia with enough water to make one gallon of general-purpose cleaner for windows, bathrooms, and most painted surfaces. (See "*Caution*" below.)

6. Mix one half cup sudsy ammonia, one pint rubbing alcohol, and one teaspoon dishwashing liquid with enough water to make a gallon of cleaner to serve as a super window cleaner for very dirty windows.

CAUTION: Some dishwashing liquid detergents contain ammonia, so please read the label or call the manufacturer's 800 number (usually shown on the label) before mixing them into homemade cleaning solutions, because mixing bleach and ammonia can cause a poisonous gas. *Always* clearly and boldly label homemade cleaning solutions with the ingredients and keep them away from children and pets.

Also, although the above solutions are usually safe on painted surfaces, it's always best to try a solution on an inconspicuous place first.

NOTE: Also, please see "Simple Home Repairs" in chapter 3.

Five Basic Cleaning Steps for Best Results

(with homemade or commercial cleaning solutions)

General precaution: Before you apply a commercial cleaning agent, read the label carefully for any mixing, dilution, or other precautions. All cleaners are not alike! Apply enough cleaner to cover the surface well; otherwise it may evaporate before it does the job.

1. Prepare the area by removing all surface dirt, food, or any other loose substances with a broom, vacuum cleaner, or dry duster.

2. Identify the dirt. Not matching your cleaning technique to the dirt can leave you with a bigger mess than you had at the beginning! For example, paint thinner will dissolve road tar immediately, whereas water-based household cleaners won't affect it at all. Most cleansers list

their dissolving agent or base (such as water or alcohol) on their labels, along with some of the substances they will dissolve. If you think a cleaner may harm the surface, don't take a chance; test in an inconspicuous place first.

3. Be sure to give the cleanser enough time to work. If you are too eager and wipe off the cleanser before it has a chance to work, you'll just have to waste more time repeating the process.

4. Remove the cleanser properly. With a clean cloth, squeegee, or sponge, soak up the mixture of solvent and dirt, rubbing stubborn areas. Then rinse if necessary and wipe up as much liquid as possible. Finally, dry with an absorbent cloth or allow to air-dry as directed.

Kitchen Sink and Dish Washing

If the sink and counters are clean, the whole kitchen looks clean.

KITCHEN SINK STAINS

To remove accumulated stains in white or light-colored porcelain sinks, pour in enough liquid bleach to cover the bottom; fill the sink with cold water; let soak for at least a half hour.

CAUTION: Colored sinks can be damaged by bleach and should be cleaned with mild liquid detergents, baking soda, or vinegar. *Also*: Protect children and pets from the bleach water.

CLEAN-AS-YOU-GO

If you don't have a dishwasher, here are some hints for hand-washing dishes.

1. Keep a recycled squirt container filled with water and a small amount of liquid hand-washing detergent so that you can squirt some of the solution on a sponge or plastic scrubber to wash your single dish, cup, or bowl after each meal. A detergent-water solution is easier to

rinse off and isn't as drying to the skin on your hands as full-strength detergent and saves you money!

If you wash each dish as it's used, you always have a clean one waiting in the dish drainer.

HINT: Put the water into the container first, then a squirt of full-strength detergent to avoid excess sudsing as you fill it.

2. Instead of a squirt bottle, make a detergent-water solution in a spray bottle and spray this solution on dishes, the sink, countertops, or anything else that needs washing with a mild detergent solution.

NOTE: The bonus is that if you mix about one third cup of hand-dishwashing *blue* liquid detergent to one gallon of water, the solution also kills some flying insects—so you have a relatively safe bug killer on hand at all times.

3. Keep a large plastic cup (recycled from a fast-food meal) of sudsy water in or next to the sink and toss all silverware into it after use so that it will soak clean by the end of the day. *Bonus*: Silverware doesn't end up down the garbage disposal.

NOTE: A variation on this is to fill the sink with sudsy water and toss all dishes (except for very greasy frying pans) into it all day long to soak; then washing dishes after your last meal is a matter of adding very hot water to revitalize the suds and doing a few wipes and a rinse.

Air-drying is certainly good enough and since there's only one person, if you hate putting dishes away, you don't have to. Many of us have a favorite mug that never gets put away in the cupboard, so why not a plate, bowl, and silverware that "live" in the sink strainer? It's your house; your rules!

DISHWASHER

If you have a full-sized dishwasher, you should rinse dishes before loading into the machine, to prevent food from drying on them since you aren't likely to run a load every day. Some dishwashers have "rinse and hold" cycles which you can use daily until the dishwasher is full enough to run a wash cycle.

1. Stains

Wet stain with water, sprinkle on instant powdered orange breakfast or powdered lemon drink mix, allow to remain for at least an hour. Wipe a bit off to see if the stain is gone; if it is, add dishwasher detergent and let it run through the cycle.

2. Mineral buildup

Mineral buildup can adversely affect the dish-cleaning process.

CAUTION: Do not combine the two steps in this cleaning method; it can damage the dishwasher. And do not put gold-trimmed glassware, dishes, or silverware in the dishwasher when you use the process; they will be damaged.

Step 1: Pour one cup of liquid bleach into a bowl; set the bowl on the bottom rack of the dishwasher and run through the "wash" cycle only. Do not dry. If your dishwasher can't be programmed to stop automatically after individual cycles, you'll need to stop the action manually after the "wash" cycle. Some dishwashers have a "cancel drain" button, which is used to stop the action at any time while the machine is running. Check your dishwasher manual for instructions on how to run only the "wash" cycle.

Step 2: Next, fill the bowl with one cup of vinegar; let run through the entire cycle. Dishes will be clean, and discoloration, film, and mineral buildup inside the dishwasher should be gone. If not, repeat steps 1 and 2.

3. Grease buildup

In some dishwashers, grease accumulates under the bottom edge of the door and prevents proper dish-cleaning action. Dishes won't look or feel clean. This problem is most likely to occur when your dishwasher doesn't receive hot-enough water and is not the type that heats its own water hot enough to dissolve detergent and grease.

CAUTION: The surface can be very sharp, so wipe it with a large handful of paper towels or a sponge. One of my readers wrote to warn others that she found a small piece of glass stuck in the grease glob she removed from the door's edge.

Hot Water Hints: Water should be hot enough if your water heater is set to 120 degrees F. *Caution*: Setting the heater to 140 or 160 degrees F. puts people at risk of getting scalded in the bath.

Run water in the sink until it's hot before you start the dishwasher to ensure hot water being available for the first washing cycle. This hint is especially important if your hot-water source is very far from the point of use.

Note: If, after cleaning your dishwasher and making sure hot-enough water is available, your dishes still don't get clean, you might want to have a plumber check the drain system; even a drain that's not completely clogged can slow down the machine's wash/rinse action and result in food specks getting baked on dishes during the dry cycle.

Garbage Disposal/Sink Drain

1. *Quick fix:* Freshen a smelly garbage disposal by tossing in citrus-fruit rinds or ice cubes and a splash of vinegar. Run lots of cold water afterwards.

Hint: Recycle the vinegar you've used to delime your coffee pot by pouring it down the garbage disposal/sink drain.

2. *Next step*: If running lemon or orange rinds or vinegar and ice cubes through a smelly garbage disposal doesn't work, unplug the unit and, if you can, remove the rubber splash guard located in the sink drain. Wash it thoroughly, especially the underside. Please see "Major problem" below.

3. *Major problem*: If there is a persistent odor coming up from the sink drain even after you've cleaned in and under it, the cause could be bacteria buildup in the drain. Try pouring bleach into the drain; allow it to remain in the drain for several hours to kill the bacteria. Then run hot water for at least sixty seconds.

NOTE: Sometimes the rubber in old garbage-disposal splash guards and sink stoppers gets so smelly and grungy that no amount of washing will help. Since these items are relatively inexpensive and usually standard in size, you may want to just buy new ones and save your time and energy for something more pleasant than cleaning a sink drain!

NOTE: Also, please see section on weekly and monthly kitchen-drain cleaning in the "Simple Home Repairs" section of chapter 3.

Stove and Oven Cleanup

If your oven isn't self-cleaning, you will have to clean it or risk the danger of fire or having the thermostat become so encrusted with gunk that your oven temperature controls won't work properly. Here are some oven-cleaning hints to make this dreaded chore a bit easier:

COMMERCIAL OVEN CLEANERS

CAUTION: If you have a self-cleaning or continuous-cleaning oven, using some commercial cleaners or abrasive cleaners will damage the oven-wall surface and therefore impede the cleaning function. Between cleanings, wipe with ordinary detergent and water or window cleaner.

CAUTION: Always follow directions carefully and exactly to prevent injury or damage. When you use commercial products containing caustics, such as lye or ammonia, always turn on the stove vent and/or open a window to protect yourself from fumes; wear good-quality rubber gloves to protect sensitive skin. Cover all adjacent kitchen surfaces, and be sure to place several layers of newspapers on the floor in front of the stove to catch drips when you open the oven door. And finally, *always* keep children and pets away from such cleaning projects.

Oven racks

Cleaning the oven racks in a self-cleaning oven cycle will discolor and dull the finish, which is not a problem if you don't care about oven-rack esthetics.

To clean racks outside the oven, put them in a large, heavy-duty plastic trash bag and spray them with an oven cleaner or ammonia. Close the bag tightly and let the cleaner work overnight. The next day, rinse in the sink or, if you can, wash off outdoors with a hose. Scrub remaining gunk off with a steel-wool pad.

HINT: After using a commercial cleaner, you may be left with a residue that stuns your nose the first time you heat up what you thought was a clean oven. To prevent this unpleasantness, spread a thick layer of newspapers on the oven floor after you finish cleaning with the commercial cleaner. Then, with a spray bottle, spray warm water on the top and sides of the oven well. Next, dry the inside of the oven with a clean cloth, then roll up the newspaper carefully and discard it.

Range-hood filters

Many metal-mesh range-hood filters can be removed and washed in the dishwasher (if they will fit). A normal hot-water wash cycle will clean even the gunkiest, greasiest one. Do wash them as a separate load to allow maximum water action.

If you must wash a range-hood filter by hand, it's an unpleasant mess at best. Try an ammonia-based window cleaner (See cleaning solutions having ammonia and detergent in this chapter.) or detergent specially formulated to remove grease. Apply the cleaner, let soak, rinse. Repeat if necessary—and it will probably be necessary—then allow to dry and replace.

QUICK FIX FOR OVEN SPILLS

To eliminate burnt odors and smoke after food has boiled over, sprinkle a little salt on the burned goo. Pour the salt into a long-handled spoon if the spill is too far back in the oven to reach easily. The mess will be easier to wipe up when you have finished baking.

HINT: Avoid mess by placing a cookie sheet or sheet of foil under foods that are likely to spill over.

RANGE-TOP CLEANING

1. *Clean-as-you-go*: Sponge surfaces with hot water and dry stainless-steel surfaces with a towel to remove water spots.

2. *Quick fix*: Stainless-steel surfaces will sparkle if cleaned with window cleaner or full-strength vinegar or a dab of ammonia on a sponge. Quick-polish stainless steel with a bit of cooking oil on a paper towel or rag—wipe all surfaces, then polish.

3. *Major cleaning*: Electric-coil units usually clean themselves by burning off spills; gas burners, drip trays, burner rims, and other removable range-top parts can be soaked in strong detergent solutions of about one half to one cup laundry or dishwasher detergent added to a gallon of hot water. Dissolve detergent, soak stove parts, rinse well after soaking, and dry well.

CAUTION: Gas burners must be completely drained and dried before replacing them; residual water can divert the gas flow! Dry unreachable places of a gas burner with a hand-held hair dryer set on HIGH *before* replacing the burner.

MICROWAVE-OVEN CLEANING

1. *Clean-as-you-go*: Wiping up spills is important because a messy oven won't cook accurately. Wipe around the door seal, door surface and frame frequently to maintain a good seal.

2. *Quick-fix cleaning*: If soil doesn't wipe up easily, heat a bowl of water in the oven so that the steam softens the spills for wipe-up.

3. *Major cleaning*: For a more serious cleaning and to remove odors

mix two tablespoons of either lemon juice or baking soda with one cup of water in a microwave-safe four-cup bowl. Let the mixture boil in the microwave oven for about five minutes so that steam condenses on the inside walls, then wipe off all surfaces.

REFRIGERATOR/FREEZER

1. Wipe inside surfaces with detergent, borax, or baking-soda solution; rinse and wipe dry for fresh smell and sparkle.

2. Wipe all door gaskets with borax or baking-soda solutions only; strong detergents or bleach may damage the seal.

HINT: To test the gasket seal, close the door on a piece of paper or a dollar bill. If the paper slips out easily, the seal may need replacement or the latch, if there is one, may need adjustment.

3. Dirt accumulated beneath refrigerators or freezers can interfere with air circulation around the self-cooling systems of the coils and motors. Either vacuum dust from the coils with the crevice tool or fasten an old pantyhose leg or sock to the end of a yardstick or broom handle with a rubber band and then carefully slip the "duster" under the fridge, moving it from side to side.

SMALL APPLIANCES

1. Blender (and some food processors)

Fill one half to one third full with water; add a few (only a few) drops of liquid hand-dishwashing detergent; put on the top; whir a few seconds and rinse.

CAUTION: Be sure to check manuals of food processors and food choppers to find out which parts may be submerged in water and which must be protected from water! *Always* unplug appliances after use.

2. Coffee Pot

Mineral buildup in the brew chamber can cause coffee to have an "off" taste. Most pots have directions in the manual for removing mineral buildup. The following vinegar method works with most pots:

Run the fullest measure the pot allows of white vinegar through the cycle one or more times, followed by three or four cycles of fresh water. Then filter the vinegar and store it to use another time. You can also pour it down the sink drain or garbage disposal, into the toilet, or use this vinegar for other cleaning.

HINT: If you brew coffee with distilled water, you won't have to clean the chamber. The coffee tastes better, too!

3. Toaster

Crumbs accumulated in the bottom of a toaster can affect the sensors that give you the right shade of brown, and they are a fire hazard, too! As with all appliances, unplug the toaster before cleaning it. Look for the latch that's on the bottom of many toasters to release the tray, then brush off the crumbs. If you can't remove the bottom, you can just turn it upside down and gently shake out the crumbs.

4. Waffle Irons

Follow manufacturer's instructions for cleaning nonstick grids. When other types of waffle irons accumulate too much burned-on grease, place an ammonia-soaked paper towel or napkin between the grids; let soak overnight; then clean with steel wool.

NOTE: To season new or newly cleaned grids, apply unsalted fat or oil; preheat before pouring on batter.

Miscellaneous Cleaning Hints

BRASS AND COPPER

To quick-clean brass and copper items, pour vinegar on a sponge, sprinkle the sponge with salt, and rub away. Rinse well and dry with a soft cloth. Polish with mineral oil, if you wish.

BLANKETS (COTTON, RAYON, SYNTHETICS)

1. *Quick fix*: Fluff in dryer on cool "air" setting with a fabric-softener sheet to freshen.
2. *Next step*: Prespot and presoak heavily stained or soiled blankets. Wash four to six minutes in cold or warm water (check the label) on a "delicate" cycle with detergent and an oxygen bleach (if label says bleach is allowed). Dry on "gentle" cycle or line-dry as label recommends.

NOTE: Electric blankets can be laundered, but *always* follow manufacturer's directions. Generally you pretreat satins, then wash on a "delicate" cycle for four to six minutes in warm water, detergent, and bleach (if allowed). Most labels say to line-dry electric blankets by hanging them over two lines.

HINT: To protect the plug during laundering, stitch or pin it into a corner of the blanket.

NOTE: Down comforters can be machine-washed unless the manufacturer's care label specifically recommends dry cleaning. Wash with a mild detergent on a gentle setting. When drying, add a clean sneaker or tennis ball to the dryer to help redistribute the down as it fluffs. (This same laundry advice applies to down jackets and vests.)

QUILTS, BEDSPREADS

1. *Quick fix*: Fluff in the dryer's cool "air" cycle with a fabric-softener sheet to freshen.
2. *Next step, launder*: Always check manufacturer's directions and

check dyes for colorfastness before washing. Wash in water temperature suited to fabric and color on "delicate" cycle. When in doubt, use cold water. Agitate gently for four to six minutes; add fabric softener to add softness and dry in automatic dryer to fluff.

CARPETS

1. *Quick fix*: To freshen a carpet, sprinkle with dry baking soda with a flour sifter; allow to remain on the carpet for twenty minutes or longer, then vacuum. To freshen or remove minor soil on upholstery and rugs, sprinkle on dry cornstarch, rub it in, then vacuum it up. This method doesn't work with heavy soil.

2. *Next-step cleaning*: White vinegar mixed with a teaspoon of mild liquid hand-dishwashing detergent and one pint of lukewarm water will remove many oily stains from carpeting. Apply a little of the mixture to stained area and rub with a soft sponge. Rinse with a towel dampened with clean water; blot dry.

HINT: To remove dents caused by furniture, place an ice cube into the dent caused by furniture legs. Allow to remain for about twelve hours, then blot up the water and gently "comb" up the carpet fibers with a fork or pull them up with your fingers.

HINT: When hairs and threads get wound around a vacuum cleaner's or carpet sweeper's rotating brush, cut across them with a seam ripper or single-edged razor blade.

CHOPPING BLOCKS/WOOD CUTTING BOARDS

Small cuts on wood surfaces can harbor bacteria, so you need to disinfect these surfaces occasionally with a mild bleach solution (two to three tablespoons of bleach to one quart of water); rinse well. Baking soda removes some stains and light burn marks; rinse after scrubbing. Rejuvenate cutting surfaces (and wood salad bowls) with an application of a thin coat of mineral oil; let soak for a half hour and buff.

NOTE: Don't substitute salad oil for mineral oil; it tends to get rancid.

Drapes and Curtains

1. *Quick fix*: Freshen by fluffing them in the dryer on the "air" setting for a few minutes.

2. *Next step, sheers*: To avoid ironing sheer curtains, wash them as directed on the label, then, in the sink or a large dishpan dissolve a cup of Epsom salts in hot water. Dip sheers into the solution and hang on rods to dry. If the sheers are too drippy, put a plastic drop cloth (old shower curtain, split-open large garbage bag) topped by old towels to protect the floor.

3. *Next step, washable draperies and curtains*: Shake or vacuum to remove loose soil and dust. Soak heavily soiled curtains in warm water and fabric bleach (if bleach is recommended on the label). Use a high water level so that curtains/drapes move freely in the machine. Wash with warm water (or cold if label says so) using regular detergent. If curtains or draperies are old or have been exposed to sun for a long time, use gentle care and cycles to avoid damage.

NOTE: Next-step cleaning for slipcovers is to wash them if the fabric is washable or dry-clean if that's recommended. Before washing, test fabric in an inconspicuous place to see if it's colorfast. To wash, remove dust by shaking or vacuuming; soak five to ten minutes in cool to warm water with regular detergent; agitate three to five minutes on "delicate" to "normal" cycles depending upon fabric and construction; remove from dryer while still damp and replace on furniture so that cover dries to fit snugly.

Dusting Knickknacks, Nooks, and Crannies

Blow dust away with a hair dryer on the cold-air setting. Or, blow dust away with a clean, dry plastic squeeze bottle pumped like a small bellows. (This works on 35mm slides, too!)

Dusting Paintings

Never wipe with rags or feather dusters, which can catch on textured parts of oil paintings and actually lift off bits of paint. Minor dust can be removed by gently dusting paintings with a soft camel- or badger-hair brush using a back-and-forth motion.

CAUTION: Don't attempt to clean valuable paintings yourself; it's a job for an expert!

Flooring Shoe-Heel Marks

Remove from resilient flooring by rubbing the marks with a pencil eraser or slice of white bread.

Kitchen Floors and Painted Surfaces Rinse

Add a splash of white vinegar to rinse water for kitchen floors and painted surfaces to remove dulling soap films.

Mattress Pads

To launder, prewash or soak heavily soiled or stained pads in warm water and bleach. Machine-wash in hot water, detergent, and bleach on "delicate" cycle. Dry in automatic dryer, if possible, to fluff, removing when slightly damp to reshape.

Miniblinds

1. *Quick fix*: Dust with the upholstery attachment of the vacuum cleaner or with an inside-out "orphan" terry-lined sock. Frequent dusting means less frequent "next steps."

2. *Next step*: Put a sock (see above) over your hand and spray it with window cleaner. Close the blinds and, starting at the top, go over them side to side. Do the same on the back side of the blinds.

3. *Major cleaning*: Take the blinds down and put them in the bathtub (be careful not to scratch) or flat on a surface that can tolerate soapy

water. With a solution of mild dish-washing soap and water and a soft brush or nylon net scrubber, clean away. Rinse well and dry immediately.

CAUTION: Take care when cleaning any blinds. They are easily scratched, and the strings/tapes can break if carelessly handled. And, it's easy to cut your hands on some metal blinds; that's why a sock over the hand is a good idea!

Pillows, Stuffed Toys

Washing these items is *not* recommended unless they can be dried in a dryer because they can mildew before they get completely air-dried. However, foam-rubber-filled pillows and stuffed toys can be washed and should not be machine-dried.

To wash: Check covers to make sure they are strong and securely stitched. Machine-wash two pillows at a time to balance the washer. Wash on a high setting of warm water for four to six minutes in slow agitation with detergent and bleach. Submerge pillows to remove air at the beginning and stop the agitation occasionally to press air from the pillows or toys so that they remain submerged.

Rugs—Throw, Scatter, Bathroom

1. *Quick fix*: Shake or vacuum to remove dust and loose soil.
2. *Next step*: Launder after removing loose soil and dust.

a. Pretreat stains and presoak heavily soiled rugs in hot or warm water, depending on the fabric.
b. Try to wash two or three small rugs together or arrange a large rug around the agitator to balance the washer. Most rugs are washed on "normal" cycle for eight to ten minutes; furry rugs should be washed on "gentle" cycle for four to five minutes. Use a "fast spin" for all rugs and add fabric softener in the rinse water to reduce static electricity and to fluff the fibers.
c. Air-dry furlike rugs or those with rubber backings; heat causes these to deteriorate.

Varnished Woodwork or Paneling

Remove fingerprints and built-up dirt with a mixture of one part vinegar to two parts water. Wring out the cleaning rag well and wipe away. After cleaning the wood, polish with a dry cloth to bring out the luster. The vinegar-water solution can also be used on some furniture finishes. Test on an inconspicuous space.

Windows

1. *Quick fix*: Wash lightly soiled windows with just water and a squeegee.
2. *Next step*: Wash more heavily soiled windows with the homemade vinegar or ammonia cleaning solutions listed in cleaning solutions in this chapter or commercial cleaners.

Smelling Clean—Air Fresheners, Potpourris

Here are some inexpensive and environmentally friendly household deodorizer/air fresheners for dealing with annoying household odors.

BAKING SODA

1. Dollar stretcher: Double the volume and still get equal fragrance by mixing commercial carpet deodorizer with an equal amount of baking soda; use as directed in the "Carpets" section of this chapter.

NOTE: Rub cornstarch into soiled spots before vacuuming, and you'll clean your carpet while freshening it.
2. When water beds get a musty odor, washing the "mattress" with a solution of baking soda and water will help if the plastic is the problem. Bacteria growth in the water inside the mattress also can cause odors; ask at a water-bed shop for a commercial product to combat odors.

NOTE: Baking soda can absorb odors and help remove stains from regular mattresses, too. Remove bedding, sprinkle liberally with baking soda, allow to remain for twelve to twenty-four hours, then remove soda with vacuum cleaner or whisk broom. If you can, it helps to air out the mattress in the sunshine, too.

3. To prevent musty odors when storing a cooler, sprinkle some baking soda into it and add some newspapers before closing the lid. Then, when you get the cooler out for a picnic, dump the soda into the kitchen sink, run water, and it will freshen the drain.

4. Sprinkle baking soda into smelly shoes after you remove them to deodorize them overnight. In the morning, sprinkle the soda into the bathroom sink or commode to recycle this wonderful deodorizer as a cleaning product.

HINT 1: To prevent foot odors, try applying antiperspirant foot spray or powder after your daily wash with soap and water. If you have a serious problem, try wearing sandals or buying shoes made from either canvas or leather so that your feet can "breathe" and perspiration is absorbed.

HINT 2: Refresh hot, tired, achy feet by spraying them with a bit of cologne or dabbing with a moist towelette. Women can do this with pantyhose still on; they dry in seconds.

5. Dust your dog with baking soda between baths, leave it on for ten minutes or so, then brush it out and enjoy a sweeter-smelling pup.

6. Often floor safes develop musty odors. If keeping an open box of baking soda doesn't prevent them, try commercial "desiccant bags," available at stores that sell safes.

7. Sprinkle a bit of baking soda or talcum powder into rubber gloves to help them glide on or off and smell better.

HINT: To prevent rubber glove odors after each use, after you've finished a chore, dry the outer surface of your rubber gloves while they are still on, then pull them off so that they turn inside out. The fingers usually stay stuck in, so cuff the end of the glove and blow it up like a balloon. Hang the inside-out gloves on a towel rack or over a bottle to air-dry. To wear, "cuff and puff" again to blow them right-side-out.

8. Keep a "tried and true" opened box of baking soda in the fridge and, every few months, replace it. Pour the used baking soda down the

sink to freshen it or put the baking soda into the bottom of a cat-litter box.

HINT: If you have a spoiled-meat odor in the refrigerator and washing the inside of the fridge with baking soda doesn't work, put dry coffee grounds on a couple of paper plates and set them on different shelves. The odor should go away in two or three days.

CAT LITTER

1. If you or your friends still smoke, a layer of deodorized cat-box filler put into ashtrays controls the odor and extinguishes cigarette butts immediately, too.

HINT: To add a fresh smell to smoke-filled (or other) rooms, soak a cotton ball with peppermint oil and put it in a small jar with a lid. When you need to scent or "de-scent" a room, remove the lid.

2. To remove musty odors from stored luggage, place a shallow box filled with cat-box litter deodorizer in the suitcase, close the lid, and wait twenty-four hours or longer. The litter should absorb the musty odor. You may also want to let the luggage sit outside, opened, so that the sunshine and fresh air can finish the job for you.

CHARCOAL

1. Put charcoal (barbecue or aquarium-filter type) in a bag made from an old sock, a pantyhose leg, nylon net, or a recycled onion/potato mesh bag, then hang the bag in a closet, basement, or storage room to remove stale, musty odors. You can also put the charcoal (or fresh-from-the-can coffee grounds) into a coffee can and place it in a corner for the same effect.

2. Pour aquarium-filter charcoal into a bag made from several thicknesses of pantyhose legs, tie a knot at the open end to seal, and tuck the bag under your car seat to prevent and absorb musty odors.

3. If you have to store books, put charcoal in an old sock and place the sock into the box with the books. Keep the books in a cool, dry place.

4. When you store a refrigerator or freezer (or when moving cross-

country), place a sock filled with charcoal or dry, unused coffee grounds in the fridge to prevent musty smells.

CAUTION: Always secure doors on refrigerators or freezers to prevent harm to curious children or pets. Push unused refrigerators and upright freezers door-side to the wall as an extra precaution.

FABRIC-SOFTENER DRYER SHEETS

1. Freshen musty-smelling stored bedding by tossing it into the dryer with one or two fabric-softener sheets; allow to fluff on "air-only" setting for about ten minutes.

NOTE: To keep stored bedding and other linens smelling fresh, tuck in a fabric-softener sheet or an unwrapped bar of pleasant-smelling soap.

2. To freshen down/feather-filled comforters and pillows, toss them into the dryer with a tennis ball and a dryer sheet and run on the "air-only" cycle for a few minutes. If this doesn't work, call to find a professional cleaner who has the proper equipment to clean feather pillows and comforters. You can also freshen non-feather-filled pillows by tossing them into the dryer air cycle with a fabric-softener sheet for about twenty minutes.

3. Place a fabric-softener sheet in the bottom of the garbage pail before putting in the plastic garbage bag.

4. To avoid musty odors in stored luggage, stuff the suitcase with newspaper and a handful of fabric softener sheets before storing it. Don't store luggage in damp places like basements or garages.

5. To deodorize a room, place a scented fabric-softener sheet between the inner and outer vacuum bags or into the bag of an upright vacuum cleaner. The scented softener sheet will put a pleasant scent of fresh laundry in the room for several weeks each time you vacuum.

6. Place a fabric-softener sheet or two on a sleeping bag when you roll it up for storage to prevent musty odors.

VINEGAR

Add one cup of white vinegar to the final rinse water to make laundry soft and fluffy with a fresh clean fragrance.

QUICK-FIX DEODORIZING

1. Toss any one of the following into the vacuum bag to make the house smell spicy and nice when you vacuum—a handful of unused spiced tea; a few whole cloves; carpet freshener or baking soda; a cotton ball sprayed with your favorite perfume or dabbed with peppermint or almond extract.

2. If you have a fireplace, sprinkle herbs, fresh or dried, cinnamon sticks, or spices on a small, gently burning fire to make a room smell festive. Or you can buy bags of scented chips in hardware stores to make the house smell spicy and sweet.

3. To remove kitchen odors like those from fish, put one cup of water, six whole cloves, and half a lemon into a microwave-safe dish. Cook in the microwave oven on HIGH for about three to five minutes.

4. Company coming and kitty just had an accident on the carpet? After cleaning the carpet, put some white vinegar in a squirt bottle and spray directly on the carpet. It will control the odor until you can take serious steps to remove the padding and replace it.

5. Make a homemade "doggie deodorant" by mixing thirty-two ounces of water with two capfuls of your favorite fragrant bath oil. Put the mixture into a spray bottle so that you can spray it on and then rub it into your pet's coat between baths.

CAUTION: Always clearly label bottles of homemade solutions.

6. Sprinkle floral-scented carpet deodorizer in the bottom of an indoor kitchen garbage can to control odors.

COMMERCIAL AIR FRESHENERS

1. Dollar stretcher for air fresheners—Tear back the foil only halfway on small plastic air fresheners to make them last longer and prevent the scent from overpowering the room.

2. To dollar-stretch and renew a room-deodorizer "mushroom," put a few drops of a liquid deodorizer or your favorite perfume on top of the mushroom.

3. To remove cigarette odors from a mattress, try an aerosol spray from supermarkets made for fabric- and upholstery-odor removal. After

spraying, allow the mattress and box spring to stay outdoors in the fresh air and sunshine all day if you can. If odor persists, you may need to clean the mattress or box spring thoroughly with a rented cleaning machine—follow use instructions that come with the machine.

Homemade Potpourri Dollar Stretchers

1. To the water in your potpourri you can add the remaining drops of your favorite perfume (rinse out the bottle with alcohol and pour into potpourri water).

2. Mix up combinations of orange or lemon peels, cinnamon sticks, allspice (or simmer some poultry seasoning for a Thanksgiving fragrance) according to "taste."

3. My favorite Heloise potpourri: Gather two cups of rose petals, two cups of rosemary, two cups of mint, four cinnamon sticks, one-half cup of whole allspice, and two whole cloves. Place all ingredients in a large jar and cover with heated white vinegar. Let the jar sit for about a week, then place some of the potpourri in a simmering pot. Experiment with different mixtures to find your favorite fragrance.

Hint: If you don't have a potpourri "cooker," you can simmer potpourri in a mug or old gift cheese crock placed on a coffee-cup warmer, put potpourri in the portable vaporizer/humidifier water compartment, or just nuke a bowl of water and potpourri in the microwave.

Care and Cleaning of Electronic Equipment

One of my favorite resources for technical information is the Electronic Industries Association Consumer Electronics Group, P.O. Box 19100, Washington, DC 20036. It offers numerous booklets about various products and appliances. You need to send a stamped, self-addressed number ten envelope and ask for a booklet on specific subjects such as Audio Tape Decks, Camcorders, etc.

AUDIO TAPE DECKS/CASSETTE PLAYERS

Bad or garbled sound can signal the need for cleaning, and maintenance means fewer repair bills. The Electronics Industries Association suggests cleaning heads after every twenty to thirty hours of playing time. Buy a commercial head-cleaning kit and follow directions exactly.

NOTE: Protect your equipment by using only tapes that offer a warranty; bargain tapes tend to shed more oxide. (When a tape moves through the machine, bits of the oxide coating that makes the tape magnetic can flake off. The bits stay on the tape path and stick to the heads—the parts that play, record, and erase sounds.) Oxide-particle buildup causes sound to deteriorate. Dust that collects in tape decks, especially car players and portable sets, also affects sound.

CAMERAS AND CAMCORDERS

Use commercial lens cleaners exactly as directed and protect your equipment from water with plastic bags or waterproof carriers.

COMPACT DISCS

Hold CDs by the rims, keep them in their containers, and follow all manufacturer's instructions to keep CDs free from skin oils and scratches (which confuse the laser and distort sound). Heat can warp CDs, so some people keep them in a clean, dry picnic cooler when transporting them by car in the summer.

To clean a CD, wipe with a soft, lint-free cloth gently in a straight line from center to outer edge, and from outer edge to the center. Or, if instructions permit, use a commercial cleaner exactly as directed. The lasers of some CD players need cleaning; check your instruction manual to find out if your player requires this.

NOTE: If you make sure your CD player is a foot or two away from the speakers, you will avoid sonic feedback that can cause "skipping" during play.

COMPUTERS

1. Clean the disk drive with a head-cleaning kit as recommended by the manufacturer or check with your dealer or service company.

2. Wipe the keyboard clean with a lint-free cloth and, if needed, spray antistatic cleaning fluid on a soft cloth or pad to wipe the keyboard. Never spray anything wet on the keyboard. If you spill a clear liquid on the keyboard, unplug it and turn it upside down to dry. If you spill sticky or sugared substances on the keyboard, take it to a service person right away.

CAUTION: Do not use window cleaner or any liquid or spray cleaner on your computer monitor screen. Dust with a lint-free cloth or use commercial cleaner pads. Always let the screen air-dry. If the commercial cleaner label says "not for use on a mesh screen," you can't use it on a screen with an antiglare finish. Manufacturers of glare-reducing mesh screens that attach to monitor screens usually recommend that you clean them with a lint-free cloth, and some come with their own cleaning cloths.

HINT: Tinted eyeglasses can reduce glare from computer screens. Brown tint reduces the glare of green text, and blue tint reduces glare from amber text. If your eyeglasses are untinted, you can get them tinted to suit your computer screen and you can sometimes get existing tints changed.

COMPUTER PRINTER

If you have a major paper jam in your dot-matrix printer, you may want to have your service person check for damage. On some machines, minor damage control after a paper jam can prevent major repairs down the road.

FAX MACHINE

Buy a plastic page "sleeve" to hold newspaper clippings and small pieces of paper to prevent paper from jamming in the machine while transmitting. Keep thermal fax paper away from heat (such as in your car while you do errands); heat damage affects print clarity.

TV SCREENS

Dust with a soft, dry cloth. If the screen is very dirty, wipe with a water-dampened cloth and dry with a clean cloth.

CAUTION: Never use window-cleaner sprays on the TV and never touch or attempt to clean a projection TV screen; you could damage it beyond repair.

VCRS

As with audio equipment, use a commercial head cleaner and follow instructions exactly. Overcleaning can cause damage. Some machine instructions recommend cleaning every thirty to forty hours, and others recommend weekly or monthly cleaning. Some suggest annual professional cleaning, lubrication, and adjustment in addition to regular home head-cleaning.

NOTE: Protect your VCR by using only "logo" tapes (Beta, VHS, etc., are logos listed by the Electronics Industries Association). Nonlogo tapes can damage VCR heads. So can overuse of old tapes. Replace old tapes if they get "dropouts" (spots with no picture or sound) or after you've used them to record/play back about two hundred times.

Shopping List of Cleaning Supplies

1. Heloise favorites, white vinegar and baking soda
2. Ammonia or window cleaner
3. Petroleum-based prewash fabric spray
4. Sponges, paper towels, reusable "magnetic" dusting cloths
5. Mineral oil
6. Bleach
7. Specialized commercial products as needed such as oven cleaner, furniture cleaner/polish, hard-water-deposit removers, etc.
8. Feather duster, soft paintbrushes

9. Rubber gloves
10. Floor-cleaning equipment: broom and dustpan, vacuum cleaner, dry mop, wet mop, bucket

Hints for Substitutes

1. One-half of a paper plate can substitute for a dustpan. A damp newspaper is a good dustpan when you are sweeping up broken glass. Cover a dustpan with a plastic grocery bag when sweeping up something messy, then remove the bag carefully so that it encloses the mess for disposal.

2. If you have no vacuum cleaner, sweep a carpet with a damp, (but not wet!) broom. It will collect dust as it sweeps.

3. If you have no bucket, use a plastic wastebasket.

4. No sink stopper? A blue rubber racquetball ball will hold water in a sink that requires a rubber plug, such as a laundry-room sink. Or, a flat rubber-disk jar opener can substitute for a sink stopper when there is a grate over the drain such as in a bathtub or kitchen sink.

5. Save "orphaned socks" for dusting, to slip on a sweaty cold-drink glass (to protect a tabletop from the moisture), or just wear them around the house for "footie" slippers.

6. Save old pantyhose and use them, among hundreds of other uses, to tie up newspapers for recycling.

Sources: Heloise files, books, newsletters, Electronic Industries Association Consumer Electronics Group.

CHAPTER FIVE

Clothing Care: Repairs, Laundry, and Spot Removal

You'll avoid repair and laundry mishaps if you make sure to read all labels *before you buy*.

Be sure the fabric and construction of a garment are suited to the kind of wear you will give it and, if you can't afford dry cleaning, buy as many washable garments as possible.

Here's a checklist of questions to ask yourself even if the item is the best bargain you ever found in your whole entire life:

- What about construction? Check for:

- even hems
- ample and well-finished seams
- firm and even stitching
- securely fastened buttons
- neatly inserted zippers
- matched stripes
- well-bound button holes.

If the fabric is puckered at the seams or if it appears stretched off center, laundering or cleaning will not fix it; it will definitely make the problem worse and the garment won't fit, look, or wear properly.

- What about the fabric? Is it suited for the purpose, such as tough cotton for sportswear and silk or rayon for dress wear? Is the fabric free of such flaws as snags or weaving defects? Is the color dyed evenly?

• How about trimmings? Will the piping, lace, buttons, bows, buckles, and linings wash the same way as the rest of the garment?

Not all buttons and trimmings can be dry-cleaned on the garment; do you really want to remove and replace them or pay for this service each time the item is cleaned? Some buttons with shanks can be pinned on from the back side, but this is not usually the case!

Beware of nylon-lace-trimmed cotton blouses that have to be ironed; to avoid melting the lace with an iron hot enough for cotton is a real challenge!

• How will this garment be worn? How dirty will it get? How will it be cleaned? For example, jeans or sweatclothes are likely to be worn where they will get very dirty and need more vigorous washing methods. If they have fancy and frail trims, they will be a problem to launder. I have my best jeans dry-cleaned after every five to six washings to help prolong that new look.

NOTE: One of my single friends simplifies her laundry sorting by her shopping system. She makes it a policy to buy light-colored tops (blouses, T-shirts) and dark-colored bottoms (jeans, shorts, etc.) so that she can sort her laundry into two piles: tops, which are usually lighter fabrics as well as lighter colors, and bottoms, which are usually heavier fabrics as well as darker colors. The third load at the laundromat is sheets and towels (all light or all dark, depending upon which set was used that week).

Repairs and Sewing—For People Who Don't Sew

QUICK SEWING

One day when you are feeling the need to organize things, thread several needles with different colors of thread cut in lengths of about eighteen or twenty inches; knot the ends. Poke the threaded needles into a pin-cushion, sponge, or bar of soap and keep them in a convenient place so that they are ready when you pop off a button or hook your heel in a hem.

Having the needles ready-threaded makes the job easier; you can even do your quickie mend as you ride to your destination. I've done this many times!

CAUTION: Naturally, only if you are *not* the driver. Just about everyone I know has seen someone driving a car while doing seemingly impossible things. I read about a man eating cereal from a bowl while driving and a woman putting on pantyhose. If that's not scary, I don't know what is! The only safe thing to do while seated at the steering wheel of a moving vehicle is to drive!

SEWING ON BUTTONS (SO THAT THEY STAY ON)

1. Jackets—Some jacket buttons just seem to break off the thread over and over again; the solution is to sew them on with fishing line, or dental floss.

2. The button "shank"—To withstand stress, buttons should not be sewn on so tightly that they are flat on the garment. Instead, they need a "shank."

When you sew the first loop(s) on the button, place a straight pin across the top of the button under the top loops, then stick the pinpoint into the fabric beside the button. The button will stay in place while you sew, and the space that the pin takes up will allow some "slack" for buttoning the garment after it's removed.

NOTE: If you really want to do a professional job, after you sew all the loops and remove the straight pin, stick the needle through one of the holes in the button and bring it out under the button but not through the fabric. Without pulling too tightly, wind the thread around the "shank" about two or three times, then poke the needle through the fabric under the button and make your knot on the inside of the garment.

You can also make a knot under the button on the "shank" if you don't want it to show on the inside of the garment, such as the first button at the neck of a shirt/blouse.

EASY WAYS TO THREAD A NEEDLE

1. Cut the thread at an angle for easier threading.
2. *Quick fix*: Buy a needle threader.
3. *Quick fix*: Prop a piece of white paper behind the needle so that you can better see the eye.
4. *Next step*: Dampen the end of the thread with a bit of starch or dab the end of the thread with a very little bit of colorless nail polish, let dry, and poke it through the needle. The trick with nail polish is to glide the thread over the brush; don't apply so much polish that you end up with a blob.
5. To thread yarn into a large-eyed embroidery or needlework needle, fold in half a piece of thread about five inches long and thread both ends through the needle eye leaving a loop on one side of the eye. Poke the yarn through the loop, then pull the yarn through the eye with the thread.
6. Embroidery needles are good all-purpose needles because they have longer "eyes," which are sometimes gold colored, and so they are easier to thread than the general-use needles called "sharps."

THREAD

1. Cut thread only eighteen to twenty inches long to avoid knots and tangles. A good rule of thumb is to have your thread three times the length needed.
2. If the thread keeps fraying, use a larger-holed needle.

MISCELLANEOUS SEWING HINTS

1. If fabric puckers or gets pulls, the needle might be bent, dull, or point damaged. Quick-fix the point by sanding it with an emery board or by poking it through sandpaper. If it's still rough, get a new needle.
2. When hemming a garment, make knots every now and then (about six to eight inches or so) so that if the hem thread breaks while you're wearing the garment, the whole hem won't come down at once.

QUICKIE CLOTHING REPAIRS

1. Fix a fallen hem with a stapler, masking tape, fabric glue, iron-on fusible tape.

2. A bit of clear-drying fabric glue on a frayed collar point will last through several washings.

3. To mend a small hole in woven fabric, cut some threads or a small piece from the seam allowance; place a small piece of similar fabric behind the hole; then glue the "patch" to the hole with clear-drying fabric glue, colorless nail polish, or fusible mending tape. Test the glue or colorless nail polish in an inconspicuous place before attempting to do the repair on a conspicuous area; with some fabrics, you could end up with a lump. Remember: a little dab of glue or nail polish is usually enough.

CAUTION: If the garment is expensive, you might want to have a professional fix it and not try home remedies.

SHOPPING LIST FOR A MENDING KIT

- Pair of medium-sized scissors.
- Pack of needles of various sizes; consider embroidery needles instead of "sharps" because they are easier to thread.
- Thimble and needle threader.
- Combination package of different colors of thread; also, spools of black and white thread.
- Small box of different-sized safety pins.
- Box of straight pins. (If your fingers tend to fumble small objects or your eyesight isn't as keen as it might be, get pins with colored ball heads.)
- Nonwoven fusible mending tape; pack of colored iron-on mending-tape strips; pack of white iron-on mending tape.
- Card of standard white shirt buttons.
- Fabric glue.
- Seam ripper. (Use this to remove sewn-on price labels, and you'll never cut into the fabric!)
- Tapemeasure and small ruler or hem-measuring gauge.

NOTE: Save every giveaway sewing kit found in hotel/motel rooms and toss one in your suitcase, desk drawer, briefcase, purse, glove compartment, and sewing box.

Doing Your Laundry: Laundromat Hints

Laundromats have two basic types of washers, top loaders and front loaders, and each is used differently.

TOP LOADERS:

Found in most homes, the top loader has a center-post agitator to provide washing action while the clothes are completely submerged in water.

1. Use any type of all-purpose detergent.
2. The machines vary according to capacity, water volume, agitator action, and cycles.

Find out the capacity of the washer you use so that you don't overstuff the machine, causing poor cleaning and rinsing and also crushing items you don't want to iron. Clothing items should have plenty of room to turn over and move freely in the washer.

Although washer capacities are often given in weight, space occupied is more important than weight. For example, six pounds of nylons or permanent-press items may take up twice the space of six pounds of cotton garments. Avoid crowding any load, especially permanent-press clothes, knits, and synthetics which will wrinkle and possibly tear if washed in an overloaded washer.

Here are some typical washer loads:

Large-Capacity Washer

Mixed load: 1 sheet (king size), 2 pillow cases, 2 shirts, 3 T-shirts, 3 shorts, 2 blouses, 6 handkerchiefs.
Heavy work clothes: 3 pairs jeans, 3 pairs work pants, 1 denim jacket, 1 coverall.

Extra-Capacity Washer

Mixed load: 3 sheets (double), 4 pillow cases, 2 shirts, 8 T-shirts, 6 shorts, 2 blouses, 8 handkerchiefs.
Heavy work clothes: 4 pairs jeans, 4 pairs work pants, 2 denim jackets, 2 coveralls.

Front Loaders

Found in many coin-operated laundries, they have a washing action that works by rotation of a circular drum that causes fabrics to tumble. This action of being lifted out of the water and dropped back into it provides more vigorous cleaning, and some say clothes get cleaner because of it.

They hold about half as much water as top loaders and may provide lower-cost laundering because the laundromat saves money on water and on heating it. If you have never used a front loader, be sure to check with the coin-laundry operator or the machine directions to find out about the proper amount and type of detergent that's recommended.

Carrying Laundry to the Laundromat

Have a laundry bag (or pillow case) for each load (whites or colors; hot water or cold water; sturdy or delicate) according to the system you use to separate the loads, and save time by putting each garment into the proper bag as you take it off. Toss the bags into a laundry basket or large box, whatever you'll use to carry the clean wash home. Then you're all set to grab a machine as soon as you walk in the door.

Powdered Detergent

Measure enough soap powder for each load into recycled margarine tubs or other containers such as plastic grocery veggie/fruit bags, or keep a set of zippered plastic bags to hold individual-load amounts of soap so that you don't have to tote a big box of laundry soap.

Buying your laundry-soap powder at the supermarket is much cheaper than buying it in the laundromat vending machines. Remember to reuse, recycle the soap containers as many times as you can.

Liquid Laundry Detergents

Measure a one-load "dose" and transport in plastic margarine tubs or jars that seal without spilling. Or, spot-treat each garment with a one-load measured amount of liquid laundry detergent at home, using it all up so that you transport the detergent absorbed by the fabric and don't need any containers at all.

Water Softeners

Buy a small size at first, and you'll have a container to transport softeners you pour out from the larger, more economical, size. Or, soften and keep static out of your clothing with dryer sheets, which are light and easy to carry.

When the Washer Oversuds

Add a splash of vinegar, a splash of water softener, or a sprinkling of table salt to cut the suds. Then remember to use less detergent next time!

Separating Loads

When a whole family's laundry gets done together, it's possible to separate hot-water whites, warm-water colors, cold-water dark colors, delicates, and so forth. But realistically speaking, unless you do your laundry with someone else, you will probably wash mixed loads to save money on coin-operated laundries.

But you won't save money in the long run if you wash everything in one load because colors fade and run, and if you mix some darker-colored garments with lighter-colored ones, you will ruin a lot of clothes. I always remember how we could tell who was a freshman at college—they wore white gym socks and underwear that had turned various shades of pinky gray from having been washed with jeans and other noncolorfast garments.

Before You Mix Any Loads

Read the labels to see if the garments are colorfast and what temperature of water is recommended.

If You Must Mix Loads

Try to combine only colorfast garments and then wash with cold water to make sure the colors don't run.

Wash jeans with dark socks, dark-colored T-shirts, and dark-colored underwear in cold water.

Avoid overloading, especially heavy garments like jeans with lighter-weight ones like blouses, shirts, delicate underwear; heavy garments will crush and snarl up the lighter ones, and you'll have to do some serious ironing!

Keeping Brights Bright and Whites White

1. Black clothing and stockings: Rinse in clear water to which a couple of glugs of vinegar have been added.

2. Colored fabrics and embroidery cottons: Help set colors by soaking washables in a strong salt water before first laundering. This is an old wives' tale that seems to help with some colors.

3. Make dingy whites white again: Add a couple of slices of lemon to a large kettle of boiling water. Add dingy socks, underwear, etc., and let soak for at least an hour; launder as usual. *Note*: This is a good way to use up those extra lemon slices left over from a party! Or, pick up a box of fabric whitener or bottle of old-fashioned bluing found in the laundry aisle of your grocery store.

4. When white fabrics turn gray: Dissolve 1 tablespoon of borax in hot water and add the solution to the final rinse to make whites get white again.

5. Yellowing of white nylon, polyester, durable press, etc.: Soak overnight with enzyme detergent or oxygen (nonchlorine) bleach, then launder in hottest water safe for fabric with detergent and bleach safe for these fabrics. Or launder with enzyme detergent/oxygen bleach added to regular detergent and hottest water safe for fabric.

HINT: Modern fabrics contain fluorescent brighteners which react to the sun; instead of bleaching them, sunlight may cause them to become permanently yellowed. Avoid yellowing by drying white fabrics away from natural sunlight.

NOTE: When stone-washed jeans yellow, it may be that the residue from the stone-washing process has not been rinsed completely from the fabric. Then, yellowing can result when the fabric is in contact with some chemicals and even sunshine. Although it's usually permanent, the yellowing can sometimes be removed by commercial laundering.

AVOIDING LINT ON LAUNDRY

1. Sort properly. Don't wash and dry lint makers like bath towels with lint collectors like synthetics or permanent-press garments.

2. Remove all papers and tissues from pockets before washing and drying clothes! Tissues seem to expand when laundered and are a real bother to remove. *Hint*: A cup or two of apple-cider vinegar in the water will help loosen tissue that has become stuck to garments in laundering.

3. Fabric softeners reduce static electricity and therefore reduce lint collection.

4. Overloading the washer prevents clothes from being properly rinsed, and overloading the dryer means it will take longer to dry the load; you'll generate even more static electricity.

5. Remove clothing from the dryer when it's still slightly damp. Lint clings more easily to overdried clothes.

6. Clean the dryer lint screen before doing each load. Toss that lint to the birds!

KEEPING TRACK OF YOUR CLOTHES

Attach cheap kitchen magnets to the machines doing your laundry so you can tell at a glance which is yours.

Also, while I believe most people are honest, I still wouldn't leave my clothes in the machines and go shopping. You might find that someone has emptied your machine and either taken your clothing home or piled it up in a snarl, which means you'll have to do major ironing.

AVOID IRONING

Hang or fold T-shirts and other garments while they are warm from the dryer, and they may require only a touch-up with the iron.

HAND WASHING HOW-TO

Some delicates and wools must be hand-washed in mild detergent—see label for instructions.

Avoid wringing and twisting garments, which can ruin the shape and make ironing difficult; some delicates are nearly impossible to iron without melting some parts of them. Get a tub drying rack so you can let clothes drip-dry in the tub.

NOTE: In my other hints books, I've suggested flattening place mats, napkins, dresser scarfs, doilies, and linen guest towels to the sides of the bathtub and letting them dry that way to avoid ironing.

Then I received a letter from an ironing-hating bachelor who carried this technique to new heights. He showers with his shirts to wash and rinse them, and then, he says, he plasters them against the shower wall to dry flat. He claims he can wash and wear his shirts with this method and needs to send them to the professional laundry only every third or fourth time that they're worn. If it works, I'm all for an idea!

Spot and Stain Removal

Most of the spot and stain removal information in this section has been published in my other books, but I have added a few new hints. Because spots and stains usually occur when we are least prepared to deal with them, I included as many ways to remove each type of spot or stain as I have in my files; some are Quick Fix and some methods take several steps. Some methods allow full-strength applications of alcohol, vinegar, ammonia, noniodized salt, etc., and others require diluting stain removers. Let the fabric's sturdiness or delicacy be your guide.

CAUTION: With all spot-removal techniques, *always* test on an inconspicuous place to make sure the method won't harm fabric or fade colors. Don't take a chance!

Of course, if a garment is useless unless a stubborn spot is removed, it won't hurt to try a variety of homemade remedies.

However, when in doubt with your better garments, take them to a professional laundry/dry cleaner for advice and help.

PROBLEMS A DRY CLEANER CAN'T SOLVE

1. Some stains can't be removed without ruining the garment.
2. Some colors bleed even in dry cleaning. "Bleeding" occurs when manufacturers don't thoroughly test dyes.
3. Some fabrics may shrink during dry cleaning because some manufacturers don't preshrink materials used in making the garment.
4. Holes or tears can appear after the dry-cleaning process if the fabric has been damaged by insects or acid spills. Although they don't show up prior to cleaning, weakened fibers may fray or come apart during the cleaning process.
5. Excess shine caused by home ironing can't be removed by dry cleaning. Place a cloth over such fabrics or iron on the wrong side, which is a good idea for all dark colors no matter what the fabric type.
6. When working on spots, always blot instead of rubbing—which spreads the stain and may damage the fabric, especially silks.

GENERAL STAIN-REMOVAL GUIDES

1. Fresh stains are easier to remove; old and set stains may not come out at all.
2. Before treating a stain, find out what kind of stain it is, the type of fabric, if it is colorfast (see label), and how old the stain is. Ordinary machine washing and drying will set some stains permanently.
3. Generally, you start with cold or warm water; hot water sets some stains.
4. When bleach is recommended, use a bleach appropriate to that fabric. Chlorine bleaches are best diluted for stain treatment. Read the container!

5. Test stain removers on an inside seam or hidden area to make sure the fabric won't be damaged or the color won't fade. It's worth the effort.

6. Putting the stained area facedown on a paper towel or white cloth and then applying the stain remover to the *back* of the stain can force the stain off the fabric instead of into it.

7. Protein stains are easier to remove if you break them down with meat tenderizer or enzyme presoaks first.

8. Always use dry-cleaning solvents in well-ventilated rooms.

Common Stains and Ways to Remove Them from Washable Fabrics

ACNE MEDICATIONS WITH BENZOYL PEROXIDE

This is not actually a stain problem; it's a bleached-spot problem that can't really be solved because benzoyl peroxide can destroy fabric dyes permanently.

To avoid damage to T-shirts, towels, and other garments (even wall paint when you grope for a towel!): after applying the medication, wash your hands thoroughly to remove any residue before you handle or touch fabrics.

HINT: Dry face and hands with white towels and switch to white bedding during application periods so that colored towels and sheets don't get ruined. It only takes a bit of this medication to bleach fabrics.

ALCOHOLIC BEVERAGES

Washable fabrics: Soak or sponge stain promptly with cool water; sponge with white household vinegar and rinse. If stain remains, rub in liquid laundry detergent, rinse, and launder as usual. See "Beer" and "Wine, Soft Drinks," below.

ANTIPERSPIRANT/DEODORANT

Ironing may set these stains.

Method 1 (light stains): Rub in undiluted liquid detergent and then launder with hottest water safe for fabric.

Method 2 (heavy stains): Place stain facedown on a paper towel and sponge the back of the stain (on inside of garment) with dry-cleaning solvent, let dry, rinse. Rub in undiluted liquid detergent and launder with hottest water safe for fabric.

Method 3 (fresh perspiration stains): Apply diluted ammonia to the stains and rinse with water. For old stains, try applying white vinegar and rinse with water or launder.

Method 4: Before washing the garment, rinse the area with plain water, then wash with the rest of your laundry in either warm or hot water with good suds.

Method 5: Soak in warm water with enzyme presoak product. Wash in hottest water safe for fabric. If stain remains, dampen and sprinkle stain with meat tenderizer. Let stand thirty minutes to an hour. Launder again.

HINT 1: Avoid buildup by washing garments in hottest water safe for fabric every third or fourth time.

HINT 2: Allowing your deodorant to dry completely before you dress may help to prevent stains from some brands.

HINT 3: If you want to use a nonstaining natural deodorant, try dabbing/dusting your underarm area with plain baking soda. Please see "Perspiration," below.

ARTIST'S OILS ON CLOTHING

Turpentine removes oil paint but can discolor some fabrics. Try removing artist's oil paint with bar face soap. *Note*: You can even clean your brushes with bar soap. Put the soap and brush under warm running water and rub the brush into the soap from side to side, making sure the soap goes all the way up the bristles. Gently rub the soap through the bristles with your fingers until all the paint is removed. Rinse with clear warm water, squeezing out the excess soap.

BALLPOINT-PEN INK

Method 1 (washable fabrics): Denatured rubbing alcohol will usually remove ballpoint-pen ink from washable fabrics. Lightly spot-clean the area with a cloth dampened with the alcohol. Keep paper towels under the stain and change them frequently because the ink bleeds when in contact with alcohol. Rub liquid laundry detergent directly into remaining stain and launder as usual.

Method 2 (washable fabrics): Apply aerosol hair spray until wet, then flush with solution of one teaspoon detergent to one quart warm water; rinse in cool water; launder as usual immediately. Apply glycerine to tough stains before washing.

Method 3 (dry-cleanable fabrics): To home-treat, place a blotter under the stained area; drip a compatible dry-cleaning fluid through the fabric; blot, blot, blot; and reapply if needed. As always, be sure to tell the dry cleaner what caused the stain and how you treated it if you attempted to remove it yourself.

BEER

Rinse with cool water first, then sponge stains with white vinegar.

BLOOD ON FABRIC

Getting to this stain ASAP (as soon as possible or sooner than possible) is the key. Always avoid hot water, as heat sets bloodstains.

Method 1 (washable fabrics): Apply prewash stain remover. Or, soak in cold water for one-half hour. If stain is stubborn, rub with detergent and rinse. Really stubborn stains can sometimes be removed with a mixture of one tablespoon ammonia and one cup water applied to stain. Rinse well before washing with chlorine bleach. Avoid hot water; it sets the stain.

Method 2: Soak stain in cold water immediately. If stain remains, pour 3 percent hydrogen peroxide over stained area. Test first; peroxide removes color.

Method 3: Dampen stained area with cold water; sprinkle with unseasoned meat tenderizer and let set. You may need to repeat the method until all traces of the stain are removed; then wash as usual.

Method 4: If fabric is bleachable, douse with hydrogen peroxide or diluted ammonia before rinsing in cool water.

Method 5 (dry-cleanable fabrics): If you can't get the garment to the dry cleaner immediately, try treating the stain with a solution of one ounce table salt to one quart cold water. The salt may help prevent color bleeding. Rinse areas and blot with towel.

BRASS/COPPER TARNISH

Rub the stain with a paste made as follows: Mix together equal parts salt and flour, then add white vinegar to make a paste. You may have to repeat applications.

BUBBLE GUM

Although bubble gum is not really a stain, it certainly is a blemish when it's stuck to clothing, hair, furniture, etc. Please see "Chewing Gum," below.

BUTTER, MARGARINE

Please see "Grease Stains" and "Oil on Fabric," below.

CANDLE WAX AND CRAYONS

Method 1 (washable fabrics): Allow wax to harden before scraping it off with a dull knife; place stain between paper towels (or brown paper bags) and press with warm iron, replacing towels or paper frequently to absorb more wax. Then place stain facedown on clean paper towels and sponge the back of the stain with dry-cleaning solvent. Let dry, then launder. If traces of color remain, wash again with bleach that is safe for the fabric. Otherwise soak in enzyme detergent or an oxygen bleach in hottest water safe for fabric; then launder.

Method 2 (dry-cleanable fabrics): Same as above for washable items. Please see "Crayon Stains," below, for more special wax-stain removal methods.

CANVAS SHOES

Stain prevention: Spray with stain-resistant fabric spray before the first wearing. They'll be easier to clean. Repeat spraying after they have been washed.

CARBON PAPER

Dampen area and rub liquid laundry detergent into the stain. Hand-wash garment in warm, soapy water; rinse and repeat steps if needed until stain is removed; then launder as usual.

CATSUP/TOMATO SAUCE

Dab off excess and soak garment in cold water for thirty minutes. Rub liquid laundry detergent or white bar soap into remaining stain while still wet. Then launder in warm water and detergent.

CHEWING GUM

Method 1 (washable fabrics):

Step 1: Rub area with ice until gum hardens, or place garment in a plastic bag and put it in the freezer for several hours until the gum has frozen. Scrape off frozen gum with a blunt knife.

Step 2: Place fabric facedown on paper towels and sponge remaining stain with dry-cleaning fluid or treat with prewash spray and launder.

Or, place waxed paper over excess gum and iron lightly over paper, changing paper as gum sticks to it; then place fabric facedown on paper towels and sponge remaining stain with dry-cleaning fluid or treat with prewash spray and then launder.

Method 2 (dry-cleanable fabrics):

Step 1: Follow Method 1, Step 1.

Step 2: Place fabric facedown on paper towels and sponge remaining stain with dry-cleaning fluid.

CHOCOLATE

Washable fabrics: Soak garment for at least thirty minutes in cold water. Rub liquid laundry detergent or a paste of detergent and hot water into the stain while still wet. Rinse. If a greasy stain remains, sponge area with cleaning fluid, then rinse and launder in warm water. Bleach will remove some stubborn chocolate stains, but use only with colorfast clothing.

Nonwashable fabrics: Take to dry cleaner.

CLEANING-FLUID RINGS

Sometimes, these can be steamed out if the garment is held over a teakettle. *Caution*: Steam can burn; put the garment, not your hands, over the steam spout!

COFFEE OR TEA

Method 1 (washable fabrics): Sponge with cold water. Simple washing will usually remove black coffee or tea stains. You can also sponge the stain with dry-cleaning fluid if you've used cream/milk in your coffee or tea.

Method 2 (washable fabrics): Immediately rinse area well in cold water. Treat stain with prewash spray and launder in warm water and detergent. Allow garment to drip-dry to make sure all traces of stain are gone. (Dryer heat will set stains.) If necessary, repeat all steps.

Method 3 (dry-cleanable fabrics): Sponge with cold water. Use dry-cleaning fluid if there is cream/milk in the coffee or tea. Treat the same as washables.

Method 4 (quick fix): Blot spot with club soda.

NOTE: Because coffee and tea contain tannin, they may cause a stain that seems to disappear after washing but returns later. When these stains set too long they may be impossible to remove. It's best to take the garment to a dry cleaner and point out the stain so that a professional can treat it with special chemicals.

COSMETICS

Method 1 (washable fabrics): Dampen stain with detergent until outline is gone and rinse well. If safe for the fabric, a few drops of ammonia, followed by a good rinse, may work on stubborn stains.

Method 2 (washable fabrics): Wet stain and rub bar soap into it. If the stain remains, use regular liquid detergent. Gently work it into the stain, then wash the garment as usual.

Method 3 (dry-cleanable fabrics): Sponge dry-cleanables with dry-cleaning fluid.

CRAYON/CANDLE WAX

Scrape off excess hardened wax with dull knife; sponge with nonflammable dry-cleaning solvent; launder.

CRAYON STAINS

When a crayon has gone through the wash cycle in a pocket, try this: Rub all crayon stains with waterless hand cleaner, then wash the garment in cold water with detergent; but after the wash cycle, stop the machine and let the garment soak overnight. In the morning, complete the wash cycle. If some spots still remain, repeat scrubbing the spots with waterless hand cleaner and a scrub brush.

When crayon stains a whole load of clothes: First wash with hot water and laundry soap, such as mild baby-clothes soap, and one cup baking soda. If color remains, launder with chlorine bleach if fabrics are bleach safe. Otherwise soak in enzyme detergent or oxygen bleach in hottest water that's safe for fabric and then launder.

When crayon-stained clothing has gone through the dryer, spray both sides of the stain liberally with petroleum-based prewash stain remover and rub it into the fabric with your fingers. Let stand for a while and wash as usual. You may have to repeat the process two or three times. If stains remain on bleach-safe fabric, follow directions on the container for the amount to use for removing stains from that fabric. If there is any wax on the dryer drum, dampen a small cloth with prewash spray and wipe out the drum.

CREAM, MILK, ICE CREAM

Sponge with nonflammable dry-cleaning solvent.

DEODORANTS

Please see "Antiperspirant/Deodorant" and "Perspiration."

DYE TRANSFER

Method 1 (whites): Fabric color remover, used according to directions, may remove dye that has "bled" on white fabrics. Launder after treatment. If dye remains, launder again using chlorine bleach if safe for fabric.

If dye has bled onto a white collar of a colored sweater, you can try a color remover just on the collar; but if it doesn't work, return the garment for replacement or refund.

Method 2 (colored fabrics, nonbleachable whites): Soak in enzyme detergent or an oxygen bleach, then launder.

EGG

Soak in cold or warm water with enzyme presoak. Treat grease stains with nonflammable dry-cleaning solvent. Then wash.

FABRIC-SOFTENER SHEETS (LOOKS LIKE A GREASE/OIL SPOT)

On polyester silk-look garments, wet the area, then rub stain with white bar soap or liquid laundry detergent. Rinse well with hot water, let air-dry. If necessary, repeat cleaning steps and launder in hottest water safe for fabric. Make sure all the stains are gone before placing the garment in the dryer, because dryer heat can set stains.

NOTE: I prefer to air-dry the garment first to be sure the stain is gone.

CAUTION: Too few or too many clothes in the dryer can cause these stains as well as too high a heat setting. If you are only drying one or two garments in the dryer with a fabric-softener sheet, add some lightweight bath towels.

HINT: Certain polyester fabrics seem especially prone to this problem. Try saving old softener sheets and using the old sheets instead of new sheets with fabrics you think might absorb the softener. Or, just avoid the dryer altogether!

Fruit Juices, Soft Drinks, Alcoholic Beverages Containing Sugar

Sugar stains must be treated immediately.

Method 1 (washable fabrics): Soak the stained garment immediately in cold water to which a few tablespoons of glycerine have been added. (Glycerine can be found in most drug-store first-aid sections.) Launder as usual.

Method 2 (washable fabrics): Rinse the garment with a mixture of white vinegar and water. Launder as usual.

Method 3 (dry-cleanable fabrics): Sometimes club soda will remove some stains of this type from dry-cleanable fabrics, but it's best to rush the item to the dry cleaner.

Fruits, Fruit Juices, Berries

Method 1 (washable fabrics): Soak immediately in cold water for about thirty minutes. Rub some detergent into the stain while it's still wet. Wash as usual. If this treatment doesn't work, apply hydrogen peroxide if the garment is bleach safe, then rinse well.

Method 2 (washable fabrics): Soak. If stain remains, apply white vinegar and rinse; stubborn stains may need application of hydrogen peroxide.

Method 3 (washable fabrics): Soak immediately in cool water; wash. If stain remains, cover area with a paste made from oxygen-type bleach, a few drops of hot water, and a few drops of ammonia; wait fifteen to thirty minutes; wash.

Method 4 (dry-cleanable fabrics): Apply a small amount of detergent to the stain and rinse if the fabric allows, or sponge with dry-cleaning fluid.

GRASS, FLOWER, FOLIAGE STAINS

Method 1 (washable fabrics): If you have no prewash stain remover, work detergent into the stain and rinse; then launder in hottest water safe for fabric.

Method 2 (washable fabrics): Try sponging the stain with one part alcohol to two parts water, then rinse. If stain persists, try applying hydrogen peroxide.

Method 3 (washable fabrics): Apply rubbing alcohol liberally to stained areas before laundering as usual.

Method 4 (dry-cleanable fabrics): If the garment is dry cleanable only, you probably wouldn't be wearing it gardening; but if you did, it may be safe to apply alcohol or sponge with dry-cleaning fluid. Test on an inconspicuous spot.

Method 5 (acetate fabrics): Sponge with nonflammable dry-cleaning solvent.

GREASE STAINS

(Car grease or oil, butter, margarine, lard, salad dressings, cooking oils):

Method 1 (washable fabrics): Pretreat with heavy-duty liquid laundry detergent or prewash spray or liquid. Launder.

Method 2 (heavy stains, washable fabrics): Place stained areas face-down on paper towels. Apply dry-cleaning solvent to back side of stain, replacing towels frequently. Allow to dry, rub in liquid detergent or dampen stain area with water, then rub with bar soap or detergent paste. Rinse and launder.

Method 3: Gently rub in talcum powder, cornmeal, or cornstarch and let set. Later, brush or sponge powder away. If fabric is washable, launder. Please see "Oil on Fabric."

GREASE ON SUEDE

Sponge the grease out with a cloth dipped in club soda or white vinegar; restore suede nap with a suede brush.

CAUTION: Test club soda or vinegar in an inconspicuous place before sponging it on. These are emergency measures; expensive suede items should be taken to a professional for cleaning.

GREASE ON TABLECLOTH

Sprinkle talcum powder or cornstarch over the stain. As the grease is absorbed, add more powder until no more grease is absorbed; brush it off. Treat the remaining stain with prewash spray and wash in the hottest water safe for the fabric. Before putting the cloth in the dryer, check the spot to make sure it doesn't need a second treatment.

GUM

Please see "Chewing Gum."

ICE CREAM

Soak garment in cold water; hand-wash in warm soapy water and rinse. If a greasy stain remains or if the ice cream was chocolate, sponge the stain with cleaning fluid. After all traces of stain are gone, launder as usual.

INKS

CAUTION: Regular laundering removes some types of ink but sets others. If in doubt, take a good garment to a professional. Also, some inks require a color remover, and some permanent inks can't be removed.

Method 1 (washable fabrics): Pretreat first by placing stain facedown on paper towels and then sponging the back of the stain with alcohol or dry-cleaning solvent. If some ink remains, rub with bar soap; rinse; launder.

Method 2: Dampen stain with water and rub with bar soap. Rinse. Soak in enzyme detergent or oxygen bleach in hottest water safe for fabric; launder. If stain remains, launder again with chlorine bleach if safe for fabric.

Method 3 (dried-ink stains): Rub noniodized table salt into the stain and dribble lemon juice over the salt. Launder after stain is gone.

Method 4 (An old wives' tale that works on some fabrics): Soak ink spots in warm milk before they dry. Rinse out milk in warm (not hot) water. Then launder as usual. Also please see "Ballpoint-Pen Ink."

IODINE

Rinse from underside of stain with cool water. Soak in solution of color remover, rinse, and launder.

IRON RUST

Moisten the stain with water, apply lemon juice, then rinse. You may have to repeat the treatment several times to get the stain out. Hanging a lemon-juice-treated item out in bright sun sometimes makes the lemon juice work better. *Caution:* Lemon juice will lighten certain colors. Test the juice in an inconspicuous place on the garment before using it. Of course, if you can't wear the garment with the rust stain, a bleach spot isn't going to matter much.

LIPSTICK

All methods are for washable fabrics.

Method 1: Place stain facedown on paper towels. Sponge back of stain with dry-cleaning solvent, replacing the paper towel underneath frequently so that color can be absorbed. Dampen stain with water and rub with bar soap, rinse, and launder. White fabrics may be laundered with diluted chlorine bleach and colored fabrics with oxygen-type bleach.

Method 2: Immediately place stained area over absorbent towel and saturate with rubbing alcohol, then rub area with cloth dipped in rubbing alcohol. Rinse and launder after all traces of stain have been removed.

CAUTION: Test for colorfastness before using alcohol.

Method 3: Try prewash spray before laundering as usual.

MAKEUP/FOUNDATION

For powdered or water-based makeup: Dampen the area and rub the stain with white bar soap. Rinse and launder.
For oily makeup: Treat with prewash spray, then dampen the area and rub to work stain out. After all stain is gone, rinse and launder in hottest water safe for fabric.

NOTE: It's best to take silk and other fragile fabrics to a professional dry cleaner for removal of all makeup stains.

MASCARA

For water-based mascara: Dampen the area and rub with bar soap or liquid detergent until suds form. When the outline of the stain has disappeared, rinse thoroughly. You may have to repeat the process.
For oil-based mascara: Apply prewash spray or stick directly to the stain and machine-wash.

NOTE: Some waterproof mascara is impossible to remove.

MEAT JUICE

Soak in cold or warm water with enzyme presoak. Treat grease stains with nonflammable dry-cleaning solvent. Then wash.

MILDEW

Old mildew stains are almost impossible to remove, and mildew fungus can destroy or weaken fabrics.

HINT: When brushing mildew off items, take them outdoors to prevent the spores from getting airborne and setting up housekeeping elsewhere in the house.

Method 1: Launder with chlorine bleach if it's safe for the fabric; if not, soak in oxygen bleach for fifteen to thirty minutes, then launder.

Method 2 (bleachable fabrics): Brush with a stiff brush to remove mold spores and soak in solution of one tablespoon of chlorine bleach to one quart of water for fifteen minutes. Rinse and launder, adding one-half cup chlorine bleach to wash cycle.

Method 3 (nonbleachable fabrics): Brush with stiff brush to remove mold spores. Flush the stain with solution of one-half cup lemon juice and one tablespoon of salt. Dry garment in the sun. After stain has been removed, launder as usual.

Method 4 (walls and floors): Scrub with a brush dipped in borax and water.

Method 5 (books and papers): Dust with talcum powder, cornmeal, or cornstarch; let set for two days; brush off.

MILK

Albumin, a protein in milk, is the culprit.

Method 1 (fresh stains): Soak clothing for several hours in water to which detergent containing enzymes has been added. Launder as usual.

Method 2 (baby formula): Soak garment in cold water. Rub liquid laundry detergent into stain and then launder in hottest water safe for fabric with enzyme detergent. If a greasy stain remains, sponge area with cleaning fluid and launder again before drying in clothes dryer.

MUD

Allow to dry, then brush off excess dirt and spot-clean with detergent or shampoo.

MUSTARD

Method 1: Dampen area and rub liquid laundry detergent into stain. Rinse, then soak in hot detergent water for several hours. Launder with enzyme detergent.

Method 2: Apply prewash spray or liquid, or dampen stain with water and rub with bar soap. Rinse and launder with chlorine bleach if safe for fabric. If not, soak in enzyme detergent or oxygen bleach in hottest water safe for fabric; then launder. You may have to repeat the process.

Method 3: Rub glycerine, which can be found in most drug stores, into the stain. Wash the area with warm, sudsy water; rinse and launder according to care-label instructions.

Method 4: Immediately rinse in cold water. Wash with hot, soapy water with chlorine bleach if fabric is bleachable. Use oxygen-type bleach for laundering colored fabrics.

NAIL POLISH

Method 1: Test garment for colorfastness and fabric safety for acetone use. If it's okay, place paper towels under the stain and sponge with pure acetone. After removing all stain, launder. *Caution*: Acetone will dissolve acetate and triacetate in fabrics. Amyl acetate is safe for acetate fabrics.

Method 2: Place stain facedown on paper towels. Sponge back with nail-polish remover, frequently replacing the towels beneath the stain. Repeat sponging until stain is gone. Launder. *Caution*: Do not use nail-polish remover on acetate or Arnel fabrics; it will damage the fabric. Send them to the dry cleaner.

OIL ON FABRIC

Method 1 (quick fix for fresh spots): Salad oil dribble on your shirt or blouse? Apply baby powder to the spots, wipe it off, apply more, and let it set awhile. Wipe powder away before laundering.

Method 2 (quick fix): Rub white chalk into the stain before laundering. (Chalk's easy to carry in a purse or bag.) Please see "Grease Stains."

PAINT

Check label on the can for cleanup instructions. Some paints clean up with soap and water, and others require solvents.

Method 1 (oil-based paint): Gently rub stain with a cloth saturated with a bit of the solvent recommended on the paint-can label (turpentine, paint thinner, or mineral spirits) if the fabric is color safe. (If label instructions are obscured by dripped paint, use turpentine.) Rinse well. Then rub with detergent paste, liquid laundry detergent, or bar soap and wash as usual. It may help to soak the garment before washing.

Method 2 (oil-based paint): Scrape off fresh paint. Sponge with non-flammable dry-cleaning solvent. Launder.

Method 3 (water-based paint): If treated immediately, water-based paints may wash out with soap and water. Rinse the stain well in warm water to flush out paint, then launder as usual. If it has set and dried, water-based paint cannot be removed.

PENCIL LEAD

Try to gently erase as much of the mark with a clean pencil eraser. Then rub liquid laundry detergent into remaining stain and launder as usual.

PERFUME

Please see "Alcoholic Beverages" and follow the same instructions.

PERSPIRATION

The International Fabricare Institute says that these stains result when you apply a large amount of deodorant and then wash the garment with cold "hard" water (high-mineral, low-alkaline water). Many deodorants and antiperspirants contain aluminum salts. When combined with laundry detergent and cold water, the salts cannot be easily dissolved and so they remain on the fabric. Please see "Antiperspirant/Deodorant" for removal instructions.

PET-URINE STAINS

Method 1: Soak stained area in warm, soapy water. If stains remain after soaking, sponge with solution of equal parts water and white household vinegar, which will also help to neutralize remaining odors. Rinse well and launder as usual.

Method 2: Dampen area with equal parts of white vinegar and water; blot dry.

PLAY PUTTY

Remove putty by rubbing liquid detergent into the spot from the underneath side of the fabric; scrub well. This should remove the putty; but if a stain remains, try sponging diluted hydrogen peroxide onto the area.

CAUTION: Always test in an inconspicuous spot first, because peroxide can remove color.

RING-AROUND-THE-COLLAR

Method 1: Rub ring with hair shampoo, prewash spray, or liquid laundry detergent. Let set for thirty minutes and launder as usual. Use hottest water safe for the fabric.

Method 2: Mark the stain heavily with chalk to absorb oils. After oil has been removed, the dirt comes out more easily. If a yellow stain has been on the collar for a long time, you may have to repeat the process; but on a new shirt, one application should do the trick.

HINT: *Avoid* the problem. It helps if you wipe your neck with astringent (or rubbing alcohol) before getting dressed, especially if you are in a big city where the air is polluted from traffic and industry.

RUST

CAUTION: Do not use chlorine bleach on rust! Commercial rust removers for fabric use are available in the fabric-dye section of the supermarket. Never use rust remover near or inside a washer; it can remove the glossy finish on porcelain outside and inside the machine.

Method 1 (few spots): Apply commercial rust-stain remover; rinse and launder.

Method 2: Dampen stain with lemon juice and sprinkle on noniodized table salt. Lay garment in the sunshine and continue to dampen area with lemon juice until the stain is gone. Launder as usual.

Method 3 (rusty discoloration on white load): Wash in phosphate detergent, if available, with one cup enzyme detergent or an oxygen bleach. If stains remain, dissolve one ounce oxalic acid crystals per gallon of water in a plastic container. Soak clothes in this solution for ten to fifteen minutes. Rinse and launder.

RUST ON LAUNDRY

When you frequently find rust spots on whole loads of laundry, sometimes it means that laundry soap has had a chemical reaction with certain local water supplies—usually due to iron or manganese in the water. Dirt and soil are washed out, but a new substance—the detergent and the soil—is redeposited onto the garment; it looks like rust spots. Change laundry detergent.

When iron is present in your water supply, use extra detergent plus a nonprecipitating water conditioner. To get best results, dissolve the detergent and water conditioner in warm water before adding to the washer.

You may also want to consider installing a water softener, chemical feeder, or special filters to remove iron and manganese from the water supply. Also, avoid overloading the washer—clothes should move freely with enough water to rinse away all deposits.

Rust stains can also be caused by a rusty water heater or rusty water lines. Your local water company or a water-quality company can test your lines for iron or manganese (rust) content.

SALAD DRESSINGS

Please see "Grease Stains."

SCORCH MARKS

NOTE: Severe scorch marks cannot be removed.

Method 1: Launder with chlorine bleach, if safe for fabric.

Method 2 (nonbleachable fabric): Soak in strong solution of enzyme detergent or oxygen bleach in hottest water safe for fabric. Launder.

Method 3 (colorfast fabrics): After testing fabric for colorfastness, dab 3 percent hydrogen peroxide (sold for use as an antiseptic in drugstores and supermarkets) on scorched area with clean, white cloth. Apply until scorch mark fades.

Method 4 (delicate fabrics): Rub scorch marks lightly with a clean, white cloth dampened with white vinegar. Wipe the area (don't rub) with a clean, dry cloth. Press if needed.

SHOE DYE/POLISH ON OFF-WHITE HOSE

Soak the discolored section of the hose in rubbing alcohol and wash as usual. You may need to use a color remover; if so, treat the entire pair because this method may change the overall appearance. *Hint*: To keep dye from bleeding onto hose, spray the inside of the shoes several times with a fabric-protector spray; respray occasionally.

SHOE POLISH

NOTE: Some shoe polishes won't come out.

Method 1: Dampen the stain with cleaning fluid, then wash in warm water and detergent.

Method 2: Sponge the stain with rubbing alcohol "straight" on white fabrics and a mixture of one part alcohol and two parts water on colored fabrics. *Caution*: Rubbing alcohol is safe on most fabrics, but test in an inconspicuous place anyhow.

SILK FABRIC STAINS

CAUTION: Do not attempt to remove stains from silk by rubbing the area with a damp cloth. Silk fibers break easily when wet; blot with a clean, dry cloth instead of rubbing.

1. Beverage spills may disappear when the fabric dries, but sugar in some beverages may cause a yellow stain that appears later. Take silk garments to the dry cleaner as soon as possible and explain what was spilled where.

2. Perspiration and body oils are silk's worst enemies; wear dress shields or spray the underarm areas with fabric-protector spray to prevent stains. Maintain all silk garments with regular dry cleaning or hand washing.

3. If there is a chafed area that has lost its color or luster, point this out to the dry cleaner, who can then give the item a special restoration bath.

STICKY RESIDUE
(*from gummed name stickers, etc.*):

Carefully dab with rubbing alcohol, salad oil, petroleum-based pre-wash spray, or cleaning fluid—whichever is suitable for the fabric.

SUGARED BEVERAGES, COFFEE, FRUIT JUICE, TEA

These stains must be treated when fresh because sugar stains become more difficult to remove as they age and are almost impossible to get out when they are completely set. These stains often show up as brown or yellow spots after clothing has been washed; I call them "mystery stains."

SWIMSUIT
(to help prevent fading/fabric damage from pool-water chlorine):

Buy chlorine remover for aquarium water from a pet store. Rinse your bathing suit after each swim in a solution of one drop anti-chlorine formula to one gallon water.

TAR

For washable fabrics: Rub spot with kerosene until the stain has been removed; wash with detergent and water as usual.

CAUTION: Kerosene doesn't take color out of most fabrics, but it's better to test in an inconspicuous place first anyway!

TENNIS SHOES, WHITE RUBBER

Clean stains off with whitewall tire cleaner. Follow directions on the container.

TIES

To prevent serious stains, spray new and just-cleaned ties several times with fabric stain repellent; spills won't always become stains. This is a favorite hint for frequent flyers! By the way, why does clothing act like a magnet when airline edibles are set before you?

Treat stains on silk ties as directed for silk fabric. Always check the label for cleaning instructions.

TOBACCO

Dampen stain and rub with bar soap. Rinse. Soak in enzyme detergent or oxygen bleach and then launder. If stain remains, launder again with chlorine bleach if it's safe for that fabric.

TOOTHPASTE

CAUTION: This method is not for silk or other delicate fabrics, because the rubbing motion can break the fibers.

Place a cloth underneath the fabric, then work with a damp cloth to remove toothpaste. After removing the toothpaste, blow-dry with a hair dryer.

NOTE: It's easy to avoid the problem by getting dressed after brushing your teeth or by putting a hand towel "bib" over the front of your clothing to protect it.

TYPEWRITER CORRECTION FLUID

Soap and water will not remove paint-based correction fluid. Most are latex based and must be treated like a paint stain. Take the garment to a dry cleaner and be sure to point out the stain and tell the cleaner what it is.

URINE, VOMIT, MUCUS

Remove solid residue from fabric. Then, soak with enzyme detergent and warm water. Launder with chlorine bleach if safe for fabric. If not, wash with oxygen bleach and detergent or all-fabric bleach and detergent.

Mattress "Accident"
(*to remove urine stain*):

1. Immediately (before the area dries) try to absorb as much of the urine as possible with dry towels. Sponge the stained area with a solution of half vinegar and half water to clean the stain. Again, remove as much of the moisture as possible with dry towels, or dry with a hair dryer on Low or Cool.

2. If the stained area has dried, try to keep it from getting larger by rubbing the stain from the outside in toward the center with upholstery shampoo. If the outer ring is still present, repeat the process.

3. After the mattress has dried, spray it with an air freshener made for fabrics to help prevent a musty or urine odor. If you can, place the mattress outside in the fresh air and sunshine to air it out.

NOTE: If you fail to remove the stain but are able to remove the odor so that the mattress is still sleepable, cover the mattress with a zippered fabric mattress cover (available in many catalogs).

WINE

Quick fix: Blot the fresh spill with a cloth soaked with distilled water or club soda. Or, apply club soda liberally, then sponge up soda and wine. To remove red wine on a garment, sprinkle lots of salt on the stain, then immerse the garment in cold water and rub the stain out before laundering.

WINE, SOFT DRINKS

Washable fabrics: Soak with enzyme detergent or oxygen bleach with hottest water safe for fabric, then launder. If stain remains, wash with chlorine bleach if safe for fabric.

MYSTERY STAINS

Flush with cold water; apply prewash spray, and rub into stain. After all traces of stain have been removed, launder as usual. These stains are usually water soluble if caught in time.

A reddish tinged area on a garment may be an acid color change, usually due to perspiration or deodorants, fruit juices, and some beverages. These areas are not noticeable immediately; instead they develop gradually when the staining substance remains on the fabric. Clothing should be washed or dry-cleaned often to avoid this problem. Depending upon how long the stain has been on the fabric, a dry cleaner may be able to minimize or neutralize the discoloration. As with all stains, removal is more likely to be possible if the garment is cleaned immediately.

QUICK FIXES WHEN YOU'RE AWAY FROM HOME

Quick fix 1: Rub stain with bar soap and wash/rinse. Or, use hotel shampoo on the stain for washing garments.

Quick fix 2: Some liquid hand soaps in restaurants can be used to quick-clean a spill.

Quick fix 3: Apply club soda, especially to wine stains. At home, clean that fabric as usual.

LAST-DITCH STAIN REMOVER FORMULA

Here is my favorite last-ditch stain remover for white and bleachable clothes (no silk, rayon, etc.). I use it when all else has failed and I can't wear the garment anyway with the spot on it.

> *1 gallon hot water*
> *1 cup powdered dishwasher detergent*
> *¼ cup household liquid chlorine bleach*

Mix water, detergent, and bleach well in a plastic, enamel, or stainless-steel container. (This solution should not be mixed in an aluminum container or come in contact with aluminum because it will discolor it.) Soak the garment in this solution for five to ten minutes. If any stain remains, continue to soak, then wash as usual.

OTHER LAST-DITCH SPOT REMOVERS

NOTE: Applying bleach full strength or in a strong solution to spots can weaken fabrics and may cause those areas to deteriorate with each washing, but, if you can't wear the garment with the stain, and a professional cleaner can't get it out, a last-ditch method is an alternative to throwing the garment out or sewing an applique over the stain. Also, note that the following two methods may bleach colors out with the stain.

1. Wet the stain and make a paste of water and dry dishwasher detergent powder (which contains a very strong bleach) and apply this.

Work the paste into the stain. Let the garment set for ten minutes and rinse.

Don't scrub too hard; the fabric may get "pills." Rinse, then launder with whites.

2. Squirt full-strength liquid dishwashing detergent into the spot and work into the fabric. Again, don't scrub too hard or the fabric may "pill." Let set until the spot is gone. Rinse, then launder as usual with whites.

Care-Label Hints

Keep a file of hang labels from your clothing and home furnishings so that if sewn-in ones get lost, you have a record of proper care procedures. You can toss all these labels in an extra drawer, manilla envelope, or a plastic bag with handles hung in your closet.

This is what care-label terms mean:

- Machine-wash, warm: Use washing machine, warm setting; hot water should not be used.
- Hand-wash, cold: Wash only by hand in cold (never warm or hot) water. Do not machine-wash.
- Bleach when needed: All commercially available bleaches are safe for regular use.
- Only nonchlorine bleach when needed: Nonchlorine bleach is safe for use. Regular use of chlorine bleach could harm the garment.
- Tumble-dry: Hot, medium, or low dryer temperature settings are safe for use.
- Tumble-dry, medium: Medium or low dryer temperature settings are safe for use. Don't use hot setting.
- Warm iron: Iron on medium temperature setting. The higher setting should not be used.
- Dry-clean: Item can be dry-cleaned by any commercial method that uses any of the available dry-cleaning solvents.
- Professionally dry clean, perchlorethylene: Item can be dry-

cleaned by any commercial establishment using perchlorethylene. Petroleum or fluorocarbon solvents should not be used.

• Machine-wash, separately: This warning must be given if the garment could cause harm to another product being washed with it.

• A garment with detachable pieces will have separate care labels for each piece if each needs different care but one label for all if all can have identical care.

• Care labels include all parts of the garment, such as lining, trim, buttons, and zippers, and should note if special care is needed for some parts, such as a warning to "remove trim before cleaning."

• When the label says to clean separately, it means that the garment has limited colorfastness and some dye bleeding may occur the first few times it's washed. This can cause fading as well as dye transfer onto other garments washed with it.

• International symbols for care meet requirements of other countries, but garments sold in the U.S. must also provide written instructions.

LAUNDRY WATER TEMPERATURES

If you have ever played "thermostat Ping-Pong" with a roommate during air-conditioning season, you know that the difference between "hot," "warm," and "cold" is a very subjective, personal opinion. Not so with laundry, where such words are translated into specific temperatures by the manufacturers.

Hot

130 degrees F. or above; for white and colorfast fabrics, heavily soiled loads, diapers.

Warm

90 degrees F. to 110 degrees F.; for noncolorfast fabrics, moderately soiled loads, manmade fibers and permanent-press fabrics, knits, silks, woolens. (Heavily soiled, colorfast, sturdy manmade fibers and

permanent-press fabrics can be washed in hot water if you use a permanent-press cycle.)

Cold

80 degrees F. or colder; for dark or bright colors that bleed, lightly soiled loads.

SHOPPING LIST OF LAUNDRY SUPPLIES FOR MOST COMMON STAINS

- Bleaches: Chlorine and oxygen; fabric color remover. Also substitutes such as lemon juice and dishwasher powder or liquid.
- Detergents: Heavy-duty powder or liquid, light-duty liquid for delicates, enzyme and presoak.
- White bar soap.
- Cleaning fluids: Rubbing alcohol, turpentine, nail-polish remover; dry-cleaning solvent (perchloroethylene, methyl chloroform, trichloroethylene).
- Miscellaneous: Ammonia, baking soda, white vinegar, club soda, rust-stain remover, oxalic acid crystals, glycerine, etc. (Bought in supermarkets and drugstores.)

CHAPTER SIX

Gardening Indoors When You Don't Really Have a "Green Thumb"

Gardening is fun, even if your garden plot is no bigger than your windowsill. And, the bonus is that potted houseplants can be more than just pretty decorations. Some, such as indoor-grown herbs, can perk up your salads and cooking as well as decorate a windowsill. Some plants can clear pollutants from the air. For example, English ivy removes the benzine of synthetic fibers and tobacco smoke; spider plants counteract the formaldehyde of plywood and household cleaners.

Because most people say they are already doing double time in their lives and don't really want extra work, I'm listing some plants that require minimum effort and skill. The list includes some plants that actually thrive when neglected. (Did you just say "That's my kind of plant?") Also, many plants on the list require only low light.

If your previous experience with growing green things has been limited to unspeakably offensive molds on leftovers you've forgotten in the fridge, and the last time you had a green thumb was when you colored Easter eggs, please don't be intimidated by the tongue-twisting botanical names. Common household plants have different nicknames in different parts of the country, so it's best to know the proper botanical names when you shop. Also, imagine how you'll impress people when you refer to your plant as an Aglaonema from the Araceae family instead of just saying it's "the one with the different-colored leaves."

You can grow your indoor or patio garden from seeds or buy small bedding plants. I like to grow plants from fruit pits and vegetables—these plants are really free because you use plant parts that are normally discarded. If the plant doesn't grow, you can just toss the starter out and begin anew!

Plants that root from tip cuttings can be given as friendship gifts. Decorate the pots according to the season, and you'll have a gift from the heart that hopefully continues to bring smiles and that's also kind to a tight budget.

Another benefit of an indoor garden is the satisfaction of making something grow from start to flower or flourish. Often our work leaves us frustrated because we don't see the end result of our efforts. If I didn't get letters from my readers or meet them when I'm on tour, I wouldn't get the satisfaction of hearing how a hint has made life a little easier for someone.

So, here's a list of easy-care plants which, if you live in an apartment that forbids pets, can also be your "pets." The bonus with "plant pets" is that you don't have to walk them or play with them at night when you're tired! I have a non-green-thumbed friend who names her plants because she says that if you name something, it doesn't die. She has Farley Ficus, Philomena Philodendron, Casper the Friendly Cactus, and so on, and she swears that her named plants thrive, no matter how they are treated! She actually named her "Mother-in-law's Tongue" after her mother-in-law, not because of the sharp leaf tips, but because it's a hardy plant that has survived for years under less-than-ideal conditions!

Easy-Care Plants

AGLAONEMA (CHINESE EVERGREEN), ARACEAE FAMILY

✔ Foliage can be plain green or variegated with silver, white, or pale yellow and will bear white flowers similar to a calla lily. The flowers are followed by green berries that turn red-orange. They can grow to about three feet high.

NOTE: Only pot-bound plants will bloom, usually in late summer or early fall.

✳ Doesn't need direct sun and will thrive as far as twenty feet from a bright window. If placed under a ceiling floodlight that is on six to eight hours a day, it won't need any natural light at all.

☞ Water about every three days. Soil should be kept between wet and evenly moist, but occasional dryness won't harm it.

❧ Grows in a mixture of two parts all-purpose potting soil mixed with one part vermiculite. Will also grow in a vase of water. Feed with all-purpose food year-round. You can root tip cuttings or plant seeds in spring or summer. Although the plant is very hardy, it may be harmed by cold drafts or by constant temperatures below 55 degrees F. Propagate by cutting stems into three-inch pieces, place in moist sand and just barely cover with soil. When bottom leaves fall off and the plant becomes leggy, you can cut off the tips and root/grow them in water.

HINT: Plant philodendron or pothos at the base to cover the bare stems.

BROMELIADS ("AIR PLANTS" OR "AIR PINES"), BROMELIACAEA FAMILY

✔ Almost care free, they come in about 2,000 species and many hybrids—most forming rosettes of leaves, some forming tubular vases of foliage that stay colorful for months. Colors include cerise, violet, chartreuse, scarlet, and some are almost black. Small flowers of various colors, including red, pink, and green edged with blue, hide in the leafy base.

✹ Bright sun makes foliage most colorful. In nature they grow in sunlight that filters through tree leaves, so they will do well in interior spaces away from direct light, on coffee tables, mantels, shelves, or wall brackets. They will also do well in artificial light.

☞ Keep the center of the plant filled with water and the potting mix just barely moist. Keep on the dry side during the winter. Bromeliads can go for weeks without water, which is why they are such favorites of busy people.

❧ Plant in osmunda fiber (like that sold for orchids) or a mixture of osmunda and potting soil. In nature, bromeliads grow in the decaying vegetable matter that collects in the crotches of trees. Don't feed and don't worry about insects—the leaves are too tough to be bothered by them. Bromeliads are very slow growing and relatively expensive, but they are also immune to all forms of neglect.

CHLOROPHYTUM (SPIDER PLANT), LILIACEAE FAMILY

✔ Grassy green leaves (also green-and-white striped, yellow-and-green striped, green with white margins), some on pendent stems, grown as ground cover in some climates and often potted to display indoors or out in hanging baskets. White flowers appear on the stiff stems in winter.

✸ Grows best in bright light but tolerates poor light. (This plant adapts well to any condition and is one of my favorites!)

↑ While it likes moisture at its roots, you can let the soil dry out between waterings. Spider plants have strong roots that store water in case you forget about them.

☙ Don't cut off the tiny white flowers that appear on the stiff stems; some will develop into plantlets. Plant in regular potting soil in large pots because roots fill the container quickly. Feed during periods of rapid growth. Propagate new plants by potting the plantlets that grow on stem runners or cut mature plants apart with a sharp knife and pot the parts.

COLEUS (PAINTED NETTLE), FROM THE MINT FAMILY

✔ Has colorful, velvety foliage in plum, red, pink, green, and yellow and gets blue flowers if placed outdoors in summer. Grows to about sixteen inches tall.

✸ Needs a bright sunny window indoors. Will grow outdoors in shade, but not very dense shade. When lacking sufficient light, growth is leggy and leaves are smaller and less colorful. Also, in very deep shade, lower leaves tend to drop prematurely.

↑ Water every second or third day. Plants will wilt if allowed to go dry, and lower leaves drop off if it gets dry too often.

☙ Will grow in regular potting soil. Grow new plants from seed or buy bedding plants. One package of seed produces many multicolored plants. You can also propagate new plants with cuttings from tips when the old plants get rangy and loose their color. Tip cuttings will root if planted in moist, sandy soil (or vermiculite); place in a sunny window.

Tips also root in water; plant in soil after a few sets of leaves show. Pinch flowers off seedlings if they appear. Pinch back tips and remove flowers frequently during growth and cut back hard before new spring growth to prevent legginess.

Mealybugs love this plant, and since most insecticides that kill mealy bugs kill coleus, badly infested plants should be destroyed after you remove tops for cuttings. Carefully remove all mealybugs by hand from the cuttings before planting.

Dracaena (Corn Plant), Liliaceae Family

✔ A tall, durable plant with leathery corn-plant-like leaves. Foliage can be lightly spotted with yellow to cream white on a dark-green background; gray-green and white striped; plain green; green edged with burgundy; or with green, pink, and white leaves. Will grow two feet to indoor-tree size.

✸ Will flourish in bright light with little or no direct sun. Some varieties do well in fluorescent light and others respond to available light with different growth patterns, such as a variety of angles and curves when placed in sun. Best light is a sunny east or west window, a bright north window, or similar brightness a few feet from a south window.

↱ Keep soil evenly moist but not too soggy. If soil is allowed to get severely dry, older leaves will yellow and fall off or leaf tips will turn brown and die. If water is allowed to accumulate on leaves, they may get spotted.

❧ Young plants need to be transplanted to larger pots as their roots fill each-size pot. Otherwise, the plant growth will be stunted. Mature plants can stay in the same container for years if fed regularly and top dressed. Plant in regular potting soil and feed according to package directions with all-purpose or foliage-plant food all year. Tip/stem cuttings can be rooted during any season. When tops of dracaena are cut off, the remaining stems produce new shoots. Canes cut from the plant can be planted horizontally in moist peat moss and sand to grow new plants.

DIEFFENBACHIA (DUMB CANE, OR MOTHER-IN-LAW PLANT), CALLA FAMILY

CAUTION: The stem juice of this plant is poisonous, and if it touches the tongue the result is painful swelling and paralysis that can last for as long as three days.

✔ Foliage is mostly green with white variegation (or spotted) or pale chartreuse with dark-green edges and veins. Most will produce a lilylike flower. The plant can grow up to eight feet or more.

✳ Best light is a sunny east or west window in winter. It needs less light in summer and adapts to a bright north light.

☞ Keep soil evenly moist and mist frequently. Severe dryness will cause older leaves to yellow and die. Needs more water in summer than in winter.

🐛 Thrives in all-purpose soil. Feed all-purpose plant food all year round. Dieffenbachia tend to get leggy, and some will lose a leaf from the bottom each time they grow one at the top. You can cut off the tops of leggy plants and root or grow them in water. The remaining trunks will send out new shoots. Stems can be cut into small sections of three to five inches and planted horizontally in a mixture of peat moss and sand, where they will grow shoots. You can root tip cuttings or air-layer best in the spring. Temperatures of sixty degrees F. or lower may harm dumb cane.

NOTE: Air layering (or layering) is a means of propagating plants that have become very leafy on top while the main stem lacks leaves or new growth shoots/stems. Here's how to do it:

1. Cut a lengthwise notch in the stem of the plant at a point where you want new roots to grow. (For example, if you have a clump of leaves on top of a single, leafless main stem, cut a notch about halfway to two-thirds the distance up from the stem's soil line.) Wrap very moist sphagnum moss around the notched area and hold the sphagnum in place by wrapping the area with plastic wrap, secured on either end with twist-ties.

2. Keep the moss moist by adding water periodically.

3. After four to six weeks, the moss ball will be filled with new roots. Cut off below the roots and place the new plant into potting soil; care as before. Save the old plant; it will produce a new top if you continue to water and care for it as before.

FICUS, MORACEAE FAMILY

✔ Among the most popular varieties of ficus are ficus elastica (rubber plant), which has broad, leathery twelve-inch oval green leaves; ficus pumila (creeping fig), a creeping plant with one-inch leaves, and ficus benjamina (weeping or benjamin fig), which is a small tree with two-inch oval green leaves on drooping branches.

✳ They grow best in bright light but will tolerate poor light.

☝ Keep soil consistently moist except in winter, when they need less moisture. Wipe leaves with a damp cloth to keep them shiny but avoid clogging leaf pores with oil or special leaf-polishing preparations.

🌢 Plant in regular potting mixtures. Propagate from leaf cuttings or by air layering. Even large ficus grow best in smaller pots. However, rubber plants will outgrow containers of any size. They will also grow to the ceiling and then bend over and continue to grow at an angle unless regularly pruned. Don't wait until your rubber plant touches the ceiling before pruning off the top unless you want a tall, bare-stemmed tree. When a rubber plant reaches a suitable height for the space you have, such as four to six feet, use the air-layering technique noted above to produce another plant.

SANSEVIERIA (SNAKE PLANT, LUCKY PLANT, LEOPARD LILY, MOTHER-IN-LAW PLANT), LILIACEAE FAMILY

NOTE: Mothers-in-law sure get a bum rap sometimes, and it isn't always deserved! The plant world is an example. While sansevieria is nick-named mother-in-law plant because its leaves look like long, sharp tongues, dieffenbachia is called mother-in-law plant because it has a poison that, if it touches the tongue, can result in painful swelling and paralysis; so it can be used as a potion to stop someone from speaking.

✔ An old-fashioned favorite: snake plants, with their sharp-pointed, thick, fleshy green leaves that are mottled with yellow, are nearly indestructible. Some are upright and others form ground-hugging rosettes. Rosette forms are often planted in dish gardens. Some long-leaf plants will get as tall as five feet. Mature plants produce sprays of fragrant pink-white or yellowish flowers, but flowering is erratic and unpredictable.

❋ Thrives in sun or shade but will survive even in a dark corner.

☝ Water every week to ten days. They tolerate moisture but will hardly change size if kept dry. Avoid overwatering, especially in winter. In fact, this plant is so hardy that overwatering is about the only way you can kill it—good news for people who just want to leave their plants to fend for themselves.

❧ Propagate from offsets of the root stock and plant in regular potting soil.

TRADESCANTIA (WANDERING JEW, INCH PLANT, TAHITIAN BRIDAL VEIL, PURPLE HEART, MOSES-ON-A-RAFT, THREE-MEN-IN-A-BOAT), SPIDERWORT FAMILY

✔ Fast-growing, the wandering jew has leaves that are oval, shiny and bright green (or green and purple, or purple and silver, or pinkish-cream and red, or red with silver stripes). The leaves are an inch long and spaced about an inch apart on spindly stems. This plant is often grown in water but will grow in any type of soil, too. It doesn't climb but grows well in hanging baskets. Planted in the yard, it forms a garden ground cover and can remain outdoors all year in warm climates. It produces lavender/pink or white blossoms in spring and summer.

❋ Tolerates poor light if growing in rich soil. However, colors are more intense if the plants get a lot of sunshine.

❧ Cuttings placed in water or in the yard will root quickly. Take cuttings from the tips when the plants get two to three feet long.

Herbs

Potted herbs are sold at garden centers in the spring, and many will do nicely on a kitchen windowsill.

Many supermarkets sell potted chives in their produce sections throughout the year. You can also buy herb kits in which you get all you need (soil plugs, pots, and seeds) to grow herbs such as oregano, chives, basil, thyme, parsley, sage, etc.

Follow the directions given on the tags that come with the plants or the kit directions—generally it's to put the plants in a sunny window, water when the soil is dry, and harvest the tips of stems to keep the plants small and bushy.

Sprouts for Salads and Stir-Fry
(*Alfalfa, Mung Bean, Wheat*)

Mung-bean sprouts are good in salads or Chinese stir-fry dishes. Alfalfa and wheat sprouts are good in salads, sandwiches, and are often baked in health breads.

1. On sponges—Sprinkle seeds on flat, wet sponges that are placed on dishes. Keep sponges moist and in a sunny location and watch the sprouts grow.

2. In jars—Turn recycled jars like those from large-size instant tea into "greenhouses." Pound holes in the jar lids to allow for draining water from the seeds and sprouts. You can also make strainer-lids with the rims of two-piece canning-jar lids. Replace the round seal part of the lid with cheesecloth or screening.

Put about an inch or so of seeds in the bottom of the jar and let the seeds soak, covered with water, overnight or over a day. Drain the water, add fresh water and then drain again, allowing the seeds to settle on the side of the jar. Keep the jar on its side as the sprouts grow.

Irrigate daily by pouring water over the seeds/sprouts and draining.

Do this until the sprouts reach the size you like. (I like mine to be two to three inches total in length, otherwise there's too much root.) Then, irrigate and drain one more time and put the jar of sprouts into the refrigerator to stop growth.

HINT: When growing mung beans for bean sprouts, it's better to use a brown-colored bottle so that the sprouts don't turn green from exposure to light.

HINT: Remove seed hulls before eating, if you wish, by putting the sprouts in a bowl or strainer and blasting them with cold water at the greatest pressure your faucet will provide. Then put the sprouts in a large bowl filled with water and swish them around so the remaining hulls float to the top. I don't usually bother to get them all off; it just takes more time than I care to spend on the process.

Plants from Kitchen "Scraps"

GENERAL DIRECTIONS FOR PLANTING PITS AND SEEDS
(*grapefruit, orange,* unroasted *coffee beans, etc.*)

1. Allow the pits or seeds to dry for three to four days, then plant them with the fat, rounded end down at least an inch deep in a mixture of three parts potting soil and one part vermiculite. Plant several, in case some don't sprout.

2. Place in a window, but not in harsh sunlight or under a plant light. Keep the soil damp but not soaked. You should be rewarded with sprouts in three to four weeks.

NOTE: I've had lots of failures with coffee beans. They are very temperamental. It must be the caffeine!

Avocado Pit

1. Stick three toothpicks into the pit at the middle. (Imagine that the seed is the Earth; put the toothpicks at the equator which encircles the seed so that the pointed end is north and the fatter, wider end is south.)

Then, put the seed into a glass of water with the fat end down. The toothpicks will hold the pit so that the water level covers about half the seed.

2. Maintain the water level and change the water often because algae tend to form. After a week or two, you'll have roots and a sprout. When you see enough roots, plant in a mixture of three parts potting soil and one part vermiculite. I've had trees grow ceiling high and last for ten to fifteen years, and the best part is that they are free!

Coconut Palm

1. Place an *unhusked* coconut on top of sandy soil in a wide-diameter pot.

2. Keep the pot warm, damp, and in good light. After the shoot emerges from one end of the husk, it will take about three years to grow a three-foot tree.

Date Palms

1. Plant the pits of *unpasteurized* dates in potting soil.

2. Keep the pot moist and warm. Be patient because dates are very slow to germinate.

Mango Seeds

1. Place each pit flat on top of potting soil, then push it down into the soil so that the soil forms a "collar" around the seed.

2. Put the pot in a warm place and keep the soil damp. In about a month, the root and seedling will sprout.

Ginger Root

When you buy fresh ginger root for Oriental cooking, you seldom use the whole piece, so cut off what you need and plant the remaining piece. (Be sure to select nice, plump, smooth-looking roots, not those that look dried up, wrinkled or shriveled.)

1. Prepare a large pot with about a twelve-inch depth of rich potting soil and good drainage. Then, plant the root just below the soil surface and place the pot in a warm, sunny spot (outdoors if possible).

2. After green shoots come up through the soil, mist the shoots often; water and fertilize regularly.

3. This plant will grow outdoors during the summer but should be moved indoors during cold winter weather. It will die down and become dormant during the winter months and grow again in the spring.

4. After the plant is growing well and about one year old, you can carefully dig up the roots from under the younger sprouts and cook with them.

NOTE: Avoid disturbing the original mature root, which is the plant's main root.

5. If the root system grows well, you may need to repot the plant into a larger pot to prevent it from getting root bound.

How to Propagate New Plants

Although most plants will root in water, many will not thrive if kept in water. Here's the easiest way to root cuttings in soil:

1. Place one to two inches of very light potting soil and vermiculite in the bottom of a "zipper" sandwich bag. Moisten the soil thoroughly, but pour off excess water.

2. Snip off cuttings at an angle with a sharp knife or shears. Wet the cut ends and dip them into a root starter (bought where live plants are sold); trim off leaves that cover the lower inch or two of the cutting; plant the tip in the soil.

3. Inflate the bag by sealing it almost across the top, then blow into the bag as you complete the seal. Air keeps the plastic from touching the leaves in this makeshift "greenhouse."

4. Leave the bag in partial, not full, sunlight until the cuttings root. Rooting may take three days to three weeks, depending on the plant. Keep the soil moist. After roots form, plant in potting soil.

NOTE: Larger clippings can be rooted in a pot filled with a mixture of vermiculite and potting soil. Clip stems as noted above, wet the ends, dip into root starter, and place in soil.

General Indoor Gardening Hints

GENERAL MAINTENANCE FOR MOST PLANTS

Pinch off tiny new shoots at the growing points of most plants to keep them bushy. (Don't pinch tops off trees, though!)

Fertilize potted plants—nutrients in the soil wash away more quickly when plants are in pots; they need to be replenished for best growth. I think that the easiest way is the feed as you water liquid-type. Turn plants frequently to prevent lopsidedness from their natural tendency to reach for the sun. Your trivia tip for today: This tendency to respond to a stimulus like light is called tropism.

DRAINAGE

When potting plants, you can provide drainage at the bottom of the pot by adding cracked walnut shells, broken pieces of clay pots, marbles, stones, fruit pits, or plastic-foam packing "peanuts" before you add the soil.

AVOIDING DRIPS

1. Place a shower cap over the bottom of a hanging planter to catch light drips when you water it; remove after an hour or so.

2. Hang an old, unused umbrella upside down with the handle hooked over the side of a hanging pot to catch drips and drainage. (At last! A way to recycle your favorite wind-damaged umbrella!)

BRACING PLANTS

Bend a wire hanger so that it makes a round trellis for ivy and poke the hanging part into the soil. Tie plant stalks to a stake with an old pantyhose leg or pantyhose "ties" made by cutting a leg into several crosswise strips. An old curtain rod can be a plant stake.

BUG CHECK

Check for bugs by giving your plants a good soaking in the shower. ("Shower" only one plant at a time to prevent spreading infestations.) Water will force the "uninvited guests" to the soil's surface so that you can see if and what kind of pests are bothering the plant and then determine how to treat the problem. Get advice on curing the plant's problem from your local nursery or call your local County Extension Agent. (Look under U.S. Government, Department of Agriculture, in the phone book.) If you think a plant is infected, keep it isolated— because the "invaders" can travel from pot to pot.

BUG DETERRENT

Planting a garlic clove in the pot repels many plant pests. Many gardeners plant garlic cloves outdoors at the bases of rose bushes to repel aphids.

SAFE BUG KILLERS

A mild solution of water and liquid detergent (one-third cup detergent to one gallon water) will kill many kinds of houseplant insects. Spray the leaves with the solution, especially the underside where bugs usually lurk. You may have to repeat the application several times.

CAUTION: Do not use on plants with velvety leaves.

To "de-bug" African violets when they get plant lice, spray hair spray into a plastic bag that's large enough to cover the whole plant. Immediately, place the plant in the bag and tie it shut with a twist-tie. Let the plant stay in the bag for a day. *Note:* Do not spray hair spray directly onto the plant.

Place a slice of raw potato on the soil surface to collect root-damaging worms.

Place a pest strip inside a plastic bag "tent" with the plant to collect insects. (Keep plants out of sunlight when in the tent, because it might get too hot in this "plant hospital.")

Make a trap for aphidlike plant bugs by applying a layer of petroleum jelly on a clean, dry, yellow plastic liquid dishwashing detergent container. Place the container next to a plant suspected of infection. The bugs, attracted to the yellow color, will get stuck in the petroleum jelly. When the container gets nasty-looking, wash, dry and repeat the "treatment."

PET PROTECTION

Cats love houseplants, but their interest is not esthetic. To prevent your cat from using potted plants for litter boxes, cover the soil with a roll of "chicken" wire or a mat of nylon net, a layer or two of marbles, shells, or anything else that makes digging impossible. Also, keep a "spritz" bottle or squirt gun filled with water nearby and squirt the kitty every time it approaches the plant—or, gently touch a vinegar or alcohol-moistened cotton ball to a cat's lips each time it goes to the plant and leave the cotton ball at the base of the plant as extra deterrent. Eventually, kitty will avoid the plant—and probably the whole area around it.

STORING GARDEN TOOLS

Unless you use old plastic or stainless-steel kitchen tools for digging in potting soil, it's best to lightly oil metal garden tools before storing them to prevent rust. Some active gardeners keep a small bucket of oil-soaked sand in which to dip tools before storing them. (If you live in an apartment, however, it could be difficult to store this mixture and a fire hazard, too.)

WATERING HINTS

1. Put water in an empty, clean plastic squeeze container so that you can squirt water beneath plant leaves. (Some plants, like African violets, don't like water on their leaves.)
2. Or, poke a funnel tip beneath leaves and water into the funnel.
3. Mist leaves with a clean, recycled spray bottle.
4. Recycle plastic liquid laundry-detergent containers; they make good and neat watering cans for houseplants. Rinse well before using.

FREE FERTILIZERS

Water from freshwater (not saltwater) fish tanks; or water drained after you have soaked egg shells in it for a day or so.

HOW TO PROTECT SURFACES

If you receive a gift plant that's in a wicker basket, be aware that, even when lined with plastic, some of these containers can leak and damage furniture, windowsills, carpets, or wood flooring. Place a saucer, plate, or tray beneath the container for safety's sake.

For more protection for carpets and floors, cut acrylic plastic sheets from hardware stores into appropriately sized squares, attach small rubber adhesive-backed protectors beneath each corner to help air to circulate, and put the squares beneath your plant pots.

PRETTY POTS

Apply a light coat of vegetable oil to the outsides of terra-cotta pots to prevent white spots. Or, if the pot is new or newly cleaned and dry, apply a coat of redwood stain. To paint a pot, place it upside down over a can that is tall enough to hold the pot rim above the work surface. Be sure that the pot is clean and dry before attempting to paint it.

CLEANING POTS

To prevent transfer of plant diseases or pests when you reuse pots, wash the pot inside and out with hot, soapy water; then soak it for five minutes in a solution of three-quarters cup of liquid chlorine bleach to a gallon of warm water. Rinse well.

POT SUBSTITUTES

A plastic wastebasket can hold a large potted plant or, if you punch drain holes in the bottom, it can be an inexpensive substitute for a large pot.

Two- or three-liter soft-drink bottles can be converted into planters and vases. Pull off the dark plastic "seats," and you'll have shallow planters with automatic drain holes in the bottoms. Punch holes along the rims, and they can be laced for hanging planters. Cut off the tops of large soda bottles at any height, and the bottoms can be vases or planters. Or, remove the dark plastic "seats," cut off a portion of the bottom, put dirt in the "seat," and plant small plants or seeds. Then replace the remaining top so that you have a small windowsill greenhouse. Leave the cap off for ventilation.

DUSTING LEAVES

Slip on a pair of soft cotton gloves or old socks, then put one hand beneath the leaf and gently dust with the other.

IDENTIFYING PLANTS

If you receive a gift plant and the name/care directions tag is missing, call the florist who delivered it or go to a garden center, find a duplicate, and then copy the directions given on the tag. Don't forget to check your local library for indoor gardening books; use your tax dollars!

Shopping List for Indoor Gardening

1. Plants and suitable pots/saucers or substitutes for pots and saucers made from household discards such as clean plastic bottles and jugs, chipped bowls and plates, plastic lids from such containers as oatmeal boxes, etc.
2. Potting soil.
3. Plant food.
4. Plant mister or well-washed spray bottle from a nonharmful substance.
5. Watering pitcher or substitute such as old coffeepot, teapot, plastic jug.
6. Other optional special equipment like hangers for hanging baskets, etc.
7. Root starter, vermiculite, etc., for starting cuttings.

CHAPTER SEVEN

Pets

Pets can be wonderful roommates for singles. They don't require their own rooms, never take the last soft-drink can from the fridge, and don't run up expensive long-distance phone bills.

In addition to companionship, pets can be beneficial to your health. Medical research tells us that pet ownership helps people live longer, that pet owners are less likely to suffer from heart disease and have significantly lower blood pressure and lower cholesterol levels than people who don't have pets.

But that's not what you think about when you look at a puppy or kitten; you see a cute little creature to take home and love which will return your love and care a hundredfold.

Some pets, such as fish, cats, small dogs, hamsters, guinea pigs, and birds, are especially suitable for apartment living.

If you choose a dog or cat, it's important to be a responsible pet owner by getting your pet all its immunizations and by having all dogs and cats spayed and neutered if they are not primarily used for breeding. Spaying and neutering pet cats and dogs makes them stay healthier longer, keeps their dispositions more lovable, and helps to eliminate annoying habits like cats that spray to establish their territories and male dogs that are amorously preoccupied.

NOTE: Although it seems kind to feed stray cats and dogs, it's really more humane either to adopt the animals as your pets and care for them as noted above or to notify your local animal-control officer so that strays get placed in animal shelters, where they can be found if their owners are seeking them. Owner-abandoned stray animals lead a sad and dangerous life on the streets, and most die from auto accidents or disease.

General Pet Care

TRAVEL WITH PETS

Some pets have to be in a carrier while traveling, and others will sit calmly on a seat or the floor of your car. If you have a pet that's especially anxious and frantic when traveling by car or being shipped by air in a crate, check with your vet to see if a tranquilizer is safe. Unless instructed by your vet, do *not* give human medications to pets! Some can cause kidney failure and death!

Always call ahead to the hotel/motel to make sure pets are accepted or that kennels are nearby. Take along the food your pet is used to and a jug of water from home.

Put an ID collar on your pet! You may also want to put on a harness and a collar just in case your pet gets loose and loses one or the other. On the collar, give a phone number to call in addition to your own since you will not be home. The number could be that of a friend, relative, or your vet.

In many cities dogs are licensed through veterinarians' clinics or city hall, and so the license tag will help identify your pet. If you are taking a pet on a long car or plane trip, tell your vet where you are going and provide phone numbers where you can be reached during the trip and at your destination. Then, if your pet gets lost and reported to the vet because of the license tag, your vet can find you.

OLDER PETS

Various breeds of dogs and cats have different life spans. An aging pet still needs exercise but may tire more easily. An aging pet's metabolism slows down, too, so you may have to watch the food intake to prevent your pet from becoming overweight, which can cause as many health problems in pets as in humans.

PETS IN KENNELS

Check out the kennel to make sure that it is clean, without strong odors, and securely fenced, that the animals appear well cared for, are separated from one another, and that the personnel really seem to like animals. When you board your pet, take along a favorite towel, rag, or toy that has the scent of home. Reputable kennels safeguard against dogs' catching "kennel cough" by requiring proof of immunization several weeks prior to boarding.

PET CARPET "ACCIDENTS"

Please see spots and stains section in chapter 5.

Cats

Cats can be wonderful, lovable pets who can live indoors without ever going out if you provide them with proper litter boxes and exercise. A cat can be a most suitable pet for a person who lives alone and has no opportunity or place to walk a dog. Cats can stay home alone when you go on vacation if someone looks in on them once daily to make sure they have enough food and water, clean litter, and are generally okay. Here are some things you need to know about cats:

WHISKERS

Never trim or remove a cat's whiskers. Cats are touchy about their whiskers because they are the sensors that help them get around in tight spaces and determine the source of odors, acting as wind socks.

IMMUNIZATIONS

Even if your cat never goes outdoors, it should be properly vaccinated and get its annual boosters. A newer vaccine, FVRCPC—Feline Distemper, Rhinotracheitis, Calici, Panieukopenia, Psittacia vaccine—now also contains immunization against chlamydia, a feline eye infection that can spread to humans if proper hygiene isn't observed. Chlamydia irritates the cat's eyelid membrane and tear glands and then causes tearing. It can spread rapidly from one cat to another if you have several in the home.

Toxoplasmosis

This parasitic disease found in cats and transmitted by their feces seldom causes symptoms in cats but can cause severe infection of the fetus in pregnant women and serious illness in people who suffer from AIDS. The organism that brings about the infection takes three or more days to reach the infective stage for humans. You should clean litter boxes daily wearing protective gloves.

Allergies

If you are allergic to your cat, it's most likely due to the allergy-causing protein found in cat saliva which, because of their constant grooming, is on the cat's skin and fur. You can reduce this irritant by bathing your cat monthly for ten minutes in lukewarm water (no soap needed). Also vacuum carpets and upholstery to get rid of old dander. If your cat hates water, ask your vet how to bathe it. If you start when it's a kitten, it will get used to bathing.

Cat Medications

To keep from getting scratched while pilling a cat, get a special pill-giving syringe from the vet. Insert the pill into the syringe, then wrap your cat securely in a towel so that it's a tight bundle. Cradle the "cat bundle" with one hand and arm and administer the pill with the other.

Flea Spray

Never use dog flea spray on cats. You could poison or at least make your cat sick with flea powder or spray meant for dogs. Check with your vet to get products that are safe and effective for each type of pet.

Cat Training

With a squirt gun or plant mister, spritz kitty every time it goes somewhere it doesn't belong. Soon, it will give up.

If you are gone all day and can't spritz your cat away from potted plants, you can keep kitty from digging in pot plants by covering the soil with nylon net, plastic craft mesh, "chicken" wire fencing that's rolled up, pinecones, a layer of marbles, or anything else that makes the soil unavailable.

Also, you can keep kitty from clawing or sitting on forbidden places by *gently* touching its lips with a cotton ball saturated with rubbing alcohol or vinegar each time it goes to the forbidden place. No need to rub or be mean, just a gentle touch will do. Then leave the cotton ball at that place as a reminder.

CAT TOYS

Never give a cat a ball of yarn or string to play with. Cats may swallow yarn or string, with disastrous results; they may choke on it or even need surgery to remove the string. Instead, let the cat bat around an old sock rolled into a ball, a tennis ball, a wad of crumpled paper, a small plastic pill bottle containing a small bell or several tiny pebbles. Hang a fishing float on a string from a doorknob and watch kitty bat it around.

CAT SCRATCHING POSTS

Train kitty to use a scratching post: Lead it to the post by dangling a toy on a string and then bobbing the toy over the post so kitty gets the idea of scratching at that spot. Or, put catnip on the post (not all cats like catnip, though).

NOTE: Cats will also scratch a piece of scrap-carpet-covered log or two-by-four wood building stud that's long enough for the cat to stand and stretch on. Just place it flat on the floor in a place where kitty likes to scratch.

CAT CARRIER

Most cats fare better going to the vet or elsewhere if they are in carriers. If you don't have one, a quickie carrier can be made by lacing two plastic laundry baskets together, one of them upside down on the other. Put several layers of newspapers on the bottom to absorb accidents. A harness and leash add security when you are transporting a frantic cat.

Cat Illnesses

See "Dog Illnesses"; the behaviors are similar.

Dogs

Whether you buy your dog from a good breeder or rescue one from the pound, do some research on the behavior of different breeds so that you'll choose one with a temperament and size to suit your life.

If you like peace and quiet, don't get a high-spirited terrier. If you live in a twentieth-floor efficiency apartment, don't get a Great Dane even if you like Marmaduke® cartoons! Life is not a cartoon—even if it seems that way sometimes!

Generally, male dogs are somewhat more aggressive than females, and female dogs cost more to have spayed. But both can be terrific pets for many years. Also, smaller dogs tend to have longer life spans.

How to Pick a Healthy Puppy

Look for a curious, alert, active, and friendly puppy with clean, thick, glossy fur; bright, clear eyes; clean ears, with pale pink skin inside. The puppy should be able to stand without wobbling and have a solid, muscular body. Look in its mouth; it should have healthy pink, firm gums and white teeth.

Avoid a puppy that seems despondent or is overly frightened, has discharging or cloudy eyes; excessive dark wax or bad-smelling ears; discolored gums, bad breath or deposits around the teeth; signs of parasites; excessive dandruff or bare or reddish patches on its skin; or signs of diarrhea near the tail.

Training a Puppy

Stock up on patience; you'll need it. Never let the pup have the run of the house while you are trying to train it; confine it to one area. (A friend of mine made door barricades from pegboard, and now when she wants to keep her dog away from something, like a certain chair or sofa, she places a pegboard in front of it for a couple of weeks and the dog sees that piece of furniture as a "no-no.")

If you have a large cage, it will help, otherwise a plastic wading pool or old baby playpen will do. Cover the bottom with an old plastic shower curtain and then layers of newspapers. The pup will get used to this restraint.

At the beginning, take the pup outside frequently and place some soiled newspapers on the area you want it to use so that it will get the scent and go to that spot automatically. Praise the pup for performing.

If the puppy makes a "mistake" and you catch it in the act, discipline it with a firm "No" and move the pup back to the area you want it in. Be consistent.

If you live in the city, be aware that many cities have "pooper scooper" laws and that it's just plain courtesy to your fellow humans to clean up after your dog. Either buy a commercial "poop scoop" or scoop up feces with a used paper plate into a plastic bag. Or, carry a small shovel or dustpan; insert the shovel's business end in a plastic grocery bag and then when you scoop up the poop, turn the bag inside out over the whole mess, tie it shut, and dispose of it properly.

IMMUNIZATIONS

Dogs need initial immunizations and then annual booster shots to protect them from distemper, parvovirus, coronavirus, parainfluenza, canine hepatitis, and leptospirosis.

Heartworm tests are usually started at six months, and medication must be given throughout the year—not just during mosquito season, as some people think. *Do not* start heartworm medication without first consulting your vet and having the dog tested. Be aware that reputable boarding and grooming facilities want dogs to have their immunizations kept up to date and won't accept nonimmunized dogs lest they harm the rest of the "boarders."

Dog Illnesses

Take your dog to the vet if it has sudden changes in behavior such as:

- irritability or viciousness, or lack of energy
- unusual discharges from the nose, eyes, or other body openings
- abnormal lumps
- limping or difficulty getting up or down
- loss of appetite
- weight loss or gain
- increased thirst and drinking
- difficult, abnormal, or uncontrolled urination or bowel movements
- excessive head shaking or scratching, licking, or biting any part of the body
- dandruff, loss of hair, open sores, and a ragged or dull coat
- foul breath or excessive tartar on teeth.

Dogs and Pills

If you can't convince your dog that the pill is a treat and you just can't bring yourself to poke a pill down your dog's throat, wrap the pill in a wad of cheese or liverwurst or smear it with a dab of butter or peanut butter.

Dogs and Hot Weather

On any trip with a dog, remember that in less than thirty minutes, a car can get to 120 degrees F. inside when the outside temperature is only 85 degrees. Even if you leave the windows open slightly, *never* leave your dog in the car in summer.

Also, in hot weather, don't tie your dog up to a tree or post and leave it there. Heat exhaustion causes brain damage and possible death! Should a dog suffer from heat exhaustion (continuous panting, agitation, and loss of consciousness), wet it down with a hose or in the shower, place an ice pack on its neck and paws until the temperature goes down, and take the animal to the vet.

Also, remember that dogs are especially eager to please their owners and will jog with you to the point of heat exhaustion just to be with you; please don't overexercise a dog in the summer.

DOGGY ODORS

Here's how to keep your dog free of normal odors between baths. Sprinkle baking soda on the fur, rub, and leave it on for a few minutes. Then brush well to remove.

CAUTION: Do not use on dogs that must restrict their sodium intake.

DOG TOYS

Many dogs like to play tug-o-war with an old jeans leg or sturdy leather belt. Make sure all toys are safe and suitable for chewing—no spongy rubber or hard plastic items that can be chewed into sharp pieces that will damage the digestive tract when swallowed. Hard rubber dog balls, rawhide toys, doggy plastic flying discs, and other sturdy toys are fun for playing "fetch."

CAUTION: A bored or frightened dog will tear up the house and eat just about anything. Some human food such as chocolate can be poison to dogs, so protect your pet by not leaving harmful things where it can get them.

If your dog tears up the house every time you are gone, get advice from your vet on "crate training." Contrary to what some people think, keeping a dog in a suitably large dog cage while you are gone is kinder to the animal than letting it run loose in a panic.

Dogs are pack animals, and their owners become "the pack" without which they just get lonely and scared. A cage can make a dog feel secure in its own "home territory."

Fish

Watching fish swimming in an aquarium is said to lower blood pressure and relax tense people. But, ask aquarium owners if that's why they got involved with underground filters, water Ph measurements, and air pumps, and they are more likely to say that their fish are pretty and interesting to watch.

Also, fish do not require bathing, flea dipping, or walking. However, they do require a proper environment for their special needs.

Before you buy, do your consumer research. You can find books that specialize in freshwater or "marine" (saltwater) fishes. Books and the advice from a knowledgeable aquarium store clerk (who is also a fish fancier) will help you set up the tank for easy care, to select fish that are compatible, and will provide advice on potential problems.

NOTE: Setting up the tank is the first step. You need to be sure that the aquarium doesn't leak and that all the equipment is working properly before you put the fish into the tank.

FISH SELECTION

The fish should look clean, with no evidence of disease such as white or black spots (that are not part of the usual appearance). Watch out for dull eyes, lethargic behavior, or floating listlessly at the top of the tank.

Don't just buy a bunch of fish and put them into the water and hope for the best! Saltwater tanks need to be "seasoned" by placing invertebrates in the bottom for a period of time to create a chemical balance in the water.

Fish-breed selection must consider compatibility of the fish. For example, many fish fanciers say you can have only one angelfish in a tank because they are very territorial, and the more-dominant fish will ultimately cause the less-dominant ones to die either by harassing them to death or not allowing them to feed.

African cichlids are very aggressive fish and will shred one another's tails periodically. However, if all the fish are about the same size and are placed in the tank at the same time, they will more or less establish a sort of harmony.

NOTE: If an African cichlid becomes aggressive to other fish in the tank, rearrange its territory (i.e. rocks, plants). The cichlid will begin reestablishing its territory and forget about the other fish, for a while.

"Community tanks" of freshwater fish function best if fish that live at different water levels, have different degrees of aggressive behavior, and various feeding patterns (top or bottom feeders) are placed in the tank.

ADDING NEW FISH TO A TANK

If you have a large tank of many fish, you should also keep a small tank for isolating new fish for two weeks to make sure they are healthy before adding them to the main tank where they can infect the others. The best aquarium stores quarantine newly arrived fish until they are sure that the fish are healthy.

If you are sure the fish are healthy and don't need quarantining, don't just dump them into the tank. Allow the bagged fish to float in the tank for about fifteen or twenty minutes so that the new fish can become acclimated to your tank's water temperature. After the waiting time, during which you rearrange tank decorations (see below), open the bag while it's still in the tank and allow the new fish to swim into their new home.

NOTE: Most types of fish are territorial and don't like newcomers to invade their hiding corners or swimming water levels. When adding new fish to the tank, rearrange the tank decorations such as plastic or real seagrasses, shells, coral, etc., to disorient the fish already living there. Add the newcomer in the confusion so that all the fish will have to find new territory at the same time.

FISH-TANK DECORATIONS

Place only items sold in aquarium stores; others, including shells, may have been varnished or have other substances on them that could harm your fish.

To clean algae off green coral and shells so that they are white again, carefully place the pieces in a plastic pail or large wastebasket and then add enough cold tap water to completely cover all the coral. Then, add one-fourth cup of chlorine bleach for each four gallons of water. Make sure it's plain chlorine bleach; the lemon-scented kind is not suitable. Soak for about a week. Be sure to rinse well!

If the coral is still not clean enough, add more bleach. After the coral and shells are white, you can either let them air-dry or rinse them with fresh water repeatedly until you can't smell any bleach. Or, soak the coral in fresh water treated with dechlorinator (used to dechlorinate water before putting it into a fish tank); add at least three or four times the recommended dose of dechlorinator relative to the amount of water.

The test to see if the coral is ready to put back into the tank is: If you smell chlorine, it's not ready. Repeat the soak in dechlorinator/water solution or allow to air-dry until the bleach smell is gone.

FEEDING FISH

Use food specifically recommended for your type of fish and feed only what the fish will eat in five or so minutes.

Some people feed twice daily, others three times, still others only once. Uneaten food left to decompose in the bottom of the tank poisons the water and is unhealthy for the fish. Ideally, bottom- and top-feeding fish keep food from being "leftovers."

FISH WATER

Water-test kits are available at aquarium stores. They are simple to use and will help you decide if the water has a proper chemical balance.

If fish become lethargic, check the water temperature (too-cold water makes them inactive) and check the chemical balance (imbalances affect fish behavior, for example, by making them lethargic or very jumpy so that they bolt wildly when someone approaches the tank). Get help at the aquarium store if you can't figure out what's wrong.

WATER CHANGES

Generally, you make a one-third water change at intervals of a week, two weeks, or whatever works for your tank.

The number and size of the fish, feeding procedures, and filter systems will determine how much care your tank needs. If you don't have a large container in which to dechlorinate/mix fish water, place a large plastic garbage bag in a large plastic (forty-gallon or so) wastebasket or kitchen garbage can and then mix the water in that. Before you mix the water and dechlorinator, you can use the garbage can to collect the old fish water from the tank when you drain it with a siphon (available at pet-supply stores).

To put fresh water into the tank, you can dip the water out of the garbage can with clean one-gallon milk jugs or a small plastic pail and pour it into the tank. The fish will usually hide at one end or in a corner of the tank while you are disturbing their environment, so you can pour water where they are not clustered.

NOTE: Fish-tank water, not from saltwater fish, is good fertilizer for plants—so you can recycle it!

Gerbils, Hamsters, Guinea Pigs

Like fish, these little creatures don't need walking and can stay alone in the house for short periods. The bonus is that they don't bark, claw the drapes, or otherwise annoy a landlord.

HOME

A ten-gallon aquarium with a wire screen or mesh cover over the top will house gerbils and hamsters, or you can buy special plastic aquarium-style habitats with tunnels and extra hiding places for the little critters.

Guinea pigs are usually kept in cages bought at pet stores. If you use a bird cage as a gerbil or hamster home, be sure to tie the lift-up door, because they can open it. In fact they will squeeze through very small openings, so you must always be sure to make their environment secure.

AS PETS

These small rodents become cuddly pets if allowed to adjust to handling. Handle them and let them burrow in pockets and sleeves for increasing periods of time to "tame" them.

ACTIVITY

Nocturnal by nature, these animals will sleep all day and be active at night. Females become very restless when in heat and will try to escape their homes; make sure all tunnel and other exits are securely fastened. Males are more docile.

An exercise wheel or perforated clear-plastic ball (sold at pet shops) will help entertain both you and your pet. They are an absolute hoot to watch! An exercise ball is a good way to transport your pet if you move.

FOOD

In addition to store-bought boxed food, feed carrots, lettuce, and various seeds.

Food can be put in metal jar lids or little ceramic dishes sold for small-animal feeding. Do not put food in plastic dishes because the animal will eat the dish, too.

Also provide chew sticks from the pet store, because these animals need to chew.

ESCAPES

Never keep a rodent pet in a paper or cardboard box for longer than it takes to get it from the pet store to home. It will chew its way out. You may want to buy an exercise ball when you purchase the pet and take it home in the ball.

A veteran owner of all types of rodent pets says the best way to find an escapee is to listen carefully, search with a flashlight where you hear scratching, and scoop him up.

If you have to leave for work, place the little critter's favorite food in its cage/habitat and then position the cage near where you think it's hiding—and hope for the best.

Birds

I usually have several birds as pets and really do enjoy watching them and playing with them. We recently built an aviary outdoors for Rocky, our pet macaw, but not everyone lives in our mild climate or has a backyard in which to keep an aviary.

BUYING A BIRD

Buy only from a reputable dealer. All imported birds must have stainless-steel leg bands, put on when they enter quarantine.

Many birds are smuggled into the country illegally without the benefit of quarantine: a practice that endangers birds in the United States with such afflictions as Newcastle disease, a devastating bird sickness. Please don't let your quest for an exotic pet lead you to do something illegal and harmful.

CHOOSING A HEALTHY BIRD

Look for a bird that seems temperamentally well balanced and shows interest in your presence or voice and its own surroundings.

A reputable bird dealer will agree that the purchase is contingent on the bird's passing an examination by a veterinarian of your choice. If the bird is not in good health, you should get a full refund. The dealer should give you a written bill of sale stating that you can return the bird, the date of purchase, and any other conditions of sale; the price paid and the bird's band number, if possible; the bird's birthdate, if known; and a full description, including the bird's genus and species, sex and color. If the bird has been imported, you should receive a copy of the quarantine certificate.

SIGNS OF ILLNESS

- Eye or nose discharges (staining of feathers above the nostrils)
- sneezing or coughing
- shortness of breath
- regurgitation or loose droppings

- soiled rectum
- fluffing up
- inactivity (looking sleepy or withdrawn)
- bald spots where feathers should be
- swelling or sores on the feet or claws (both feet should grip the perch or your hand firmly)
- protruding breastbone
- white crusts on the beak (which should be in good alignment)

TYPES OF BIRDS

Finches, canaries, budgerigars, and cockatiels are easiest to care for and to train.

Hand-raised, domestic Amazons and African grays are good talkers. Domestic, hand-raised macaws will talk but not as much as the Amazons and African grays. Domestic, hand-raised cockatoos are bought for their beauty and acrobatics rather than speech. Lovebirds are not easy to tame or train.

With some birds, you will be making a long-term commitment. Macaws, like our Rocky, can live for sixty to seventy years; African grays, sixty to seventy years as well; canaries, budgerigars, lovebirds, and cockatiels, ten to twenty years; finches, five to ten years.

CAGE PLACEMENT

Never keep a bird in the kitchen. Nonstick pans accidentally burning dry can give off toxic fumes that can be fatal, especially to small birds. Birds are also sensitive to hair sprays, deodorants, and flea powders and sprays. Put the cage out of drafts, away from air-conditioning or heating ducts, and not near a window where the sun will shine directly on it for long periods of time, especially in the summer. The bird needs plenty of light and circulating air. Cover the cage when the sun goes down.

CAGE CLEANING

Food and water bowls should be cleaned and disinfected daily. The cage needs a good cleaning weekly. Remove all dirt and debris, scrub with soap, hot water, and disinfect to kill all bacteria, spores, and viruses that can harm your bird. You can buy various brands of disinfectants from your avian veterinarian or mix up a solution of one ounce of chlorine (bleach) to one quart of water. (Do not use granulated chlorine meant for swimming pools.) Soak items to be disinfected in the bleach/water solution for thirty minutes, rinse, and dry.

FEEDING

Some birds are finicky eaters. To get a bird to eat the healthy variety of foods that it needs, it should be hungry at feeding time. Don't keep food dishes filled all day. Instead, set up feeding times and give it fewer seeds and more fruit and veggies. Having a regularly scheduled feeding time makes it a special bonding time between owner and bird, too.

ACTIVITY

Birds, although in cages, are not like fish. They need companionship and will pluck out their own feathers when they are lonely or bored. If your bird is alone all day, leave some toys, bells, and mirrors so that it can amuse itself, and don't forget the radio as company.

GETTING A BIRD TO TALK

Repetition is the key to teaching a bird to talk. Put the word you want it to learn on a cassette tape and then play it for your bird when you don't have time to chat or when you are away.

LOVESICK PARAKEETS

A lonely parakeet may preen endlessly in front of a mirror or a toy and may even regurgitate food onto the mirror or toy. This is courting or nesting behavior usually performed for a mate. To cure "lovesickness," remove the "love object" from the cage for two to three weeks and give the bird more exercise and attention.

NOTE: Regurgitation by parakeets and other birds can also be a symptom of digestive ailments. If your bird regurgitates often but has no other "lovesick" symptoms, check with your vet.

TRAVELING WITH A BIRD

Generally, changing locations is stressful to birds, and it is better to leave your bird at home with a sitter. You might be able to find a caretaker by contacting a local bird club, if your city has one. If you need to board the bird and if your veterinarian does not have a bird-boarding service, ask your vet for a recommendation.

If traveling by plane, check with the airline ahead of time to make sure that you will be allowed to take the bird aboard. Get a certificate of health from your veterinarian; some cities require it. Small birds may be carried on board in a cage, box, or other container. Large birds must travel with other large pets in specially designated areas of the plane. In both cases, there is a charge for each change of planes you'll make enroute. If traveling abroad, check with your travel agent for regulations at your destination; some countries have quarantine periods of up to six months.

If traveling by car, take your bird's cage, cover, food, and toys. You may want to take bottled water, too, because changes in water from one locale to another can upset the bird's digestion and cause loose droppings. *Do not* leave the bird in the car in hot weather!

As with all pets, call ahead to make sure the hotel/motel accepts pets.

PETS CHECKLIST

- Keep the radio on when you're gone to keep pets company.
- Buy dogs a new toy every week or so.
- Hide goodies for the dog.
- Keep outside water in a shaded area.
- Outdoors, put water in angel food cake pan, drive a wooden stake through the middle to hold in place.
- Put ice cubes in water to make cool when hot.
- Never keep an animal in a car in the summer.
- Keep a chart with vaccinations dates on it.
- Keep a medical record that shows all vet visits.

CHAPTER EIGHT

Your Car

Car Care for Nonmechanics

Many auto dealerships in major cities are offering free car-care classes as part of their advertising and public-relations programs. Taking advantage of a class won't make you a mechanic, but it will introduce you to "auto-speak" so that you can communicate with your mechanic, understand your repair bill, and probably save some money!

Interpreting What Your Car "Says to You"

1. *Tick, tick, tick:* First check to see if oil is low. Other causes can be checked by a reliable service person. Ticking when the engine idles could be a valve-lifter problem. Ticking from under the car can be a faulty belt or exhaust leak.

2. *Thump, thump, thump*: Check for worn areas on tire treads. Smooth spots can be caused by the tire's being out of alignment or by tread separation. (This can be very serious because it can cause a blowout!)

3. *W-h-i-n-i-n-g*: Have transmission fluid and power-steering fluid checked if a car whines as you go from standstill to regular driving speed. It could also be a wheel bearing or axle bearing that needs immediate attention.

4. *Knock, knock, ping, ping:* Car needs tune-up if you hear knocking or pinging under the hood as you accelerate. Sometimes this malady is cured by using a higher-octane gasoline.

5. *Clunk*: A clunk when you back up or move ahead could be a universal joint problem.

6. *Click . . . silence*: Could be problems with the starter or the battery and charging system. Could also be loose or corroded connections.

7. *Growl, grind, squeal, scrape*: Brakes make lots of noises to say they may have worn linings or pads, or damaged brake drums or motors.

8. *Screech!*: Worn drive belt or belt that's loose or glazed.

Car Care and Cleaning

INTERIOR

1. Clean fabric upholstery with a "dry"-type upholstery cleaner found in most grocery or discount stores. Follow instructions on the container. Or, sprinkle dry baking soda on spots and stains while the spills are fresh, then brush or vacuum it off after the moisture has been absorbed.

Wipe vinyl seats with a solution of about four tablespoons of baking soda and one quart of water, rinse, and dry. Dry baking soda sprinkled on a damp sponge or cloth can be used to scrub off stubborn spots or stains on vinyl. Rinse well with a wet cloth or sponge and dry.

2. If rubber or plastic floor mats are removable, scrub them with a solution of half vinegar and half water, rinse well, and dry in the sun if possible.

3. Shampoo or clean carpeting with a spray-type carpet cleaner, making sure not to let the backing get wet.

WHEN CARS HAVE MUSTY ODORS

Quick Fixes

1. Keep some charcoal knotted in a sock or several thicknesses of pantyhose legs under one of the car seats to keep odors under control.

2. Tuck a fabric-softener sheet under a front seat of your car to mask unpleasant odors in your car. However, this is not a permanent solution. To remove odors, you may need to have the upholstery cleaned.

3. Spray the ceiling, carpet and trunk with a good spray deodorizer made for automobile interiors.

Next-Step Solution

Clean upholstery, floor mats, and carpeting as directed in "Car Care and Cleaning," above.

EXTERIOR

1. Protect the finish on your car exterior by washing it with products made for that purpose. Some commercial products wash and wax at the same time.

Many regular household detergents can be too harsh and will dull auto paint finishes. If you have no commercial cleaner, mix only a small amount of mild liquid detergent in a large bucket of water.

NOTE: Even some detergent-based car-wash products can dull paint finishes. The best way to avoid paint damage is to wash with cleaners labeled zero-pH and always rinse well with cold-to-lukewarm water. (The pH factor denotes acidity or alkalinity in a solution; high pH signifies high acid and low pH signifies very alkaline. Both extremely high and extremely low pH are bad for the paint finish.)

Also, do not wash or wax a car in direct sunlight. Do not use alcohol-based cleaners and polishes or abrasive or chemical cleaning solvents on plastic parts of the car such as light-bulb lenses, decorative stripes, panels, bumpers, etc.

2. To remove road tar from your car, spray the spots with an oil-based prewash spray, let set for a few minutes, and scrub carefully with a piece of nylon net or plastic scrubber.

Or, remove tar or oil with a cloth soaked with lighter fluid or turpentine. Check an inconspicuous place first and remember, they're flammable. You may need to rewax this area.

Or wipe with dry baking soda sprinkled on a damp sponge. Rinse and dry with a soft cloth. (Baking soda on a sponge will also shine headlights, taillights, mirrors, license plates, windshields, and wiper blades. Rinse thoroughly and dry.)

3. Always remove tree sap, bird droppings, insects, and gasoline

residue from tank overfill before they dry or harden on the paint. Wash with lukewarm car-cleaner solution.

NOTE: After applying any cleaning fluids to the car paint or chrome work, always wash with a lukewarm soap/water solution and apply a new wax coat.

NOTE: Use only clean cloths to wash a car. It takes only a bit of grit to scratch lines in the finish. Terry-cloth or knit-underwear rags are good for washing, and plastic or nylon-net scrubbers can help get stuck-on soil off without scratching the finish.

HINT: Make a disposable plastic "scrubbie" for the nasty jobs of removing road tar by wadding up a plastic onion or potato bag.

4. After washing and rinsing your car, wipe it down with old terry towels to remove droplet marks left behind by hard or chlorinated water. Who wants water spots on a shiny car?

5. A good heavy-duty paste wax applied after the car is washed usually lasts six months or more and provides better protection than many liquid waxes.

However, many new products are placed on the market each year, and it's a good idea to get advice at an auto-supply store or check out the automotive section of your supermarket or hardware store. If you have a new car, your dealer or manual may recommend specific types of car cleaners and waxes.

Checklist for Winterizing Your Car

1. Battery: Check for corrosion on terminals and have a mechanic replace loose or frayed cables.

Quick-Fix/Self-Help: If you haven't cleaned corrosion from the terminals recently:

• pour a can of carbonated soft drink over them
• use a solution of one or two tablespoons of baking soda mixed in a quart of water.

Scrub with an old toothbrush, if necessary.

NOTE: After removing the connection to the terminal and cleaning it well, rub a little petroleum jelly around the post and the inside of the terminal and then reattach. The petroleum jelly will help prevent corrosion, which is a major cause of not being able to recharge the battery.

2. Windshield-wiper blades: When they screech a lot or don't clean properly in the rain, they won't work in the snow either.

Quick-Fix: Try cleaning the wiper blades with window cleaner to remove car wax or road dirt.

Next-Step: If that doesn't work, replace the wipers. Improperly working wipers are a major safety hazard.

3. Belts and hoses: Frays, cracks, and bulges are warning signs of trouble down the road. When the engine is turned off and cold, check for proper fan-belt tension by pressing down on the middle of the belt. It shouldn't give more than a half inch.

NOTE: If you can't tell one belt from another, get out the manual from your car and be prepared to find all sorts of useful information as well as identification of car parts!

4. Lights and turn signals: Replace all bad bulbs. You don't want to be in a collision because someone didn't see your turn signal; and, equally important, it's the law!

5. Tires: Check your car-owner's manual for recommended cold-weather air pressure. Information about tire size and inflation pressure may also be noted on a sticker placed on the edge of the driver's door, on the door post, or on the inside of the glove-compartment door. If you can't find the information anywhere and you don't have the manual, call a dealer who sells your type of tires or your make of car.

NOTE: Many states have special winter-tire requirements. Call the highway department of your area to find out what's correct. You'll be avoiding a ticket as well as making your winter driving safer!

6. Radiator: Clean with a garden hose, spraying from front to back so fins are cleared of grease, dirt, and debris. Radiator caps and thermostats should be replaced after four years or sixty thousand miles. Coolant should be changed every two years or after thirty thousand miles. (Coolants' proportions are mixed half coolant to half distilled water.)

Safe Driving

Winter Safety

The National Safety Council says that you can increase visibility in hazardous cold-weather driving conditions such as fog and mist by doing the following:

1. Slow down gradually if the fog rolls in and turn on *low*-beam headlights.
2. Open the window slightly and use the defroster and fan. Run the windshield wipers and washer as needed.
3. The pavement line on the right side of the road can be your guide to keeping your car headed in the right direction. If the fog becomes too thick, pull off the road and turn on your emergency flashers.
4. To provide friction for getting started on slippery surfaces, keep the following in your trunk for emergencies:

- plastic one-gallon milk or detergent jugs filled with cat litter or sand to provide traction
- jumper cables
- flashlight (check the batteries periodically to make sure they work)
- tire chains, if your state allows them.

HINT: Recycle those sturdy plastic antifreeze jugs as containers for tire chains.

5. Keep an old blanket in the car to keep you warm if stranded in the snow and to place under tires for traction if you are unable to get started on slippery ice.

SAFE DRIVING IN DUSK AND AFTER DARK

1. Keep headlights clean for maximum illumination.
2. Keep windshield clean to prevent glare.
3. Before driving full-speed-ahead, allow time for your eyes to adjust after leaving a brightly lighted building.
4. Turn headlights on as soon as daylight begins to fade and adjust your rearview mirror to reduce glare from vehicles behind you.

NOTE: Keep a spray bottle of one-half vinegar and water and a roll of paper towels in the trunk just for these quick cleanups.

PERSONAL SAFETY WHEN DRIVING

1. To prevent car-jacking:

- Lock doors and roll windows up high enough to prevent anyone from reaching inside.
- Keep the car in gear at stop signs and lights.
- Travel on well-lighted busy streets.
- Always keep purses and other valuables out of sight even when driving in a locked car.

HINT: If you put the seat belt through the handle of your briefcase or purse before you snap the belt in place, it can't be removed from the car by anyone but you! One of my readers hooks her purse handles to her shift stick and lets the purse rest on the floor—purses can easily be stolen from a car seat when you stop at intersections.

2. Car breakdowns: If your car breaks down and you can't drive it to a safe place, get off the road and out of the traffic path—even if you have to ruin a flat tire.

- Turn on your emergency flasher light.
- Raise the hood.
- Tie a handkerchief to the aerial antenna or door handle.

If you can't get to a roadside phone or call-box, sit in your locked car to wait for help. If someone stops to offer aid, roll the window down just enough to ask to have help sent to you while you remain in the car. (Also, if you see a motorist in trouble, send help without stopping.)

3. If you think someone is following you, don't go directly home. Instead, drive to a safe haven (police or fire station, twenty-four-hour gas station, convenience store) while you sound your horn and flash your lights. Do not leave the safe haven until you're sure the follower is gone. If you can, write down the license-plate number.

When you move into a new neighborhood or drive a new route to work, check out possible safe havens in advance. Having a plan such as this will help you stay calm and think clearly so that you can help yourself.

4. When you park your car, always lock it when you leave and check the backseats and floors before entering it when you return. If security guards are available at public places, such as some workplaces, restaurants, and hotels, take advantage of this extra help and have them walk you to your parked car.

Car-Pool Hints

1. Develop a code with the others in your car pool for a predesignated signal, like a sheet of colored construction paper or poster board, to be placed in a front window or on the outside of the front door to let them know that, because of last-minute circumstances, you won't ride with the pool that day.

2. Try a round-robin call system to help early-morning carpoolers keep on time. Each person is notified when the car-pool vehicle is on the way. The driver calls before leaving for the first stop, lets the phone ring once, and hangs up. The first-stop person calls the next one prior to leaving, and so on.

3. Car-pool courtesy means respecting the wishes of the driver.

Don't assume that eating, drinking or smoking is okay in someone else's vehicle. Always ask first.

4. Check with your auto-insurance company. You may receive a discount if you carpool.

CAR KEYS

You'll never forget whatever it is that you need to take with you—a "doggie bag" of food from Mom's that's in the fridge, a jacket or hat, the gift for a birthday party, etc.—if you put your car keys on the thing you have to remember to take. To get the keys is to get the item!

NOTE: When this hint first came in, everyone in my office said, "Why didn't I think of that?" Many Heloise hints are in that category.

AUTO CHECKLIST

- Keep cooler in trunk for frozen foods when shopping.
- Put potpourri in ashtray for pleasant smell.
- Keep can of flat tire fixer in the trunk.
- Keep bag of cat box filler in car for icy weather.
- Make a folder and keep all car paperwork in it.
- Keep emergency kit in trunk.
- Make wiper fluid: mix 3 parts water and 1 part vinegar.
- Have an extra car key made.
- Keep a flashlight and road flares in the car.

CHAPTER NINE

Managing Your Money

We all know someone who is always broke no matter how much money he or she makes and we all know someone who still has the first dollar that ever came to him or her!

My sources say that background and upbringing affect the way we deal with money. Our parents or grandparents who survived the Depression of the 1930s may do without pleasures they can afford because they still feel insecure and afraid to spend lest they become destitute again. In contrast, people who have always had unlimited resources may not even think about saving to have an umbrella for that proverbial "rainy day."

Some couples don't share financial responsibilities, decisions, or information; and then, if the less-informed partner is suddenly widowed or there is a divorce, he or she (and typically, in traditional husband-head-of-the-house situations, it's she) has serious problems.

The reality is that when you have control over your money, you have control over your life. It's a good idea to review annually your:

- credit history
- investments
- insurance
- retirement and money-management plan

Pick a date, your birthday, tax time, or the beginning of the year—whatever works for you.

Regardless of your income, you need good bookkeeping habits and some sort of financial plan.

Here are some simple guidelines to help you organize your records, check your cash flow, and complete a net-worth statement to help you formulate a financial plan.

CASH FLOW

A cash-flow statement shows you where your money comes from and where it goes. If you check your cash flow each time you pay your monthly bills by going back over your records, you'll get a good idea of your spending habits and where you can save money or cut back.

NET WORTH

Review your net worth annually so you know how you are doing financially. Your net worth is the total of what you own—such as your home, other real property, cash, savings, motor vehicles, furniture, jewelry, and other personal property—minus what you owe on such things as car payment, mortgage, credit accounts, loans, taxes, etc.

NOTE: Your insurance agent can tell you the cash value of your policies. If you own a home or other real-estate property, you can get its approximate value by comparing your property to the selling prices of comparable houses or land in the neighborhood.

Financial Plan

After you know your net worth and your cash flow, you can make a blueprint for future financial needs and set goals for meeting those needs. This blueprint doesn't need to be an elaborate chart or graph, but it does need to be written down so that you can clearly see what the plan is. The questions to answer on your plan are:

• Where am I now, financially? What's my net worth? How much money is coming in and going out? Do I have a "cushion" of savings or investments for emergencies?

• What are my future financial needs? Am I planning to return to school or finance a child's education? Am I planning a vacation, to buy a house or car? Do I plan to retire in a few years? What else will I need money for in the future?

• How can I ensure having enough money for the future? Do I need to cut household expenses (find a lower-rent apartment or move to a smaller house, take my lunch to work instead of buying it, be more frugal to reduce utility bills, etc.)? Most of the experts agree that you should "pay yourself" in the form of savings on a regular basis, even if it is only a few dollars. Then you'll have "liquidity" when you need to let cash "flow" in an emergency.

• Do I need to increase my earnings? Do I need to get a part-time job? Can I convert a hobby into an income-producing business to supplement my regular income? If I'm at retirement age, do I need to postpone retirement?

NOTE: To find out about potential Social Security benefits, call your local Social Security office and ask for Form SSA 7004. You'll get an estimate of your retirement benefits about six weeks after you send in the completed form.

Making a Budget

Here is a sample budget showing the different expense categories as determined by the National Foundation for Consumer Credit, Inc. It's based on a total income of $2,500 per month (after taxes), but the percentages can apply to a lesser income with some variation for individual situations and expenses. One variation to consider is housing, which, if you live in some cities or regions of the United States, will cost more than the typical 20 to 25 percent of your income.

Keep track of your spending according to the following categories and then determine which will always have the same percentage and which you can change to meet your goals or requirements by cutting back spending and/or adding to earnings and savings.

Expense	Percentage of Income	Amount
Housing (Mortgage, Rent)	20–25%	$500
Food (Groceries, household items, and all meals, eating out, tips, alcohol, lunches)	20%	$500
Transportation (Car maintenance, auto insurance, public transportation, parking fees, maintenance of other forms of transportation such as bikes, motorcycles)	10–15%	$250
Household (Maintenance, appliance repairs, and utilities, such as gas, electric, water, sewage, garbage, cable TV)	10%	$250
Clothing	5%	$125
Health (All medical costs not covered by insurance)	5%	$125
Personal (Personal-care items, entertainment, haircuts, hobbies)	5%	$125
Insurance (Life, health, renters, personal property, disability)	5%	$125
Savings	5%	$125
Debt	15–20%	$375
		$2,500

Personal Bookkeeping

Good records will save you lots of trouble at tax time and are the only way you can see where your money is going and where it's being wasted. I know you probably hate it, but at least give it a try.

If you put 65 cents into a vending machine every working day to buy a candy bar, your sweet tooth chews up about $169 a year! And people who quit smoking who reward themselves with the money that they would normally spend on tobacco are often stunned at how much money literally "goes up in smoke" in a year. Pennies, nickels, and dimes really do add up.

Here are some hints for keeping money records:

ORGANIZING FILES

Buy an accordion file that's already labeled for personal expenses or label envelopes or file folders with the different money-use categories, such as:

- bank accounts (checking, savings, money-market accounts, certificates of deposit)
- entertainment
- food
- household expenses (supplies, maintenance, etc.)
- mortgage or rent costs
- retirement plans (IRAs, Keoghs, pension, etc.)
- Social Security
- taxes (federal, state, property, etc.)
- utility bills
- stocks and bonds
- transportation
- travel
- miscellaneous (where you record the vending-machine money and other expenses that don't fit in the ordinary categories)

If you're the kind of person who loses bills, also make a "hot file" of bills to pay.

PAYING BILLS

Pay bills on time to take advantage of discounts, if offered, and to have a realistic idea of how much money you actually have.

You don't really have as much as the balance shown in your checking-account register if you haven't yet paid your utility, credit-card bills, etc.; so you can't really buy that coat on sale, no matter how much it looks like the real you!

Your record of payment for each bill, all shopping receipts, and your bank statements should be filed appropriately. If your bank sends you canceled checks, you can staple them to the bills for which they were issued.

Although bill paying is never a really pleasant experience, my readers have sent me a lot of ideas for making bill paying easier and more efficient.

1. Note due dates of bills on a monthly or yearly calendar as a reminder.
2. Enter the phone number of the billing company into your check register so that it will be handy if you have to call about a payment problem.
3. Checks or money orders are the safest ways to pay bills. Most bills and invoices direct you to send no cash. If you must send coins or cash through the mail, tape coins on the bill, on a piece of paper or index card, with proper identification and write on the bill how much cash you have enclosed.

Be aware that most companies use automated envelope-opening systems, which may process as many as forty or forty-five letters per minute; coins or cash can fly out of the envelopes at that pace!

4. If you want special attention given to an order, wrap mailed checks in a blank piece of paper; then, the automated system assumes that there is correspondence in the envelope and sends it to another place than the one where checks and orders go. Although diverting your order from the

automated system slows up its processing, it's a "necessary evil" if your order is to get any special attention.

5. If someone else pays a bill for you with his or her personal check, be sure that your name and account number are included for proper crediting. Also, if you move and are still using checks with your old address, be sure to correct the address on the check and order new checks as soon as possible.

6. When you mail-order or pay for magazine subscriptions, make sure the payment is properly recorded on your account by putting your code number on the check. The code or account number is located on the mailing label, usually above your name.

Bill Paying Checklist

- Put due date under envelope flap.
- Put stamp and address label on return envelope.
- File in a folder by due date.
- Write bill due dates on the calendar.
- Put bills in chronological order in a napkin holder.
- Clip the company address and paste it on an envelope.
- Keep stamps and address labels with bills.
- Keep bills to mail close to the door.
- Write bills out as they are received and mail when due.
- Pay in person when possible to save the postage.
- When paying a bill, always include your account number.
- Mail bills several days ahead to avoid late charges.

Check-Register Bookkeeping

Your check register is a good record of deposits and spending *if* you record all transactions in it. Be sure to include date, check number, name, and invoice number or date of invoice.

I realize that most check registers have only a small space for this information, but you can squeeze more information on the line if you use a very fine point pen or use every other line as I do.

1. In the register, mark all tax-deductible payments with a *T* (such as medical/dental bills, prescriptions, car registration, mortgage payments, charity donations, property taxes, etc.).

2. When making a payment on an account, note on the check's "For" line on the bottom left of the check, the before-payment balance or "third payment of 10" so that you have clear records of the payments and balance due.

3. When paying for magazine subscriptions, club dues, utility or other service bills that are due annually or monthly, note the period covered by that payment on the "For" line.

4. If you write a check for something, especially if it's to a person or business that you don't regularly deal with, note the item on the "For" line. After all, that's what a "For" line is for! This will help you later!

CHECKBOOK CHECKLIST

- Keep a spare check in your wallet.
- Paper clip the checkbook on the page you are working.
- Write check numbers in register ahead of time.
- Color code in the register, use red for tax deductibles.
- Round up check amounts to the nearest dollar amount.
- Cut addresses off deposit slips for address labels.
- Fill in the new year on several checks ahead of time.
- Keep a small, thin calculator in your register.
- Use black or blue ink; colored ink doesn't copy as well.
- Keep track of monthly expenses at the back of the book.

If You Lose Your Income

When you have an unexpected job layoff and don't have enough savings, bills will pile up and you may find yourself deep in debt. The National Foundation for Consumer Credit, Inc., offers the following advice on how to survive a layoff or temporary loss of income:

- Make a budget that reduces spending to bare essentials.
- If you can't make ends meet, get help early before you are very deeply in debt.
- If you have outstanding credit or charge accounts that you can't pay off, contact the creditors, be honest about your situation, and try to negotiate reduced or extended payments. (It really works! Don't think those obligations will go away.)
- Don't try to get more credit to pay bills. It's a trap that doesn't work. But, if you are certain that the layoff is temporary, a small, relatively low-interest bank loan to tide you over is okay.
- Protect the assets that will help you get income again such as your home, car, and tools of your trade by making sure those bills get paid.
- Try not to let insurance policies lapse, and find out how you can continue health and life-insurance benefits.
- Get professional help. (See "Credit Emergencies" in this chapter.)
- Sell what you can to pay bills while you look for work. (See "How to Have a Successful Garage Sale.") For advice on looking for a new job see chapter 11.

HOW TO HAVE A SUCCESSFUL GARAGE SALE

When you move or clean out a house you've lived in for a long time, a garage, patio, carport, or sidewalk sale is a good way to make some money. Remember the saying, "One man's trash is another man's treasure." Here's a checklist for selling your "treasures":

1. Advertise on supermarket or coin-laundry bulletin boards, in shopper weekly papers, and in at least one daily newspaper.

2. Organize items by type and make a sale table of small things with a sign such as "All items on this table 50 cents."

3. Or, place large, colored dots on each item with each color signifying a price and make a big sign (on poster board) that says Red dot = $3, Blue = $2, etc., and then, when you want to have a markdown later in the day, you can just cross off the $3 on the poster and make red-dot items $2.50 or $2. The act of crossing off and reducing prices can make your garage sale more interesting to bargain hunters.

4. Catalogs from discount or department stores will help you fix prices.

The rule of thumb is to mark most items at 20 to 50 percent of retail value. Clothing usually sells for about 10 to 20 percent of retail. Books may cost 25 to 50 cents for paperbacks and $2 for hardcovers. Your objective is to sell, so prices must be reasonable—and remember, haggling is part of the game, especially for volume sales.

5. Remember that yard-sale income is not taxable if the items sell for less than their original price, which is what you'll charge unless you're selling antiques.

6. Give the leftovers to someone who can use them, like the Salvation Army, etc.; get a receipt if your donation to a nonprofit organization is tax deductible.

Credit

CREDIT HISTORY

Generally, to get a loan or a credit card if you've never had one in your own name, you need a credit history. Here's how to get it:

1. Apply for a credit card at a local store, even the lowest limit counts, or a small loan at a local lending institution (bank, credit union, etc.) that reports to a credit bureau. Then pay the debt back regularly and always on time, and you have started establishing a good credit history!!

2. If you cannot get credit on your own, ask someone with an established credit history, like a relative, to cosign for it. The cosigner must promise to pay if you don't. After you repay the debt promptly, try again to get credit on your own.

If you are ever turned down for credit, ask why and request a copy of your credit report. It could be that you have not worked at your job for a long-enough time or that your salary may not be high enough. Reapply when the situation changes.

Don't equate good credit with the number of credit cards you acquire. Anyone can be denied a loan just on the basis of his or her credit cards' potential charge power if it seems excessive to the lender. For example, if you have a lot of gold or platinum cards with the potential of tens of thousands of dollars of debt, the lender may be wary, lest you actually accumulate that much debt along with the loan you are requesting.

CHECKING YOUR CREDIT HISTORY

If you have been turned down for credit, you have the right under federal law to get a free copy of the report that caused the denial if you request it within thirty days of the denial. (The industry practice is generally within sixty days, which is more generous than the law requires.)

The lender who turned you down is required by law to tell you which credit bureau was contacted and what information on your record led to your being refused the loan.

You can call the credit bureau to have the report mailed to you. If you want to check on your rating before applying for credit, which is a very good idea, you can also call credit bureaus to find out which one has your file and ask to see your credit file. (You get a free report if you have been turned down for a loan but may need to pay a small fee, usually about seven to twenty dollars, for extra reports requested because you are checking on your credit for your own records.) Look for "Credit" or "Credit Rating and Reporting" in the yellow pages of your phone book.

NOTE: You can get one free copy of your credit history once each year. It will not be sent to you automatically; you have to request it with a letter (no phone calls, as allowed by local credit bureaus, and no fax).

Your request letter should include:

- your full name (including middle initial and Jr., Sr., etc.)
- Social Security number
- date of birth
- spouse's name (if you had/have one)
- current address and zip code
- if you've moved in the past 5 years, previous addresses in that time with zip codes
- a photocopy of a current driver's license and current credit-card billing statement to verify that the address you give is correct and current. (A post-office box number or an outdated driver's license does not serve as verification of a current address.)

Be sure to sign the request. Send it to:

TRW Consumer Assistance
P.O. Box 2350
Chatsworth, CA 91313-2350.

NOTE 2: If you find an error in your credit file, advise the credit bureau in writing and explain the error.

Back up the correction with copies of any documents that support your case, such as canceled checks, bills marked "paid in full," etc.

The credit bureau must delete or change the information you have challenged if it cannot prove it. Your letter will become part of your credit report.

Only time will remove negative information from your record. Credit bureaus can report such information for seven years; bankruptcies are reported for ten years. Sometimes, however, certain negative information remains on the record indefinitely.

A common scam is for a phony "credit repair company" to promise that it can "repair" or "clean up" your credit history. Although errors can be corrected, the past cannot be changed. Don't waste your money or get your hopes up!

JOINT CREDIT ACCOUNT PROBLEMS

Information on a joint credit card account goes on both cosigners' credit histories.

1. Married Couples

When a married couple opens a credit-card account, they should state that it is a joint credit account; and it's best if each name is listed such as John J. Smith and Mary M. Smith, or a married couple's joint account could be listed as John J. and Mary M. Smith, depending upon the card issuer's policy. This is especially important for older couples when the wife does not hold an outside job.

Depending upon the contract, an account in which the husband's name is listed and the wife also signs but is not listed as a joint card-holder might not provide a credit history for the wife if she is widowed or divorced. *Always* read the whole contract for anything you get involved with! Call your card issuer to find out exactly what your status is if your signature is valid on cards that are imprinted only with one name.

2. Divorced Ex-spouses

Negative information on a joint credit-card account goes on both spouses' credit histories.

If there is a divorce, the credit-card accounts should be paid in full and closed after the divorce is final. Otherwise both parties are still responsible for the debt. For example, if a couple divorces, even if the judge declares who is responsible for which debts, the third-party lender (credit-card company) can still operate on the original contract under which both spouses were responsible for paying the credit-card debt. If the account is not closed, one spouse could continue to run up charges and the other would still share responsibility for paying them.

Please understand that the information above is not intended to be legal advice. This problem should be discussed with one's divorce lawyer to get proper settlement in accordance with individual state laws, individual situations, debt contracts, and divorce decrees.

COSIGNING A LOAN AFFECTS YOUR CREDIT RATING

If a friend or relative asks you to cosign a loan, be sure you know what is involved before you agree, because your own credit rating may be affected if the borrower defaults.

1. In most states, if your friend or relative misses a payment, the lender can collect from *you* immediately, without chasing the borrower first!

2. The amount you will have to pay may include late charges as well as the full amount defaulted.

3. If you refuse to pay and the lender takes you to court, you may have to pay legal fees and, if the lender wins, your wages and property may be taken.

Credit Cards

CHOOSING A CREDIT CARD

All credit cards are not alike! The promotional enhancements and the fees vary widely. Here's a checklist to help you choose the right one for you.

1. APR

Annual Percentage Rate (APR) may be the easiest way to compare different credit-card issuers. It measures the cost of credit on an annual basis and includes the interest rate and other costs such as service charges or loan fees. If you don't expect to pay the full amount charged each month, look for a card with a low APR because you'll have to pay finance charges on unpaid balances. And, boy, this can add up!

2. Annual Fee

Some companies charge an annual fee which remains the same regardless of card use. If you expect to pay your bill in full each month, you may be better off with a card that has a low or no annual fee than with one having a low APR.

3. Grace Periods

Some cards have grace periods from twenty-one to thirty days in which there are no finance charges if you miss paying before the bill's due date. Others impose finance charges from the day you first use the card. Cards with longer grace periods may be an advantage if you pay all your charges each month.

4. Other Charges

Extra fees may be assessed for paying your bill late or charging more than your credit limit. These fees may be in addition to the interest.

To Save Money on Credit-Card Charges

Here are some hints from Bankcard Holders of America:

1. Shop for the lowest rate possible if you expect to carry a balance.
2. Pay off your balance in full each month.
3. Avoid cash advances from cards that charge high cash-advance fees.

4. Pay bills on time to avoid late fees.

5. Avoid making only minimum payments, which cost more in the long run. Paying only an extra $10 or $15 each month can reduce the amount paid over the long term.

6. Instead of waiting until the end of the month to pay your bills, pay as soon as the bill arrives. Early payment reduces your average daily balance, the interest compounding, and the total amount of finance charges you pay.

7. Read your card-holder agreement carefully and call the issuer to get an explanation in plain English of things you don't understand. When in doubt, call!

MISTAKES ON YOUR CREDIT-CARD BILL

Always read your credit-card statement carefully and compare charges to your receipts.

Also read the brochures that come with your bill to make sure there have been no changes in interest rates, reduction of promotional enhancements such as insured purchases, etc.

Recently, there has been a decrease in some of the extras like duration of coverage and amount of insurance on credit-card purchases and medical coverage while traveling. If you rely on these goodies, you need to be aware of changes. Don't assume that your auto rental is covered. If you find an error on your credit-card bill:

1. Send the card issuer a letter immediately to the special "billing error address" on the statement; you have sixty days in which to complain. Only a letter protects your rights; phone calls do not.

2. The letter should include your name and account number; date, type, and dollar amount of the questionable charge; and your explanation of why you think it's a mistake. You may have to sign a statement under oath testifying that you did not make the purchase.

3. The credit-card company must notify you that your letter was received and the mistake corrected or explain why the company believes the bill is correct.

4. Do pay the charges that are not in dispute.

NOTE: Most card companies will "hold" the charge based on your call and track down the retailer to determine if an error was made while they await your written statement.

HINT: An easy way to provide a written statement is to run a photocopy of the bill and circle or highlight the charge in question.

CREDIT CARD LOST OR STOLEN

1. Call the card issuer immediately! Use the phone number stated on a bill from the card company. Then, be sure to follow up the call with a letter that states your card number, when it was missing, and the date and time you called in the loss.

2. By law, you can be held responsible for up to but not more than $50 of unauthorized charges for each card if the card is used before you notify the issuer. In practice, most banks do not charge you the allowed $50 if you notify them properly.

CREDIT-CARD SAFEGUARDS

1. Never lend your card to anyone! Don't leave your card or receipts lying around.

2. Tear up all carbons and incorrect receipts.

3. Never give your number on the phone unless you made the call and are absolutely certain of the company's reputation.

Many credit-card phone scams exist all over the country. (In one common scam, a caller says the bank is checking your records and asks for your credit-card or bank/checking account number. If you get such a call, ask for something to be mailed to you and then check with your bank.)

Also, never write your card number on a postcard or the outside of an envelope.

4. Sign your new credit card in ink as soon as it arrives.

5. Keep a record of the card number, expiration date, and the phone number and address of the card company in a safe place, not in your wallet with the cards.

HINT: If you have several cards, photocopy all of them together on one page and write in appropriate telephone numbers and addresses below each card.

CAUTION: Remember to remove all the cards and any extra copies you may have made from the machine so that nobody else gets the information.

6. Never sign a blank receipt. Draw a line through any blank spaces on charge slips above the total so that it can't be changed.

7. Open billing statements promptly, compare them with the receipts, and call and write immediately if there are questionable charges.

USING ATM CARDS FOR QUICK CASH

Be aware that when you use automatic teller machines there is usually a fee if you use machines not owned by the bank that has your money.

A friend's college student son ran up nearly $30 in ATM charges in one month on $5 and $10 withdrawals because he used campus ATM machines as if they were electronic piggybanks. There is usually no fee if you withdraw money from your bank's machines.

Credit Emergencies

Overuse of credit, faulty planning and lack of money management can dry up your cash flow. When your expenses and payments are more than you earn, you can have your salary attached or have other legal action taken against you. If you are so unfortunate, there is help.

Contact the Consumer Credit Counseling Services local offices. The CCCS is a nonprofit organization affiliated with the National Foundation for Consumer Credit and is supported with contributions from banks, consumer finance companies, credit unions, merchants, and other community services. It is not a lending institution, charity organization, or government program. Its service charge is based on the user's financial circumstances and may be free in some cases.

The CCCS will help you set up a realistic budget and a debt-management plan to liquidate the debt, which is an option to declaring bankruptcy.

NOTE: With or without the CCCS, try to work out a payment plan with your debtors that's modified to allow lower payments for a longer time. If you are temporarily jobless but know you will have income soon, try to arrange for a short delay before the next payment.

NOTE: If you are behind in car payments, financing contracts may let the lender repossess your car with no advance notice. That's why it's best to try to work something out as soon as possible when you have a problem.

CCCS services are available throughout the country. To locate the Consumer Credit Counseling Service nearest to you, look in the white pages of the phone book or call toll free from a touch-tone phone 1-800-388-CCCS.

CAUTION: Be wary of debt-counseling services that might charge you $50 or $100 a month to straighten out the mess.

Savings

We've all been told at one time or other that it's important to save regularly, even if you save only a few dollars, because "paying yourself first" establishes saving as a habit and provides the security of having a "cushion" for emergencies.

Note on Payroll Tax Deductions: Many people have excess amounts of money deducted for federal income taxes because they like to get a big lump-sum refund after filing their return.

Most financial advisors recommend that you have deducted only as much as is needed to cover the actual amount of tax you will pay because allowing excess deductions is merely letting the government hold money for you without paying you the interest or profit that you would get if you put the same money in other savings or investments.

Payroll Deductions into a Savings Account: When you have direct-deposit service, you can divert some money from your checking account into a savings account. Money in a savings account is immediately accessible in case of emergency whereas other accounts, such as Individual Retirement Accounts (IRA), Moneymarket, etc., charge a penalty for early withdrawal. Ask your banker to explain the various savings accounts and the interest they accrue. Bank services vary, and you may want to shop around to find the bank that offers savings programs that suit your needs.

Individual Retirement Account (IRA) and 401K: You can save as much as $2,000 tax free annually in an IRA, and a 401K may allow more than $2,000 to be placed in a tax-sheltered account. You will, however, pay penalties for early withdrawal of IRA or 401K accounts. Because the laws governing these accounts can change, it's best to consult your accountant or financial consultant about current tax law.

Saving to Invest: The following save-to-invest hint comes from a financial consultant and friend. It's for people who say they don't have money to invest, and it's a means of dipping your toe into the investment pool before you take the plunge. If you like a certain product and buy it frequently—for example, a popular soft drink—calculate what you spend on that soft drink each month and put that amount aside to buy stock in the soft-drink company. Do the same with fast-food chains or chain stores. Then, each time you drink the soft drink, buy the fast food, or shop in the chain store, you'll feel as if you are increasing your own profits.

Investments

Most of the experts say that although managing and saving money is absolutely necessary, investing money protects its current purchasing power and earns more for your needs in the future.

Financial experts also advise diversifying investments. For example, the average person may participate in one or more mutual funds, stagger maturity dates on bonds and CD's for security and flexibility, and, as retirement comes near, adopt more conservative strategies. Before you part with your money, the AARP Booklet, "A Single Person's Guide to Retirement Planning" says you may want to analyze every investment option with the following guidelines:

1. Yield: What yield or return can you reasonably expect to get after commissions, service charges, other fees, and taxes are subtracted from your investment?

2. Safety: How safe is the principal (the basic amount, not including interest or revenue)?

3. Liquidity: How fast can you cash in your investment? What are the penalties? What are the fees?

4. Guarantees and Insurance: Are your yield and principal guaranteed? By whom or what?

5. Term: Does the term of the investment coincide with your future needs? Or, are you tying up money that you will need?

6. Inflation Hedge: Will the value of your investment keep up with inflation?

CAUTION: Real estate is the most significant investment made by many people. Also, home equity can be tapped as a line of credit. However, you should be aware that any financial arrangement that involves your house can jeopardize your financial security. Always get good legal, tax, and financial advice before doing anything with your home/real estate property.

A Few Types of Investments

The following are some of the types of investments available and a brief description so you will at least be familiar with them. The return on your investment and the interest and taxes paid vary greatly and are affected by many factors, including changes in federal laws and the general economy. This list is in no way a recommendation, because financial markets fluctuate and tax laws change. Please see "Choosing Financial Planning Services."

1. Treasury Securities: Includes bonds, bills, and notes which are debts of the U.S. government. They are bought through banks, brokers, and/or the Federal Reserve bank. Series EE bonds also can be bought through payroll deductions.

2. Federal Agency Securities: These are debt offerings by federal agencies. The best known is Government National Mortgage Association (GNMA), a.k.a. "Ginnie Maes."

3. Bank Offerings: You are lending money to banks, savings-and-loan, or credit unions in the form of a savings account, money-market deposit account, or certificate of deposit.

4. Corporate Bonds: Money borrowed by a corporation at certain specific interest rates and for terms ranging from one to thirty years.

5. Municipal Bonds: Often referred to as "tax-free" bonds. Here your money is being borrowed by a state, city, county, or subsidiary agency of any of these.

6. Preferred Stocks: Similar to common stocks in that they signify ownership instead of debt but like bonds because they usually bear a specific dividend rate, preferred stocks are usually paid off before common stocks if a company goes out of business.

7. Common Stocks: Fractional ownership shares in a corporation which fluctuate with the economy. They are usually considered speculative.

8. Mutual Funds: Fund managers invest your money in a variety of enterprises with risk factors ranging from very conservative to speculative, including such funds as GNMAs (see above), corporate or municipal bonds and stocks.

9. Annuities: These are issued by insurance companies and can include "fixed annuities," in which the rate of return over a given period is specified, or "variable annuities," in which your money is invested in mutual funds whose performances determine your return.

Choosing Financial-Planning Services

If you don't think you know enough about investment alternatives to make your own financial-planning decisions without help, ask friends, relatives, and business associates to recommend a financial planner whom they have found satisfactory. Look for such credentials as licensing, extensive education and/or professional experience, a successful track record, and a philosophy that matches your own. For example, if you are conservative, you don't want a risk taker! Here's a checklist of what to expect from a financial planner:

1. Your opinions and needs should be considered.

2. You should get a clear written analysis of your financial situation and a written summary of services and fees. (Fees may be hourly, a flat fee for specific services, percentage of annual income or total assets, a commission on financial products you buy, or the fee may be offset by commissions on investments made for you). Don't sign anything, including checks for services until you understand exactly what you are getting for how much.

3. Be sure the planner documents reasons for decisions, has access to other experts and sources, and will discuss and implement small investments as well as large ones.

You will have to give the following information to the planner: All names, addresses, birthdates, etc., of people in your financial plan; names and phone numbers of your attorney, accountant, and banker; lists of all assets (bank accounts, stocks, bonds) and purchase dates and value of each; description of financial commitments; copies of property and valuables' appraisals; salary records, tax returns, and expectations of future earnings; your budget of fixed and variable expenses; retirement plans; statement of goals and priorities, including how much, for how long, and why you are investing and how much risk you can afford.

Scams and Frauds

In addition to saving and investing, it's important to protect yourself from scams and frauds. The oft-repeated rule is valid: If it sounds too good to be true, it probably is.

The Alliance Against Fraud in Telemarketing, a coalition coordinated by the National Consumers' League, has predicted that the following will be the scams of this decade. Beware of:

1. 900-Number Con Artists: Often targeting people with credit problems, they offer worthless products, conceal the cost of calls, and keep you on hold to run up higher phone charges.

2. Boiler Rooms: Pushing such "investments" as precious metals and penny stocks, these illegal fly-by-night operations use high-pressure telephone salespeople and move around the country or overseas where they can operate freely to con unsuspecting "marks."

3. Bogus Health-Care Promotions: Telefrauds and health scams capitalize on our interest in health products, especially in arthritis remedies and quick-weight-loss gimmicks.

4. Bank-Financed Precious Metals: The investor pays for 20 percent of a quantity of gold or silver in a deal arranged by the con artist with a bank. After the con collects commissions, storage fees, and dealer markups, the investor gets nothing.

5. "Blind Pool" Penny Stocks: These are offered to you, but you get no real information about how the company uses the money you invest. Americans lose $2 billion annually in this scam.

6. Look-Alike Envelope Promotions: You get an envelope that resembles mail from a federal agency which may be printed with "official business" or "open immediately" on the outside. It's really a private-firm sales pitch.

7. Accelerated Mortgage Scalpers: Con artists arrange for you to pay off your mortgage more quickly, but you lose money in service charges and late mortgage payments.

8. "One-Sort" Credit Cards: You get a phone call that makes you think charging a $35 or $50 catalog order will get you a VISA or MasterCard, but when you get the credit card, you find out that it can be used only for that catalog.

9. "Guaranteed" Time-Share Resales: A telemarketer fraudulently offers to sell your time share within a year or give you your money back for a fee of $300 or $400. You don't sell the unit, and you don't get the fee back either.

10. Phony Foreign Banking Schemes: You are told that you will get extremely high rates of return from an overseas banking institution because foreign banking laws allow it.

When You Shop

Just about everyone likes a good sale, but it's possible to "go broke saving money" if you sale-shop impulsively. Generally, the definition of a bargain is: something you want or need that's being sold at a price you can afford. Before you whip out your plastic and start dashing toward the cash register as you yell "Charge!" take the Heloise Bargain Test below.

The Heloise Bargain Test

(If you can't answer "yes" to *all* of the following questions, you don't have a bargain.)

1. Do I really want or need this? A $300 suit for $75 is not a bargain if it really doesn't suit you.
2. Does the item meet your specific requirements? If you measured your apartment living area before you went shopping and decided that it could accommodate only a love seat, will the "fabulous-buy," greatly reduced fifteen-foot sectional sofa be a genuine bargain?

NOTE: The armless unit of a bargain sectional sofa might fit in another room, such as a bedroom, and so the remaining units would still fit in the living room as a love seat.

3. Is the price significantly lower than normal? By that I mean, is it *more* than 20 percent off prices in your area, not just at that particular store? You can usually get 10 or 15 percent reductions by paying cash for larger items and/or by shopping around at other stores.

4. Can you really afford that price? If all you can spend on new shoes is $30, then a $100 pair marked down to $50 is still not for you.

5. Will you use the item enough to justify the cost? Just because it's 50 percent off, should you buy a super, high-tech tent made to be comfy in the Arctic if you only camp out once a year during the summer?

6. Have you considered other factors such as dry-cleaning costs for bargain clothing, service and maintenance availability on appliances bought at a discount store?

7. If the items are sold "as is" or are "seconds," are the flaws acceptable? For example, a towel with a pulled thread will get you dry after a shower, but a coat with a hard-to-match missing button or torn sleeve may cost too much time, effort, and money to fix.

8. Can you return the "on sale" item? If not, have you answered "yes" to all the other questions?

Sale-Shopping Savvy

The Federal Trade Commission says that a sale must offer "substantial, not merely nominal reduction" from the usual or original price. Although most businesses offer genuine sale prices, it's still best to research prices in your area before you sale-shop. Here are some definitions of "sale-speak" to help you sale-shop.

Storewide: Usually held after Christmas, Easter, and July Fourth. Everything in the store is reduced. Some items may not be reduced by much, however. Watch out for shopworn goods from holiday handling.

White: Originally known as White Sales because they were on white sheets and towels, now they include all kinds and colors of bed linens, towels, bath mats, mattress pads, etc.

Red Tag: Sale items are identified by red or blue or green or any other color tags or stickers. Be sure to know the regular price, because reductions may not be that terrific!

Preseason and Promotional: New items such as seasonal fashions or new cars are being offered to the public for the first time. Stores use such sales to arouse interest and test response to these new products. However, stores may also use such sales to get rid of items that didn't sell as well as expected.

Clearance: Stores are clearing out the current season's unsold merchandise to make space for the next season's items. Savings can be as high as 70 percent, but remember: These items didn't sell during the regular season. Ask yourself why?

Holiday: Items on sale are specific to a particular holiday, such as Christmas or Easter. It may also be a general or even storewide sale on a holiday such as President's Day or Labor Day. Sometimes, such a sale is a collection of items at nearly regular price which are suitable for a certain holiday such as Mother's Day.

Closeout: A manufacturer offers a discontinued line to the retailer at a large discount, which is, in turn, passed on to the consumer. Savings can be high, but if it's on appliances or electronics, you may have spare-part problems in the future.

Special Purchase: Similar to closeout sales, these are held when a retailer gets discounted goods from a manufacturer or wholesaler. Although top-quality but overproduced products may be offered, it may also be seconds. Check carefully before buying. *Always* try on clothing; sometimes garments have wrong-size labels.

Inventory: The retailer is trying to reduce stock for a variety of reasons. Savings can be as high as 75 percent. However, some so-called inventory sales are only promotions; compare prices before buying.

Where to Shop

Discount, off-price, surplus, and outlet stores are popping up all over the country. But how can you tell one from the other? By their products, you shall know them!

Discount Store: Basically inexpensive merchandise in a budget atmosphere; some items are brand name, most are not; prices are kept low by volume buying and taking advantage of manufacturers' closeouts.

Factory and Manufacturers' Outlets: Goods are from one manufacturer, usually located in the same area. Good buys are due to low overheads, no middleman, and no advertising. Seconds and irregulars may be mixed with top-quality goods. Inspect each item carefully, and try on clothing.

Off-Price Stores: It's the same clothing as that found in fine department and specialty stores; name labels are frequently left in the garments. (When labels are cut out of garments, it's to avoid conflicts with department stores which may be selling the same designer's fashions at higher prices.) Low prices are due to buying cleverly, either before or after the big retail stores do their buying or due to volume purchase.

Mail-Order Catalog Surplus Stores: Serve as dumping grounds for mail-order companies; discounts may be as high as 80 percent.

CHAPTER TEN

Single Living

Living alone is an exciting rite of passage for most people. Moving into your first apartment is a big step, especially if you've always lived in a house with your parents or a spouse. You have to deal with rental leases, getting homeowner's insurance, security, and a lot of other responsibilities you didn't have when you shared a home with family.

Some people opt for a roommate either for security and/or companionship or to help pay the rent and living expenses. Others prefer to live alone.

If you're divorced or widowed after having been married for a number of years, finding a new social life, traveling alone, and sometimes just daily living present added challenges to coping with your loss. Also, there are some very practical matters that people don't like to talk or even think about, but that are very important to consider in the event of divorce or widowhood.

Your First Apartment

GETTING AN APARTMENT

Most major cities have apartment-locater services that charge no fee. They are listed in the yellow pages of the phone book. Generally, they want to know the area you prefer, how much rent you can pay, and other special needs—furnished, handicapped access, near public transportation, school or work, etc.

Colleges and universities have student/faculty housing assistance and information. They can even help with finding a roommate if you need one. One of the best resources is a network of friends, relatives, and coworkers who can help you find an apartment and suitable roommates, too.

In addition to the usual housing rental and sales advertising, most major city newspaper real estate sections have editorial information about apartment complexes and subdivisions to help you get familiar with what's available in the different parts of your community.

HINT: It's easy to get confused after you've visited many possible locations. When you are responding to newspaper ads, clip each ad and tape, ste, or staple it to an index card or a notebook page. Then, as you visit 1 apartment/house, write down what you like or dislike about the place and any other pertinent information that you'll need when you make your final decision. An instant camera can help you remember details, too.

Read the Lease Before You Sign

Always remember that leases are drawn up by landlords, so you know whose side the lawyer was on!

Here's a checklist of notations in the lease that will affect your life for better or for worse:

1. Most leases require you to pay the first and last months' rents and/ or a security deposit. Be sure to find out what the security deposit will cover. A few nail holes in the wall from pictures may prevent return of the security deposit! (Please see the quick-repair and cleaning ideas elsewhere in this book.)

2. Which repairs will be made by you and which by the landlord? Tenants should keep all receipts for repairs or major cleaning (such as carpet cleaning) for reimbursement if the lease allows or if you have to go to small-claims court to get your security deposit back.

HINT: Take photos of your apartment's flaws when you move in so that you have proof of preexisting problems and wear. This is especially important if you are renting a furnished apartment and might be blamed for excess wear of upholstered furniture or carpeting. You may even ask your landlord or apartment manager to stand in the photo with you and include a sign or newspaper with a date to prove when the photos were taken.

3. Get the lease's definition of "Clean" spelled out so that you and your landlord are speaking the same language when you do your final cleanup on moving day.

4. Find out what happens if you have to move before the lease is up. Can you get permission to sublet and therefore get released from legal obligations under the lease? Also, find out what changes in the lease must be made if you decide to get a roommate.

5. Novice apartment renters often ignore the lease's "fine print" and, unfortunately, that's where you'll find those restrictions that most affect your daily life. Restrictions can include:

- children (living in or visiting)
- pets
- using an apartment for a home office
- appropriate dress in the lobby/common areas
- cooking on balconies
- potted plants on windowsills
- radio/TV antennas
- extra charges for use of pool/recreation facilities
- regulation of storage and parking areas
- right of the landlord to enter your apartment with or without notice whether or not you are home
- any additional services provided by the landlord
- conditions for eviction and terminating the lease.

NOTE: Property/liability insurance is necessary even when you are not the homeowner. Please see "Property and Liability Insurance," chapter 12.

SECURITY WHEN YOU LIVE ALONE

Although no apartment or home is burglar-proof, when you do a "security survey" of an apartment, here's a checklist for you:

1. Are entrances, walkways, and parking areas well lighted?
2. Do trees and shrubbery obscure doors, windows, or pathways?

3. Are there any unprotected openings to the apartment such as skylights, crawl spaces, or vents?

4. What sort of security is provided regarding locks for lobby, basement or other common-area doors, parking-area gates or garages, laundry-facility doors?

5. How secure is your apartment door? Your door should have a "peephole" and deadbolt lock or locks with a minimum of a one-inch throw. The door and its hardware should also be strong enough to withstand excessive force. Sliding doors or windows should be secure against being lifted from the frame. All window latches and locks should be secure and work properly.

6. Are smoke detectors placed strategically? Where are fire extinguishers and alarms? What is the fire-evacuation plan for the building if your apartment doesn't have direct outside exits?

CHECKLIST FOR PERSONAL SAFETY

Safe Places to Go When You Have Trouble

When you move into a new area, check the potentially safe havens along your daily routes such as twenty-four-hour gas stations, convenience stores, police and fire stations.

Sounding an Alarm

When traveling alone, avoid high-crime areas; and, my sources say that if you are attacked, shout "Fire" instead of "Help" or "Rape" because it elicits a better response. Also, carrying a shrill whistle and blasting it can unnerve an attacker and alert assistance.

Emergency Phone Numbers

If your area doesn't have 911 emergency service, write emergency numbers on a label and stick the label to your phone or program them into a programmable phone on "Number One" or at the buttons that have the symbols for fire, police, and ambulance.

Opening Doors

Remember what your parents taught you about opening your door to strangers! Don't! Some doors, especially hollow wooden ones, can be forced open even when chained!

Phone Safety

Don't advertise that you live alone if you are a single woman; have your name listed in the phone directory with first and middle initials only such as J. A. Smith instead of Janet A. Smith. If you are receiving annoying or harassing phone calls, contact your local phone company service representative to find out your options. Generally, you are advised to hang up at the first obscene word or if the caller is silent after you say hello.

Numbers Safety

Never give any personal information over the phone unless the caller has been properly identified in a way that you recognize as valid. And, never ever give any of your important numbers (credit card, social security, checking/savings account) to any caller for any reason. Scam artists continue to profit from use of these numbers despite all the publicity warning against them. If someone calls and asks for these numbers "to verify your account" or "because you've won a sweepstakes," tell them to send you something in writing. Then, check with your local Better Business Bureau or the U.S. Postmaster (who deals with mail scams) before responding in any way.

Safety When Driving Your Car

Please see safety hints in chapter 8, "Your Car."

Suspicious Persons and Activities

Call the police if you see any of the following:

- people loitering in front of a closed business or unoccupied house
- anyone loitering around parked cars and peering into them
- anyone loitering around schools or parks
- people in pairs going door to door in a residential area, especially when one goes to the back door as the other is in front
- someone forcing open the door of an unoccupied house
- people selling bargains on the street
- people in parked cars or in slow-moving ones along residential streets, especially if it's an unusual hour
- people removing property from a house at an unusual hour or removing parts of a car
- people who show unusual mental or physical symptoms that indicate the influence of drugs.

When You Call Police

Be prepared to tell what happened, where and at what time, if anyone is/ was hurt, description of suspect person and/or vehicle, license plate number of the vehicle (if you can remember only the first three letters or digits, it's still helpful), the time and direction the suspects went when they escaped, and any additional details asked for.

Residence Sharing

People share homes or apartments to help cut living expenses, for companionship, security and, in an increasing number of multigenerational shared living arrangements, for exchange of services. For example, elderly or disabled persons can stay in their own homes if they get help with household chores in exchange for room rental, or a single parent can share a home with someone who will care for children after school.

IF YOU DECIDE TO SHARE

Community Zoning Ordinances

While different communities have zoning ordinances or deed covenants designed to preserve the ambiance of neighborhoods by banning group homes (for the elderly, for handicapped persons or others), as of 1987, thirty-five states have enacted laws to preempt local zoning.

Most of the problems have revolved around the definition of the term *family* and the number of people involved. Generally, the definition of family includes: A relationship among the members that is either biological or legal; a single head of household; a single household; and, a numerically limited number of unrelated people living together. Some communities define "family" as "one individual" or "a number of individuals living as a single housekeeping unit."

Information about zoning restrictions is usually available from a city's zoning or housing board or commission. Home-sharing problems of the past due to zoning are decreasing as the need for this type of "family living" increases, especially as a means for elderly or disabled people to avoid placement in a nursing home when they are still capable of some self-care. It's a viable solution as people live longer and nursing home care costs escalate.

Finding a Suitable Share Through Community Agencies

Many communities have organized programs for home sharing. State agencies on aging can help elderly people and others to find home sharers.

The national agency, The National Shared Housing Resource Center, will help you find a local agency that has a house-sharing/roommates program or can help elderly or disabled persons find a group home operated by a nonprofit organization. (A group home is defined as one in which each person has a private bedroom but common living areas are shared like a family.) Write National Shared Housing Resource Center, 431 Pine St., Burlington, VT 05401, or call 802-862-2727.

Advertising to Find a Home Sharer

If there is no shared-housing program in your community, spread the word among your friends and relatives, at your church or synagogue, at work or other organizations you belong to.

If you decide to advertise in newspaper ads or by putting up cards with basic information on bulletin boards of community centers, social-service agencies, churches, universities, or other suitable places, it's best to list a post office box number for replies for your safety's sake. Ground Rules for Harmony—"A Consumer's Guide to Homesharing," from the American Association of Retired Persons (AARP) and National Shared Housing Resource Center suggest the following checklist to help you determine if you and your prospective housemate will be compatible:

• Did we discuss what we expect from home sharing? What are each person's socializing and privacy preferences?

• Have we discussed service exchange, if any? If there is a service exchange, what are the services and what are they exchanged for—rent reduction, free rent, free room and board, free room and board plus compensation?

• Have we discussed music preferences; television habits; home entertaining; overnight guests; work, sleep, and wake-up schedules; temperature preferences for summer and winter months; privacy needs; pets, smoking, alcohol use, etc.?

• How much will the common rooms, kitchen, and outdoor space be shared? Will personal television, stereo, cookware, dishes, linens, tools, etc., be shared? What about storage space?

• Do we agree on meal preparation and schedules? What about use of refrigerator, freezer, pantry and kitchen storage space? What about food preferences and special diets?

HINT: Some roommates assign a refrigerator shelf or side of shelves for each person or just write their initials on soft drinks and other food containers stored in the fridge. Drinking someone's last cold can of soft drink can be a terrible transgression on a hot day and one of those little things that destroy friendship!

• Do we agree on who does what household chores? What are the cleanliness standards for *all* rooms of the house? What about laundry?

• Do we agree on financial arrangements? Who pays utility, phone, and food bills? Will they be shared and if so, how?

- What do we like most about each other?

- Do we have similar values and needs?

- What don't we like about each other?

- Can we overcome our differences?

- Have we offered each other personal references and have we checked each other's references, or talked with each other's acquaintances?

- Do we feel satisfied that there are no important unspoken needs that might come up in the future? How will we make changes in the agreement if they are needed?

- Have we exchanged information about medical conditions, medications, and arrangements to be made in the event of injury or illness, including emergency numbers to call?

- Can we agree to a trial period of living together before making permanent obligations to live together?

- Will we consider using a written agreement to specify rights and obligations? The agreement should note how long the arrangement is in effect and how much notice is needed to terminate it.

If sharers both enter a leasing agreement at the same time (when the apartment or house has not been previously occupied by either person), there should be agreement on who signs the lease and the ramifications if one of you chooses to move out. For example, if only one person signs the lease, that person is responsible for the full rent payment if the other person moves out. The notice to terminate the agreement should provide enough time for the lease holder to find another roommate or for both to terminate the lease and move elsewhere.

- Finally, if you are moving into a home-sharing agreement, in addition to the points listed above, you should also consider the same things you would if you were renting a place to live in alone: Do you like the neighborhood? Is it close enough to family, friends, and transportation? Can you afford it?

Traveling Solo

Don't let the prospect of traveling solo deter you from having an adventure or a much-needed vacation. If you have never traveled without family, a spouse, or close friends, ask yourself the following questions before you decide to do it.

1. Do I talk easily to strangers?
2. Can I assert myself if I feel I'm being overcharged or given poor service?
3. Is my health good? Can I carry my own bags?
4. Can I plan my own days easily?
5. Do I have a good sense of direction?
6. Do I dine alone comfortably?
7. Am I comfortable going out alone at night? For example, if you get yourself tickets to evening entertainment, can you get yourself to the show, opera, etc?
8. Do you enjoy being alone for long periods?

(From The AARP booklet "A Single Person's Guide to Retirement Planning")

Group Travel

Often travel agents can help you arrange special group or companion travel. But there are also special trips and travel clubs for certain age or special-interest groups such as insurance travel clubs, senior-citizen organizations, church groups, ski clubs, bird-watching societies, and theater, zoo, or museum "friends" groups.

Group travel is often discounted and includes all or most costs so that you can better budget for the trip. For example, two national organizations that offer group trips are the Smithsonian Associates and the Sierra Club.

THE PROS AND CONS OF GROUP TRAVEL

1. You follow the tour company schedule.
2. Cannot usually deviate from the tour itinerary.
3. Many extras included in the package price.
4. Prearranged meals.
5. Full schedule, minimal leisure time.
6. Travel with strangers, but there is companionship.
7. Pace preestablished and includes many early-morning departures.
8. Tour company assumes responsibility for safety, security, and also, safety in numbers.
9. All of most arrangements handled by tour leader.
10. Little chance to get to know the country or people if the tour is arranged to be an exhausting sightseeing whirlwind of seeing a lot superficially.
11. Hype may include travel time with the vacation time, standard hotels called deluxe, etc.
12. Tour guide's expertise available; tour company can back this up.

THE PROS AND CONS OF INDEPENDENT TRAVEL

1. Make your own schedule.
2. Higher air fare and hotel rates.
3. Pay for each extra service as needed.
4. Flexible meals and mealtimes.
5. Free time; unlimited leisure-time activities.
6. Your choice of traveling companions, if any.
7. Security and safety is your responsibility.
8. All needed arrangements, such as getting through customs, transportation, meals, etc., are your responsibility.
9. A better opportunity for unique, close contact with the people in the country or area you visit.
10. No exaggerated claims about activities, atmosphere, etc.
11. You have to rely on your own knowledge and ability to deal with situations.

Traveling Independently

If you decide to travel independently, you will find many free sources of information.

Research

Check out the public library's travel books, guidebooks, and videotapes. Many libraries now have videos that are wonderful and help you see where you are going, what to do, and how you need to be dressed.

Other information sources include:

Road Atlas

Even if you don't plan to drive, a road atlas can give you a lot of good travel information and help you locate places of interest.

Tourist Information Sources

If you are traveling in the United States, call 1-800-555-1212 to see if your destination state has an 800 toll-free number for its tourist bureau or traveler's and visitor's information department. Most states offer free brochures on what to see and do, including information on free tours of special factories, museums, and similar places to help you have fun on a budget. Information is usually included on how to contact visitor information sources in specific cities that you plan to visit.

Hotel/Motel Information

Most hotels and motels have 800 numbers to call for reservations and information.

Ask what the facility offers in the way of pool and spa services so you know if you should pack spa clothing, robes, swimsuits, etc. If you need hair dryers, ironing equipment, or anything else, ask about these, too. If you are traveling to the destination by air, find out if the hotel has any limousine service from the airport that can save you an expensive taxi fare. If you are traveling with a pet, you need to find out if pets are accepted or if pet boarding facilities are nearby.

Free Admission and Shopping Discounts

If you belong to a local museum, zoo, or arboretum "friends" association, your group may be offering tours at reasonable prices. Sometimes membership in one association gives you free admission and/or discount shopping opportunities in other cities' facilities. For example, many arboretums offer each others' members free admission under the World-Wide Reciprocal Admission Program for Arboretums. It always pays to ask!

General Travel Information

Economical Lodging

Save hotel costs by trading off homes with people in other cities or countries. A directory for vacation house swaps is available from the Vacation Exchange Club, Inc. (Call 1-800-638-3841), or check your phone book yellow pages to see if there are exchange groups in your area. Often travel agents know of exchange clubs, too.

Cruise Vacations

Many cruise lines offer year-round discounts of as much as $300 per person if bookings are made several months in advance. If your time is flexible and you don't have specific preferences, you may be able to take advantage of low "season" rates (also referred to as "peak value" or "economy sailing dates") at various times of the year. Contact a travel agent. If your time is very flexible, ask a travel agent about standby travel in which you get discounted accommodations in the event of cancellations or if a group has not been able to book its required capacity.

Packing a Suitcase

If someone else always packed your clothing, you may arrive at your destination with nothing to wear because it's all too crushed! Here are some of my favorite packing hints.

GENERAL PACKING HINTS

1. Distribute weight in the suitcase evenly.
2. Place heavy items toward the bottom near the hinges.
3. Leave some space for purchases.
4. Cushion folds with other garments to lessen wrinkles.

For example, fold pants flat-out lengthwise, carefully on the natural crease; place pants waistband to side of case. Then place a sweater folded in thirds lengthwise, facedown on pants, letting half the sweater hang out at right angles to the pants. Fold pants back over sweater, once, then fold rest of sweater back on top, before folding last part of pants legs back. Use underwear to pack folds of garments, too.

5. Zip, button, and fasten each item you can.
6. Wrap shoes in mitts or bags. Place them heel to toe in the mitts and then along the hinge of the case so they won't shift and crush things. Tuck soft things like socks and underwear inside shoes to help keep their shape.
7. Unpack as soon as possible, even if only for one night to let clothes hang free and prevent severe wrinkling.
8. Moisture and heat may remove some wrinkles. Bring a travel iron or steamer, or hang an item in the bathroom and run the shower to steam wrinkles out. Sometimes you can "iron" wrinkles from some fabrics by blowing them with a hair dryer, running across creases with a curling iron, or by running creases over a hot light bulb of the hotel lamp.

CAUTION: Be careful with fragile fabrics like silk and polyester which can melt if subjected to too much heat from a curling iron or light bulb.

9. Leave plastic dry cleaners' bags over clothing when packing a hanging-style garment bag to help cushion garments, prevent major

wrinkling, and protect garments from moisture that can seep in through some zipper closures of soft-sided luggage.

10. When packing a regular suitcase, lay each garment flat and face up on a plastic dry-cleaning bag so that the plastic overlaps on each side. You may have to cut the bag open to a single layer if you need more surface area.

Then, button two or three buttons and fold in sleeves of blouses, jackets, and sweaters; fold slacks and skirts in half vertically.

Starting from the top, roll the garment and plastic together tightly to form a cylinder, making sure each garment is completely covered with plastic. Then, arrange rolled garments closely together in neat rows and layers in the suitcase.

Travel Items Checklist

My checklist may differ from yours, but here it is:

1. Toothbrush, toothpaste.

HINT: I save the smidgens at the end of a big tube and use that for travel or buy the smallest-size tube.

2. Makeup and something to remove eye makeup.

3. Dusting powder, deodorant, perfume in small sizes or sample sizes sold in drugstores and pharmacy sections of supermarkets.

HINT: Be conservative about perfume and scented deodorants or hair sprays when you travel on a plane, or avoid wearing any scent. So many people suffer from allergies!

NOTE: Bear in mind that wearing a scent for a long time desensitizes you to it; you may put on too much without realizing it, but your seat companion's nose knows it!

4. Facial tissues, individual packets of "wipes," a few cotton balls and swabs.

5. Shaving equipment, a pair of tweezers, small scissors (folding

embroidery scissors are nice because they won't poke holes), safety pins, and a small sewing kit.

6. A few adhesive bandages and/or felt adhesive pads in case a shoe rubs you the wrong way.

7. I always pack a plug-in nightlight when I'm on book tours and spending each night in a different city. It helps me to get oriented when I wake up in the middle of the night.

NOTE: I usually leave the bathroom light on and the door ajar, but sometimes that provides too much light or, with some types of lighting fixtures, it heats up the bathroom.

Special-Items Checklist

In addition to toilet articles and appropriate clothing and accessories, you'll need the following:

1. Medications: Always pack medications in your carry-on bag in case your checked luggage gets lost. Take along enough prescription and nonprescription medications for the time you'll be gone, plus a few days' more in case you have transportation problems. Keep medications in their original containers, especially when traveling out of the country. Make a list of medications and dosages to keep in another place just in case you lose your medications and have to get refills.

2. Eyeglasses: Pack a spare pair even if it's a drugstore special. It's easy to lose or break your glasses en route, and what a miserable time you'll have without them! You might also carry a copy of your lense prescription so that you can have a pair made in an emergency.

3. Passports and Visas: Get these well in advance and be sure to ask your travel agent what papers you will need. Different countries have different requirements. Also, ask if you need any special health or car insurance for your destination. Take along extra passport photos just in case your passport is lost or stolen. I know of at least one instance where the American Embassy in a Third World country was able to speed up

issuing a new passport to a traveler who was robbed just because his wife had kept his extra passport photo in her wallet. She did it because she thought he looked so handsome! Love is really grand! And convenient, too!

4. Credit Cards, Travelers Checks, Cash, Plane Tickets: Always keep these in a safe place and not in checked baggage. Do keep a list of your credit-card information, your travelers check receipt, and copy of your plane ticket/schedule in a second safe location just in case you lose the originals.

5. Camera and Film: Most film goes through the airport x-ray equipment without damage, but some of the newer fast films do not. Ask before sending the bag through. Stick your address labels on all camera equipment and film canisters in case you forget them. Readers have written to tell me that they have had lost but labeled film canisters returned—so there are a lot of nice people in this world!

6. Travel "Office": Address labels will identify all your possessions, and you can also put them on postcards so that you'll know if the card doesn't go to the person for whom it's intended because it will go to your home. Take along extras to stick on airline luggage tags or on packages if you need to ship home a purchase. Pack a small roll of package sealing tape and a black marker for mailing yourself packages or for identifying packages you check with the airlines.

Also, take along a notebook or spiral index card pack to use when you want to write down your thoughts and other to-remember information.

7. Forget your last-minute doubts and worries and have a good time!

CHAPTER ELEVEN

Special Needs, Special Circumstances

Butterflies are the symbol for "new life." Their delicate beauty emerges from an unattractive, almost ugly cocoon stage and, especially in the case of the migratory Monarch butterflies, their fragile appearance belies their strength and endurance. Perhaps butterflies can be inspirational symbols for people who are recently widowed or divorced or for those embarking on a job search, especially if they haven't been in the market for many years or if their job security has been destroyed by business failures and/or the general economy.

Being Widowed

Each state has different laws about financial and other decisions you have to make despite the shock and sadness of being widowed. And most people say that even prolonged illness of a spouse doesn't diminish the shock or sadness. It may be painfully difficult, but here's a checklist showing the steps that have to be taken:

1. Make funeral or memorial service arrangements. The Social Security Administration and Veterans Administration provide burial allowances, so check to see if you qualify to receive aid from one or both. Traditional funerals can cost more than $2,000—or even $10,000—but cost is not a measure of your love for the deceased, and you should make the arrangements that work best for your family. Burial of veterans may be at no charge in areas where a national Veterans Cemetery is located.

2. Gather all important papers (wills, power of attorney, birth, baptismal, and marriage certificates; divorce decrees, military discharges, mortgages, insurance and other financial documents, etc.). Don't throw anything away. If you are too grief-stricken to do this ask a trusted friend or relative for help.

3. Joint bank accounts are automatically frozen in some states. Ask your bank to release funds to you and immediately set up a new account to handle funds received after the death.

4. To establish claims for Social Security, life insurance, and veteran's benefits you will need several copies of the death certificate, marriage certificate, spouse's birth certificate, military discharge papers, Social Security card, tax forms, and birth certificates of any minor children.

5. Each company that insured your spouse must be notified of the death, and each needs a statement of claim and death certificate before survivor benefits are paid. If you do not need all the money immediately, ask your insurance agent for payment options and choose the best for your circumstances.

6. Social Security benefits are not automatically paid; you must apply to your local Social Security office for them. Spouses of veterans apply for veterans' benefits at the nearest Veterans Administration office.

NOTE: The benefits available to veterans' spouses vary according to circumstances. Call your nearest regional Veterans Administration Office (from any part of the U.S.), at 1-800-827-1000. The regional offices have V.A. counselors ready to help you.

7. Send a formal letter to your spouse's employer, union or other group or professional organization with which he was associated. Many such organizations have insurance policies in which the spouse is the beneficiary.

8. Advise all creditors, credit-card issuers, and holders of loans that your spouse has died. Find out if the loans or mortgage are insured; if so, they are paid for.

9. Find a lawyer who specializes in wills, estates, and probate whom you can trust and discuss fees *before* you hire legal help. Ask widowed friends or family for a reference but not for legal advice. They may mean well, but you need professional advice to avoid trouble.

10. Postpone any decisions that can be put off until you are healed emotionally such as moving, including in with other family members, quitting your job, selling your house, or any other drastic changes.

The following are just a few ways to help you delay making final decisions and occupy your time during the healing period:

Instead of moving, take a long vacation from home and/or visit family before deciding what to do. If you plan to be gone for an extended amount of time, rent out your home instead of selling it.

If you need money to maintain your home, consider a reverse annuity mortgage, taking on a roommate, or other options before selling it.

Take a leave of absence from work instead of quitting your job.

If you have no job, consider getting one or, if money is not a problem, consider doing volunteer, nonpaid work. If you haven't had a job in a long time, volunteer work can count toward getting employment. Volunteer activities can help you work through your grief and ease into a single life-style.

Being Divorced

Nobody likes to even think about divorce but if you have explored all options, including professional counseling, and still decide that it's the only solution to insoluble marital problems, there are some practical matters that must be considered even during the emotional turmoil of divorce.

First of all, seek professional counseling. Your priest, minister, or rabbi can be a resource. If your city has a women's center, it can refer you to counseling and legal resources. If finances are a problem, some universities that train social workers offer family counseling by student-interns at rates determined by income. If alcoholism is/was a problem, Al-Anon, the support group for relatives of alcoholics, can help you cope during and after the divorce.

If all attempts to reconcile your differences fail, you need to consider taking the following steps *before* you begin the legal divorce process so that you will be more in control of your future and the divorce. A publication developed under the auspices of AARP's Women's Initiative called "Divorce After 50" recommends the following checklist of steps to take in case of divorce at any age:

1. Start saving money. You'll need it for legal counsel, and once the process begins your spouse may discontinue all support.
2. Open a checking and/or savings account in your own name if you don't already have one so that you have sole control over your money.
3. If you have not already established credit in your own name, obtain a gas, store, or major credit card in your own name. (A credit card that has your spouse's name on it that you can sign for is still not a credit card in *your* name.)
4. Keep a record of personal expenses and of normal household expenses to help resolve discrepancies that may arise when you negotiate a settlement.
5. Gather as much information about your joint financial situation as you can and make photocopies of the documents if you can't retain the originals. When you negotiate a settlement, you will need such papers as wills, life-insurance policies, mortgage deed, car and/or other loan documents, credit-card agreements, pension and investment information, checking and savings statements for the past three years, and a list of the contents of your bank security box. Also make a list of your and your spouse's financial advisors.

NOTE: The above seems cold and calculating, but, nationally, it's been shown that women come out of divorce with a serious decrease in their standard of living. Older women, especially those who have not worked outside the home, often find it difficult to get jobs, and the divorce process is complicated by their rights to pension, social-security, and life-insurance benefits and health-insurance coverage. Often, when one spouse is in charge of all financial matters, the other knows little or nothing about their investments, income, savings, etc., and so the emotional trauma over the divorce is exacerbated by financial and legal issues and problems.

6. Get good legal counsel. An attorney you have used for other matters but who is not familiar with matrimonial law may be able to refer you to a good divorce attorney. Or you can get a recommendation from newly divorced friends, from a lawyer-referral service, from orga-

nizations or unions you belong to that offer legal services or from your local legal services organization for public legal assistance. If you can, interview two or three attorneys before hiring one. But, before the interview, find out if there is a fee and how much for initial consultation. Bring all your information and documents to the consultation, but don't leave them with the attorney. Here's a checklist of characteristics your attorney should have:

- Experience in matrimonial law.
- Be familiar with current pension, retirement and tax issues relevant to late-life divorce, if that's your situation.
- Be affordable or willing to allow you to pay in increments.
- Be sympathetic to your personal values.
- Can negotiate with your spouse's attorney and litigate in court if necessary and will be comfortable advising you if you decide to seek divorce mediation.

NOTE: Divorce mediation is a process in which you and your spouse work out the settlement with the aid of a neutral party/mediator. It allows a couple to resolve differences without becoming adversaries and can settle all or parts of the divorce agreement out of a courtroom setting. The mediator helps both parties identify their needs and rights; define the issues to be resolved; balance their bargaining positions; develop solutions to intractable disagreements; negotiate settlement of emotional disputes. A suitable mediator knows family law, the emotional, tax, and other financial issues of divorce, and is trained in communication and negotiation skills. Some states provide mediation services free; some communities also offer mediation services. Or, get a listing of private divorce mediators in your area by writing to: Academy of Family Mediators, P.O. Box 10501, Eugene, OR 97440, or call 503-345-1205.

7. After the Divorce Is Over: Don't hesitate to seek additional counseling. The various emotional stages are similar to those felt when you experience the death of a loved one, including sense of loss, depression, anger, guilt, and other anxieties. Avoid making major decisions until your emotional wounds are healed.

If You Are Looking for a Job

If you haven't been in the job market for several years or if your background and training are not compatible with your local market's needs, you may have to use some ingenuity in your job search. While newspapers, personnel departments, and employment agencies are traditional job sources, there is also a "hidden" job market. The AARP Booklet "Working Options, How to Plan Your Job Search, Your Work Life" suggests you check out the following "hidden" job markets:

1. Newspaper business-section stories about new and expanding businesses.

2. Yellow pages of the phone book for companies that employ people with your skills.

3. Local Chamber of Commerce publications such as a Manufacturer's Directory.

4. Former co-workers, employers, or supervisors who know about job openings *before* they are advertised.

5. Your friends, relatives, and acquaintances and their friends, relatives, and acquaintances. Tell people in this network that you are looking for a job and ask them to call with leads.

6. Community and religious groups. *Note*: Many volunteers have become paid employees in the nonprofit organizations that they served for free simply because they knew what was going on and what needed to be done about it!

7. College placement offices and membership associations, professional and trade publications can give you information, ideas and contacts. Many professional organizations have "job lines" that provide members with inside information about personnel changes and new hires.

APPLYING FOR A JOB

1. Resumes

Should be brief, one page if possible; organized with your skills and places of employment; give enough information, not just job titles and dates; note what you accomplished on each job; be concise and make sure the pages are accurately proofread and typed or typeset neatly. Omit personal information such as marital status, age, height, weight.

2. Cover Letter

Should be addressed to the person hiring you with name and title spelled properly; show you are familiar with the organization in the opening line; show how your skills will help the employer; use language of the field in which you are applying; ask for an interview in the closing paragraph. Follow up your letter with a phone call.

3. The Interview

Be aware of clothing, hairstyles, and business appearance of the other employees of the business and present yourself accordingly. Answer questions clearly, concisely, and relevantly, in a positive manner. Be prepared to answer questions, such as those listed below, by making points in your favor.

Why did you choose the organization? Research the company prior to applying for the job so that you can talk about it, its goals, and how your goals match the company's.

What can you do for the employer? Know what the organization needs and how you can meet its needs.

Have you done this work before? Tell concisely how your skills match the employer's needs.

Will you fit in here? Tell briefly how you coped with taking direction from supervisors, coped with a hectic pace, and emphasize that you evaluate people based on ability, not age, especially if you are an older worker who may end up with a supervisor who's younger than you.

What salary do you want? Find out the salary range before the interview and try to postpone salary discussion until a job offer has been made.

NOTE: Find out rates from employment agencies and other network resources. Hourly salaries are usually advertised with job descriptions for low entry-level positions. However, for mid- and upper-level positions, salaries may be discussed at the second or third interview.

HINT: Working for a temporary agency that places full- and part-time workers is a good way to learn about different work environments and helps you get training, work experience, and more contacts for your job search.

CHAPTER TWELVE

A Few Practical Matters

Although the subjects aren't pleasant to think about, life has its perils such as auto accidents, fires, wind storms, and vandalism; sickness and death are part of the life cycle.

We all need to plan for emergencies and their accompanying financial consequences. Physical or mental incapacity is not just a problem for older people; it can happen at any age.

Loved ones and health-care providers should know your values, beliefs, and personal preferences. If you want to be an organ donor in case of a fatal accident and/or have strong feelings about life support for terminal illness, your desires must be put in writing and the documents given to the proper people so that your wishes can be carried out.

Where to Keep Important Papers

Make sure your lawyer, family or close friends know where you keep your life-insurance policies, wills, living wills (declarations or directives for terminal-illness care), and other important documents. These documents need to be in a safe place, but don't put the originals in a safe deposit box because the box may be sealed at the time of death, causing confusion or delay that could result in your wishes not being carried out. Give copies of your important papers to trusted relatives or friends, the executor of your estate, your physician, and/or anyone else who might be in charge of your affairs if you are incapacitated.

Organ Donations

If you want to donate organs to help others in case of a fatal accident, you need to indicate it on your driver's license and in your health-care directive.

Terminal Illness, Physical or Mental Incapacity

If you have convictions about types of life support for terminal illness, you need to put them in writing and into your medical records so that your physician, relatives, and close friends know your desires.

Two types of documents will help others to make decisions if you become incapacitated: living wills and durable power of attorney for health care.

1. Living Wills (Health Care Declarations, Directives): Recognized in most states and the District of Columbia as evidence of a patient's wishes, living wills usually say that life-prolonging treatments may be kept from a patient who is terminally ill or if death is imminent. They may not apply if a patient has Alzheimer's Disease, stroke, a degenerative disorder, or if a patient is in a coma or persistent vegetative state. Not all allow medical personnel to withhold food and water.

You can get a living will form from your state medical society or from Concern for Dying, 250 West 57th Street, New York, NY 10107.

2. Durable Power of Attorney for Health Care: Durable powers of attorney delegate power to act in financial and personal matters; or they may be for certain powers only, such as for health care.

An increasing number of states are supporting a variation of the "Durable Power of Attorney" which is a separate "Health Care Power of Attorney" in which you can specify your treatment preferences in specific situations and have life-prolonging treatments continued or terminated by the person appointed to make these decisions for you.

However, you need to know that some states forbid certain persons, such as health-care providers, from acting in your behalf if you become incapacitated.

Also, you need to make sure your physicians or other health-care providers understand and agree with your wishes. If they object due to their personal convictions, you can select different health-care providers who share your viewpoint.

To get Durable Power of Attorney for Health Care forms contact an attorney or Concern for Dying. (See address above.) If you do not have an attorney, contact your state or local Office on Aging, which is usually a good local resource for this type of information.

CAUTION: According to the American Bar Association's booklet "Health Care Powers of Attorney," if you cannot think of anyone at all whom you trust to act as your agent with power over your health and personal care if you become incapacitated, you may be better off not creating a Health Care Power of Attorney.

NOTE: If you have created a Health Care Power of Attorney and change your mind, you can terminate it at any time by notifying your agent and health-care provider verbally and in writing. Then destroy the original document itself.

Estate Planning for Singles

Some tools useful to a single person for estate planning are a will, gifts and contributions, joint ownership, trusts, and life insurance.

1. Wills

Singles without children are likely to choose as heirs other family members, close friends, or favorite charities.

If you die without a will, most states award your estate to your closest relatives. Some states can claim your estate if you don't appoint an heir! If you don't have a will, make a commitment to get one by the end of the year.

NOTE: The importance of a will can't get too much emphasis because settling the estate without one can be a very costly, chaotic, and time-consuming affair.

2. Gifts and Contributions

A single person can give up to $10,000 per person per year to as many persons or organizations as he or she wishes without being subject to paying federal gift taxes. Upon death, the entire estate may be bequeathed to a charity free of estate-tax liability.

3. Joint Ownership

Only someone who is trusted should be made a joint owner or account holder. Any single person considering joint ownership of property, bank accounts, home, or car should get legal advice first! (See "Durable Power of Attorney.")

4. Trusts

There are many types and procedures of trusts. Get good legal advice on what's appropriate for your situation.

5. Prenuptial Agreements

Midlife singles considering marriage would be wise to consider a prenuptial agreement to spell out precisely who owns what. This is especially important if there are children from a previous marriage.

Life Insurance

According to the American Council of Life Insurance, most people buy life insurance for three reasons:

1. To have cash for immediate needs and expenses, including final illness, burial, taxes, and debts.

2. To provide money for family members during the readjustment time when they are making important decisions such as moving or finding a job.

3. Money to replace the deceased's support for dependent family members—children, spouses, others.

If you have no heirs and no responsibility to support anyone other than yourself, you probably don't need expensive life-insurance policies, only enough to cover debts and burial costs.

If you decide to buy life insurance, have several agents explain the types and costs of different insurance plans to you in terms that you can understand. You need to compare similar types of insurance and characteristics of each and then base your decision on your special needs. It's a good idea to review your insurance policies each year to make sure that the coverage remains adequate for current needs.

Three Basic Types of Life Insurance

Listed below are the three basic types of life insurance and some characteristics of each. All policies are variations on one or more of the three basic types. When you shop for a policy, use the characteristics of each type of policy as a checklist for comparison when the different agents make their presentations to you.

1. TERM INSURANCE

Term insurance is "temporary." It stays in force for a term of one or more years and benefits are paid only if you die during the term.

A term-insurance policy has no cash value but usually offers the largest immediate death protection for the premium dollar. Term policies are usually renewable for additional terms up to a stated time limit, but premiums usually increase with age. The characteristics of term insurance include:

- Low initial premium
- Protection for a specific period of time

- May be renewed or converted
- Premium rises with each new term
- You or your dependents get nothing back if you survive the term.

2. WHOLE-LIFE INSURANCE

Whole-life insurance is "permanent." Usually, you pay the same premium as long as you live. Whole-life policies develop cash values, which you can use to buy continuing insurance, take as a loan against your policy, or withdraw as cash.

The characteristics of whole-life insurance include:

- Protection for life
- Fixed premium
- Growing cash value (A sum that increases over the years which you receive if you give up the insurance. It can be collateral when you apply for a loan.)
- Higher initial premium than term
- You or your dependents always receive benefits
- Available as universal, variable, and adjustable life
- Should be bought with the intention of keeping it for life or a long period of time.

3. ENDOWMENT INSURANCE

Endowment insurance emphasizes accumulating money while providing insurance protection.

After a stated number of years, the endowment "matures" and pays the amount of the policy to the policyholder. If the policyholder dies before that time, the full amount of insurance is paid to the beneficiary. Because the emphasis is on accumulating money, premiums are higher than other life-insurance plans.

- Insurance plus rapid cash accumulation
- Higher premium than term or whole life
- You can arrange the policy to coincide with future events. (For example, you can arrange it so that after a stated number of years

or attainment of a certain age, you, the policyholder, will be paid the amount of the policy. The beneficiary receives the amount if the policyholder dies before the stated years or age.)

PROPERTY AND LIABILITY INSURANCE

Property insurance protects you against losses or damage to your property by such perils as fire, smoke, windstorms, and vandalism.

Liability Insurance

Liability insurance protects you against financial loss due to liability to pay for injuries to others or for damage to their property, including the costs of defense in the event of lawsuit.

Homeowner's Insurance

Homeowner's insurance is a package policy that protects against such perils as fire, windstorm, theft, and your personal liability for injuries to others. It also covers your additional living expenses while your damaged home is being repaired.

Special policies are available for insuring expensive art, jewelry, and other personal valuables and to protect against perils not normally included in policies, such as flood or earthquake.

NOTE: Many apartment dwellers think that the apartment owner's insurance covers all their losses in case of fire, etc., but this is not so! You need to have your own insurance when renting. The cost of renter's insurance will vary depending on the contents of your apartment and is very affordable and worth looking into. Walk around your place and mentally add up what it would cost to replace just the major items.

Automobile Insurance

Auto insurance covers damage to your own car and protects you against claims when the car you are driving injures others or damages their property. Having auto insurance is mandatory in most states.

Here are some hints on lowering your automobile insurance rates:

- Install an antitheft device on your vehicle. Make sure to notify the insurance company once it's installed.
- If your car is old and worth less than $1,000, dropping collision and/or comprehensive coverages will save money.
- If you have a good driving record with no tickets or accidents in the last three years, your insurance company might offer a discount.
- Check your deductibles; raising them will lower your premium.
- Persons fifty-five years of age or older might be able to receive a discount. Check with your agent to see if your company does this.
- If you have adequate health insurance, get rid of duplicate medical coverage on your auto insurance. Read the policy well and discuss options with your agent.

A Final Word on Friendship

"Make new friends, but keep the old;
One is silver and the other gold."

The sentiment in this old song frequently sung in rounds by Girl Scouts of America applies to all life-styles but is especially important if you are single either by choice or if the single life is thrust upon you through widowhood or divorce.

Like most people, I get by with a little help from my friends much of the time. Without them I'd feel pretty empty.

MEETING PEOPLE IN YOUR NEW LIFE OR ENVIRONMENT

Students can make new friends in classes, school sports, and other activities, but what about other singles?

Many divorced people find that those who were friends when they were "a couple" will drift away from either the ex-wife or the ex-husband—or both parties, if they can't decide where their loyalties lie.

Older divorced or widowed women whose social life was connected to their husband's work are especially vulnerable. Often people don't know how to deal with a widowed person's grief, so they avoid doing anything at all.

If you find that when you need people the most, they just aren't there for you, take heart! Sometimes your old friends are just waiting for you to make the first move toward getting back into the swing of things—call and let them know you still want their friendship.

If old friendships just don't work out, the world is full of possible new friends; finding them can be fun and rewarding.

1. Volunteering

Volunteering helps you meet some of the nicest folks in town and helps you feel good about yourself for helping others while you help yourself ease into a new life. Look in the yellow pages of your phone book under Social Service Organizations or in the white pages for your local Volunteer (Center/Bureau/Action Center) or whatever your community calls its local clearinghouse.

In most city newspapers there are weekly pleas for volunteers to help as museum or zoo guides, ecology workers, scout leaders, nonprofit agency clerical helpers, readers for visually handicapped people, and so on.

If you can't find your local agency, write to: The Points of Light Foundation, 736 Jackson Place, Washington, DC 20503, or call 1-800-879-5400. The Points of Light Foundation will direct you to your area's volunteer-referral center and will take your name and address so that your local center can mail information to you. (Please note that this organization used to be called the National Volunteer Center.)

2. Returning to School

Call your local colleges and universities to get information about adult education. You can start working on that degree you always wanted or just take courses for personal enrichment and/or you can audit classes. (No exams!) Some universities offer seniors classes for audit at no cost at all. Some communities have special education, travel, physical-fitness, and social programs for senior citizens.

3. *Joining Specific Interest Groups*

Major city newspapers publish activities of special-interest groups such as those involved with ecology, senior citizens, church, or sporting events, etc.

If you are divorced or widowed, now's the time to pursue those interests your ex-mate just didn't care about—take aerobics or dance classes, bowl, bird-watch, join a literary group, botanical society or travel club, play bridge or canasta, lick envelopes for *your* favorite political person or cause.

If you don't like eating alone, organize a "Wednesday Afternoon Lunch Bunch," start a weekly or monthly neighborhood potluck meal, or organize a fruit-and-vegetable co-op that buys bulk foods at a local farmer's market which will help save you money while you meet new people and get better nutrition!

Other ways to meet people include: teach others your special skills such as woodworking or needlework; organize or join a walking group; join your Neighborhood Watch Committee (which helps make you feel secure, too!); walk your dog!

4. *Meeting New People if You Are Homebound*

If you are homebound due to health or physical limitations or transportation problems, you can:

- offer to call and check on other homebound people on a regular basis
- write to relatives, friends, or join a pen-pal organization
- offer to help write or get information for a local senior citizens' newsletter.

Also, you can contact community or civic groups to get a daily call to make sure you're okay.

Some communities have transportation for seniors or disabled people and adult day-care programs and activities. To find out about such helps for seniors (and other age groups, too), contact your state's office on aging or other local agency such as the Department of Human Services to get information about community services.

FRIENDSHIP MAINTENANCE

When you have relied upon a spouse or your parents to maintain contact with relatives and friends, you may not realize that you are cutting yourself off from the very people you need by not acknowledging birthdays, anniversaries, and other life events and by not keeping up with general contact and correspondence.

It's up to you to "take pen in hand" to write and to return phone calls promptly. Some people aren't even aware of the need to do these things, and others just need help getting organized.

Here's how to remember birthdays, anniversaries, and other card-sending occasions, especially if you are a devout procrastinator:

1. Mark your calendar at the beginning of the year with all the dates you need to remember. Then remember to check the calendar on the first of each month!

2. Buy all your cards for the month at one time; address and stamp them so that they are ready to go at the right time. If you plan to add a note, don't seal them. However, don't procrastinate sending the card until you have more time to write a note! We know what happens when we wait for *more* time—*nothing!* There will always be only twenty-four hours in each day, no more and no less!

3. Buy cards you like when you see them and keep a stack in your desk drawer so that you don't have to make a special trip when you need them.

4. Buy blank, no-message cards so that you can write "Happy Birthday" or "Happy Anniversary" and personalize them yourself. The bonus is that you will have written a note, however short, and feel good about it!

5. Buy postcards in a pack and carry the pack around so that you can write brief notes to friends while you are waiting in doctors' offices, beauty shops, etc. But then, remember to send them out. If

you stamp and address the postcards ahead of time, you'll be more likely to send them.

6. Don't wait for friends to call; pick up the phone yourself! And return all phone calls, too. I put stick-on notes either on my phone or my fridge when I want to remember to call someone. Check your fridge for stick-on notes each day as you prepare your dinner and make those phone calls while the food cooks or even while you eat, if it's a close friend who doesn't mind hearing a bit of crunchy munching in between sentences and/or being your dinner companion via the phone lines.

And don't forget to write to me if you have any more good ideas to help other singles.

Hugs, Your Friend,

Heloise

Heloise
PO Box 79500
San Antonio, TX 78279-5000

Heloise's column "Hints from Heloise" is syndicated in over five hundred newspapers internationally; in addition, she writes a monthly column for *Good Housekeeping*.

Index

		U.S.	Canada
___All-New Hints From Heloise®	399-51510-0	$ 9.95	$12.95
___Heloise® Hints for a Healthy Planet	399-51625-5	7.95	10.50
___Heloise® from A to Z	399-51750-2	10.95	14.50
___Heloise® Household Hints for Singles	399-51811-8	7.95	10.50

Subtotal $_____

Postage and handling* $_____

Sales tax (CA, NJ, NY, PA, Canada) $_____

Total amount due $_____

Payable in U.S. funds (no cash orders accepted). $15.00 minimum for credit card orders.

*Postage and handling: $2.50 for 1 book, 75¢ for each additional book up to a maximum of $6.25.

Enclosed is my ☐ check ☐ money order
Please charge my ☐ Visa ☐ MasterCard ☐ American Express

Card #_____ Expiration date _____

Signature as on charge card_____

Name_____

Address_____

City_____State_____Zip_____

Please allow six weeks for delivery. Prices subject to change without notice.

Source key 50

0440